W9-CBA-210

STORIES TO TELL

A MEMOIR

RICHARD MARX

SIMON & SCHUSTER

NEW YORK   LONDON   TORONTO   SYDNEY   NEW DELHI

Simon & Schuster
1230 Avenue of the Americas
New York, NY 10020

Copyright © 2021 by Richard Marx

All images courtesy of author's collection except where indicated.

All rights reserved, including the right to reproduce this book or
portions thereof in any form whatsoever. For information, address
Simon & Schuster Subsidiary Rights Department,
1230 Avenue of the Americas, New York, NY 10020.

First Simon & Schuster hardcover edition July 2021

SIMON & SCHUSTER and colophon are
registered trademarks of Simon & Schuster, Inc.

For information about special discounts for bulk purchases,
please contact Simon & Schuster Special Sales at 1-866-506-1949
or business@simonandschuster.com.

The Simon & Schuster Speakers Bureau can bring authors to
your live event. For more information or to book an event,
contact the Simon & Schuster Speakers Bureau at 1-866-248-3049
or visit our website at www.simonspeakers.com.

Interior design by Kyle Kabel

Manufactured in the United States of America

1   3   5   7   9   10   8   6   4   2

Library of Congress Cataloging-in-Publication Data

Names: Marx, Richard, author.
Title: Stories to tell / by Richard Marx.
Description: First Simon & Schuster hardcover edition. | New York : Simon & Schuster, 2021. |
Summary: "Legendary musician Richard Marx offers an enlightening,
entertaining look at his life and career"—Provided by publisher.
Identifiers: LCCN 2020056706 (print) | LCCN 2020056707 (ebook) |
ISBN 9781982169428 (hardcover) | ISBN 9781982169435 (paperback) | ISBN 9781982169473 (ebook)
Subjects: LCSH: Marx, Richard, author. |
Singers—United States—Biography. | LCGFT: Autobiographies.
Classification: LCC ML420.M2739 A3 2021 (print) |
LCC ML420.M2739 (ebook) | DDC 781.63092 [B]—dc23
LC record available at https://lccn.loc.gov/2020056706
LC ebook record available at https://lccn.loc.gov/2020056707

ISBN 978-1-9821-6942-8
ISBN 978-1-9821-6947-3 (ebook)

This is dedicated to Ruth and Dick,
for being the best teachers of love and humanity,
simply by example.

CONTENTS

CONTENTS

CONTENTS

OCTOBER 2019

"Fucking hell. I'm going to be found dead in a shitty hotel room in Montclair, New Jersey."

It started four days ago.

I had returned slightly less than a week before from a two-week tour in South America, doing concerts with my band in Argentina, Chile, and Brazil. My wife, Daisy, had accompanied me (as she does as often as her schedule permits), and in addition to the tour being very successful and getting to play for lots of amazing and passionate South American fans, we'd had a blast. Daisy and I always have fun on the road. We can be in the most obscure, dumpy town and we'll find a way to enjoy it. Staying in cities like Buenos Aires and São Paulo made it even easier, thanks to their choices of wonderful restaurants and beautiful hotels.

We arrived back home in Los Angeles knowing I had a fairly quick turnaround before returning to the road for a five-shows-in-a-row run on the East Coast. Daisy and I rested up a day or two and then resumed one of our favorite activities, hiking. Living in Malibu means lots of options for being in nature. The beaches, when not packed with people in the summers, are glorious, and there are numerous hiking trails that will give you breathtaking views and intense physical workouts. The day before I was set to head out on the road again, we hiked in Solstice Canyon, a popular trail we frequent regularly. This particular hike, however, was not like the others.

While Daisy and I are both pretty fit, I tend to have a bit more strength hiking the steeper inclines and usually put a bit of distance between us before I stop and wait for her to catch up. But on this Tuesday afternoon, it was I who was dragging. My energy was really low. I couldn't keep up with her, and so we ended up cutting the hike short and driving home. I wasn't feeling any better when we walked through our front door, but I figured a hot shower and chugging some H2O would set me right.

Now, mind you, I never get sick. *Never.* Though in my twenties and thirties I battled constant colds and sore throats, the removal of my tonsils in 1993 at age thirty turned everything around. I've had maybe two or three bouts of a twenty-four- to forty-eight-hour case of sniffles and cough in the past ten years. I'm so generally healthy and immune to illness I'm kind of a cocky dick about it, as my previous sentence or two would indicate.

I stepped out of the shower, threw on a bathrobe, drank down a cold glass of water, and curled up in one of the oversized white chairs in our master bedroom. Within minutes I started having cold chills. *Chills??* I don't get *chills!* For some stupid reason I did not take my temperature, but rather simply threw a blanket over myself and waited for the chills to subside.

Daisy came into the room, took one look at me, and said, "My love, are you okay? You don't look so good. Are you sure you can do these shows starting tomorrow?"

I said I'd be fine by morning. Just needed a good night's sleep. My flight to Dayton, Ohio, was early—7:00 a.m.—to get me there in time to do a sound check and relax before the concert. I awoke at 4:30 a.m. to finish packing and get to LAX in plenty of time.

When I opened my eyes, I realized my theory of simply needing a good night's sleep was just wishful thinking. I felt like a truck had hit me. Extremely lethargic. It didn't feel like a typical cold or flu, but I assumed it was something in that family of maladies. Being on tour when you're sick sucks. It's the fucking worst. You can't really look after yourself properly going from town to town, hotel room to hotel room. And the fear that whatever illness I might have could attack my throat and compromise my singing is always a real one. As I said, I've been incredibly fortunate to have had few to no health issues at all, let alone on tour, but doing concerts when you're physically not well is stressful and a total drag.

This particular run of five shows in a row would all be part of my solo acoustic tour. I started doing shows like this around 2009. The initial idea of it, performing alone with just my acoustic guitar and a piano and no band, scared the living shit out of me. But as I continued to do this type of show, I started learning layers of stage performance I had never known before. Telling stories, making the audience laugh, and attempting to make the whole experience feel like a chill evening with friends was an art form quite different than my previous life of playing with a band and delivering a high-energy rock and roll show. Over time I found that as much as I still love band shows and playing with other musicians, it's the solo show I love doing the most.

The first show in Dayton was a charity gig sponsored by a local radio station that had always been a great supporter of my music. Because my performance was part of a bigger overall event, I was requested to play only forty-five minutes instead of my usual two hours. As I arrived at my hotel from the airport, still feeling at least five shades of shitty, knowing I only had to play forty-five minutes was a relief. I decided I'd play, get right into my hotel bed, get a great night's sleep, and wake up having conquered this flu-like nonsense. This was not to be.

The gig went fine. My voice was strong. The radio station personnel couldn't have been more grateful and kind. But I was exhausted. My tour manager, Sam Walton (who, unless Daisy is out with me, is my only traveling companion when I do my solo show) got me immediately back to my hotel room to rest. Daisy had work commitments in LA and couldn't join me on this run but was texting me constantly from the time my early morning flight landed in Dayton. She was worried and regularly monitoring me from afar. I assured her I was okay and that I'd feel "better by tomorrow."

The next morning, however, I did not feel better. At all. Much worse, in fact. My voice was fine, but I felt like an even bigger truck had hit me. I pulled on a pair of jeans and a sweatshirt and met Sam in the lobby to make our way to the airport and fly to city number 2, Philadelphia. When Sam saw me, he became concerned.

"Don't take this as an insult, but you look like shit. Are you okay?"

I said, "I look exactly like how I feel, but my voice is okay so let's get me to Philly so I can rest as much as possible before the show. It'll be fine."

We arrived by noon and headed straight for the hotel where I bolted to my room, curled up under the covers, and slept for about two hours before waking up drenched in sweat. Like, seriously drenched. Like, just walked right from an hour in a steam room directly into this bed. At first, I felt a slight sense of relief thinking, *Ah, I had a fever, and it broke, and now I'm all good.* The problem was that unlike my previous experiences with a fever breaking, I could feel my fever was still very much present. I also started having pretty intense chills.

I texted Sam and asked him to bring me a thermometer. Moments after he arrived with it, I saw a number staring back at me I'd never seen in my life: 104°. I was burning up.

Sam said, "Oh, my god! We need to cancel these shows and get you home to a doctor."

I said, "Whoa, whoa. Hang on. I don't cancel shows. Just get me some Advil and it'll pass. All these theater shows are sold out, and my voice is still totally fine. I think I can get through it. I just really need to rest in between."

In my text and actual conversations with Daisy, I downplayed what was going on, not wanting her to worry. But Daisy's really smart and she suspected she wasn't getting the whole story, so she called Sam, who ratted me out.

I said, "Dude!!! What the fuck?? I don't want her to worry."

"First of all, I won't lie to Daisy," he responded. "Secondly, we're *both* worried about you and feel you should cancel these gigs and reschedule them."

Stubbornly, I refused.

"Sam, I love you for caring most about my well-being, but I know my body and what I'm capable of. Now, let's go soft-rock the shit out of these Philly fans."

The Philly gig, like the others on this run, was in a beautiful theater holding about two thousand people. This is the perfectly sized venue for my solo acoustic show: intimate but still very much a concert experience. I walked out onstage to a pretty ecstatic welcome of applause, whistling, and "wooooooo"s, and kicked right into my opening song, "Endless Summer Nights."

The show was a blast for me. My voice was strong, and my stories and jokes went over just as I like. I felt a little dizzy a couple times walking between the mic stand, where I play guitar and sing, and the piano, but nothing crazy. I also noticed that unlike a normal solo show where I might get the slightest bit perspired, sweat was pouring out of me like a human fountain.

I waved good night to the incredible Philly fans, climbed the stairs just offstage that led to my dressing room, and collapsed in a chair, my clothes soaked with sweat. I'd brought the thermometer from the hotel, and it gave me another reading of 104°.

Sam knocked on my dressing room door, opened it, and gave me the biggest smile. "Boss, I don't know how you did that just now, but holy shit. That was an incredible show." By the way, although Sam is my employee, you'll have to take my word for it that he's not a suck-up. There've been shows where something here or there was just off a bit and he'll always acknowledge it. The truth matters.

Sam could see that despite a great show, I was not in great shape, and he got me right back to my hotel room where I somehow got a decent night's rest. The next morning we headed to Staten Island, New York. It's only a ninety-minute drive from Philly so I'd have a good chunk of the day to rest before my show there. As if imitating a scene from *Groundhog Day*, we arrived at the Staten Island hotel, and I headed straight under the covers.

Again, about two hours later, I awoke drenched in sweat and with another fever of 104°. On this afternoon, however, my illness decided to add something new to the mix. It began as another intense bout of cold chills, with my body soaked in sweat but my hands and feet cold as ice, but within a few minutes I started con-vulsing in bed. The chills and fever were giving me a seizure of some kind that I could not stop. I was shaking out of control under the covers for about fifteen straight minutes before it slowly and slightly subsided enough for me to painstakingly make my way to the bathroom and turn on a hot shower. I'd never convulsed like that. Ever. It was incredibly frightening, and I was grateful it had passed.

I needed to get up and get dressed and ready for my performance. Before I even left the hotel room I was perspiring under my clothes. I didn't tell Sam about the seizure and *certainly* didn't volunteer it to Daisy. She was already beside herself with worry and about to cancel her work commitments and fly out to take care of me.

I somehow convinced her it would be okay and that if it got much worse, I'd reschedule the remaining shows and come home. But, truthfully I had no real intention of doing that. I've done concerts under very dicey health situations: strep throat, near-total laryngitis, sinus infections. It's a rare occurrence, and I just figure out how to get the job done.

Once, in 1992, I was juggling concert dates, shooting a video for my hit single, "Take This Heart," and about to produce a track I wrote for the great R&B singer Freddie Jackson. What began as a head cold got considerably worse until I was having trouble breathing and was diagnosed with pneumonia.

While it didn't affect any concerts or the shooting of the video, my diagnosis happened just as I was committed to three days in a recording studio producing the song for Freddie. I ended up not canceling the sessions but having a nurse hook me up each day in the studio's control room to a portable IV, which fed me medication and much-needed hydration while I produced the sessions. Seeing me sitting in a chair hooked up to an IV, Freddie Jackson looked at me and said, "I don't know whether you're the most dedicated producer I've ever met or the fuckin' dumbest."

The point is: I . . . don't . . . bail.

But now, here I am in city number 4, Montclair, New Jersey. After an even quicker drive from Staten Island of forty-five minutes, I gingerly climbed into this bed late this morning in what is probably one of the better hotels in town, but not exactly the Four Seasons. When you've toured all over the world your whole life on the level I have, it's easy to become a bit of a hotel snob. I'm not at all a diva about it. I'm totally comfortable in any hotel where the rooms are clean and comfortable. This room is clean (I think) but not so comfortable and just a little . . . sad.

The gray, rainy weather outside isn't helping the vibe. I just need to sleep as much as I can to try to muster enough energy for another show tonight, and one tomorrow night and I'll have done it. I'll have gotten through a sold-out run of five shows without canceling. I drift off to sleep, feeling the fever that's making Advil its little bitch.

A couple hours later, I'm awake, sweat-soaked, hands and feet freezing, and my teeth chattering. I slowly feel the return of yesterday's seizure, but before I can embrace the fear of it, it is on me. My body is shaking and convulsing uncontrollably.

I realize it's worse than yesterday. I'm legit scared. I become acutely aware that I cannot physically do anything to stop this. It's already lasting longer than the last time. It's got to be twenty minutes of this by now and it's still going. What's happening to my body is violent and out of control. As I continue to thrash around in this bed, I have the thought that even my strong and healthy heart probably cannot withstand much more of this. Am I about to have a heart attack? I can't even reach my phone to call for help. Will I just die here in Montclair, New Jersey? It's not as bad as being found next to a toilet with your pants down, Elvis-style, but it's pretty fucking grim.

Just as I am reluctantly resigned to whatever awful fate awaits me, the shivering has slowly started to subside. A few minutes later, I am in a new state of terror. I realize I have to get up and try to pull it together enough to get showered and dressed for tonight's show. The problem is my body is again drenched in sweat under the covers, and the idea of even putting my pinky finger out into the room, which is seventy-two degrees but feels to me like forty-two degrees, fills me with panic.

Eventually, I start to rise from the bed but am too weak from the seizure. I dry heave but have been unable to eat solid food in over two days so there's thankfully no disgusting mess for the maid to discover. I actually crawl across the floor to the hotel bathroom before pulling myself up and starting the shower.

I'm shivering but not seizing. As the hot water covers my head and body, I am consciously grateful to still be alive. Somehow, once again, I manage to make myself presentable (funny enough, I'm having a particularly good hair day) to stagger out of my room, into the hotel elevator, and meet Sam in the lobby to head to the gig.

My face is ashen and I'm already sweating again. As we drive to the venue, Sam says he really feels we need to seek medical attention for me. I tell him, "It's been a really rough day, but I can get through this show."

We arrive at the venue a mere ten minutes before showtime. The room is packed and I can hear the din of the crowd talking and laughing over the preshow music that starts playing every night as soon as the doors to the venue are open. (Side note: If you ever come to see me live in concert and become aware of whatever song is playing overhead as you settle into your seat, know that it's a song I personally chose. I fill each night's playlist with the music of my heroes and friends. Songs I love and admire but songs I also think set a good tone for my performance, which is about to begin. Everything from Vertical Horizon's "Broken Over You" to Tove Lo's "Not on Drugs" to Post Malone's "Circles" to the Tubes' "She's a Beauty.") I have just enough time to sip some tea that Sam has made me and do a last mirror check before it's time to head to the stage. I'm already perspiring again, and I have some chills so despite knowing the lights that illuminate me to the audience will get hot, I wear a sportcoat over the open-collared black dress shirt I have on.

There's a narrow hallway leading from my dressing room to the side of the stage from which I'll walk out, and as I walk I slightly lose my balance twice and have to touch the walls to steady myself. I stand in the wings facing the stage until I hear the cue that prompts me onto the stage every night, and I briskly walk out to greet the audience. The place erupts in cheers and whistles and even with the spotlight in my eyes, I can see the first few rows of people and the smiles on their faces are like a shot of pure adrenaline.

As I strap on my Gibson sunburst J-45 and begin the intro to "Endless Summer Nights," the crowd is still hooting and cheering, until I sing the first notes. "Summer came and left without a warning . . ." As the audience hears those familiar lyrics to a song I know they were hoping I'd play, the feeling in the room is that of love. Love between strangers, but love made up of mutual gratitude. My voice feels great. It's effortless for me to sing and play. Pure joy. I end the song to thunderous and extended applause before kicking right into the next song, "Satisfied." It's already like a party with a huge group of friends.

By the third or fourth song, while I'm thoroughly enjoying the energy between us, I'm starting to feel a little woozy. I normally have a martini onstage, which I sip throughout the show, but feeling the way I do, I have told Sam to fill the martini glass with ice water. Still, I feel like I'm on my fourth martini. I pull up a stool and rest my guitar on my lap. I talk to the audience as I always do. I make a quip about being a bit under the weather but exclaim it's nothing some Benadryl and vodka can't cure.

I begin the next song, "Hazard." This song has a very specific rhythmic meter, which means my hands on the guitar are playing a quite syncopated pattern but my voice is singing longer, fluid notes on top of that. It's a musical juxtaposition I find very satisfying. It required much concentration in the early days of me playing it live, but now, having played it about six hundred times, it's more muscle memory.

I start to sing the first verse, which is the story of a young man in a small Nebraska town accused of murder. As I'm singing the lyrics, I realize that although what's coming out of my mouth is a completely error-free performance, what's going on in my mind is wondering why my ancestors chose to spell our last name with an x instead of Marks. Did it have to do with Nazis? No, it couldn't be that because my great grandfather's birth name was Emanuel Marx, and he was born in 1855. So, who made this decision and why?

My train of thought is interrupted by wild applause. I've just played the last chord of "Hazard" and the audience is cheering my performance, which appears to have been pretty flawless. I just wasn't mentally present. Two songs later, I started hallucinating mid-song that the sweat dripping from my hair onto the tip of my left ear was actually warm water leaking from the ceiling above me. Again, the song was performed without a single mistake musically or vocally. Never even screwed up a word of the lyrics.

Somehow I finished the show in this compromised state and took my bows with a most wonderful audience lovingly cheering me as I bid them good night. I staggered my way back to the dressing room and collapsed in a chair, staring at the wall in front of me. Moments later, Sam walked in with a huge smile to congratulate me on another great show, but seeing my colorless, sweaty face and lifeless body, his smile turned to a somber expression. He stood in front of me and said, "Richard, that was yet another incredible performance, but if you don't let me take you to a hospital right now, I will resign." I knew he wasn't kidding, and I knew it was out of sheer concern for my well-being.

I spent the next three and a half hours in a Montclair ER. They took a chest X-ray. They drew a bunch of my blood. We got a few answers fairly quickly. I was severely dehydrated and was immediately put on an IV for fluids. There was no trace of pneumonia or flu, and my chest X-ray was clear. The test for malaria was negative.

The doctor on call suggested I see an infectious disease doctor right away to test for everything from Lyme disease to West Nile virus. She said, "I would normally insist on admitting you to the hospital, but what you need most is rest and you won't get much of that here." She made me wait for a third bag of fluids to make its way into my bloodstream before releasing me, suggesting that I cycle Advil and Tylenol every six hours to try to control the fever.

"Multiple days of a fever of 104 is dangerous. It means your body is in a state of extreme inflammation. I strongly suggest you cancel your show tomorrow and fly home to see your doctor instead."

I nodded, knowing full well that was not going to happen.

The fluids made me feel a bit better, and though I generally avoid pain relievers, they kept the high fever at bay. Despite both Sam's and Daisy's pleas for me to cancel tomorrow's Boston concert, the last of the five shows, I told them I was really feeling up to it.

Truthfully, I am exhausted. I am also both relieved I didn't have pneumonia or malaria and concerned about what I *could* have.

I finally enjoy a decent night's sleep (beginning at around 4:00 a.m., thanks to the ER visit) and wake up in the best condition I've been in for five days. We arrive in Boston in the afternoon, and when I nap in my hotel room, I do not experience any seizures. Just some chills as the fever soon works its way north before being diverted by some Advil. I am spared any hallucinations at this evening's show and the love from the audience, once again, is like a Z-Pak of vitamins. As I drift off to sleep later in yet another hotel bed, I'm confident that I'm past the worst of whatever this is, but I still need to know what I'm dealing with.

I arrive back home in Malibu, grateful to have survived and ecstatically happy to be back in Daisy's worried arms, and set up an appointment the next day through my primary physician with an infectious disease expert whose nurse draws enough of my blood to fill a thermos. I consult with him in his office as he goes through with me all the results of the blood taken in the New Jersey ER.

He says, "They tested you for a whole bunch of things, and I'm going to test you for a bunch more, but so far every test is negative. Your ANA test [antinuclear antibody test, which shows inflammation in the body] was one of the highest numbers I've ever seen, so you definitely had or still have an infection or virus. We just can't determine what it is."

A week later the doctor calls me and says, "Every test is negative. I'm afraid you have what we call a 'fever of unknown origin.' But the great news is that your new inflammation levels are coming down and you feel much better. I just wish I had an answer for you."

I rest at home for a week and begin to get my strength back. I've lost an alarming twelve pounds (I'm a fairly thin guy to begin with), and my face is gaunt, but my appetite returns. Within ten days I'm completely back to normal. Working out, running on the beach, hiking in the mountains. Like nothing happened.

I perform twenty-nine more shows over the next three months, and despite the constant travel, the grind of the road and being fifty-six years old, I have the energy of a man thirty years younger. In the back of my mind, however, I find myself thinking, *What the fuck was that all about? And . . . is that awful thing going to somehow come back?*

WHERE DO I BEGIN?

To say I had a pretty idyllic childhood would be to say Pavarotti could carry a tune. I had no particular trauma. I had two parents who were loving and affectionate with me and who gave me consistent structure but also always let my voice be heard, as long as it was voiced respectfully. I didn't grow up "rich," but we lived in a beautiful home and I wanted for nothing. The word I'd use for the relationship I had with both my mother and father is *extraordinary*. My wonderful upbringing alone disqualified me from ever being on an episode of the tragedy-centric *Behind the Music*. I'm okay with that.

I was born on September 16, 1963, in Chicago. My mother, Ruth, had been a singer with a traveling big band when she journeyed to the Windy City from her very small hometown of East Liverpool, Ohio, seven years earlier to take vocal lessons from a man there who'd been recommended to her as the best in the country. His name was Dick Marx and, great as he was at it, vocal lessons were actually only his side gig. From the late 1950s, Dick had garnered worldwide praise as one of its finest jazz pianists and certainly the most respected in the city. He juggled dates between the top three jazz clubs in Chicago: the Palmer House, the Lei Aloha, and the darling of the scene, Mr. Kelly's.

When they met, Dick was several years into his first marriage and had three children. After coaching my mother for a few weeks, he took an initial liking to her as a friend. Knowing she was an innocent, small-town girl in a big city where she knew no one, he invited her to his home to spend Thanksgiving 1958 with his family. His marriage had been crumbling for years, and he wanted out but was torn about leaving his young kids. Eventually, though he had lifelong love and concern for his children, his relationship with his wife became toxic and bitter, and he left it.

In the years he'd known my mother, he had developed romantic feelings for her and now he was free to pursue her. He married Ruth in 1961, and I, their only child, came along two years later. That same year, my father also resigned from the jingle company where he'd been writing and producing music for TV and radio commercials and opened up his own operation, Dick Marx & Associates. Within a year, he was getting the lion's share of work at a time when the jingle business was exploding.

In addition to his business booming, this was work my father adored. No matter how crazy the schedule was, he would wake up every morning excited to go to the city and write and record what would become these thirty- and sixty-second hits, selling everything from peanut butter to automobiles. He had an incredible knack for creating a musical hook, a term that over the years has transformed into the word *earworm*, and soon not only was he dominating the field in Chicago, he was also getting work from New York, LA, and San Francisco. The majority of these jingles required studio singers, and my mother became one of several local vocalists who did practically every session.

My most indelible memories of my childhood are of both my parents in the studio my dad had built to accommodate the huge volume of work he was getting. Located on the top floor of a building in the middle of the Magnificent Mile, he named it Sound Market, and it was in a constant state of activity. Sometimes it would be just a rhythm section of a drummer, bassist, guitarist, and keyboard player. Other times, sessions would require a full orchestra, and my dad would hire members of the Chicago Symphony. Later, the singers would arrive to record vocals to the just-recorded music tracks, followed by voiceover talents narrating the advertising slogans.

A "normal" day for my father would be one session beginning at 8:00 a.m., another at noon, and another at 4:00 p.m. He rarely went out to lunch but preferred having a quick bite in his nearby office balancing a plate on his Wurlitzer electric piano, composing between bites. Despite the often grueling pace and pressure to keep creating, he never seemed not to enjoy his job. Possibly his most overused phrase was, "It sure beats working for a living!" I vividly remember being aware of his joy from making music and having this vague sense that whatever I ended up doing, I wanted to feel that way about it.

My father's attention was mostly on his work. He'd come home every evening around six, and we'd have dinner as a family, the three of us, and he'd then head to his home office where a second Wurlitzer took up residence, and he would compose the music for the following day's sessions. It was like this every day. I never once heard him complain or even express fatigue.

This meant that his time with me was pretty limited. On the weekends, he would occasionally take me to a park down the street from our house and play catch with me for a while, and when I learned to ride a bike, we would cruise our neighborhood now and then. But mostly, my father was someone I was aware was dedicated to his career, and though it would have been nice to have more fun time with him, I never felt deprived of his attention. Whenever I needed to talk to him or had a problem, even if he was at his desk intently writing notes of music on staff paper, he would look up and see me and down went that pencil.

Though my mother also had a busy career singing on the jingles, she was a very hands-on mom and a consistent, loving, and attentive caregiver. She was a bit overly protective of me, but I think that had as much to do with me being an only child as it did us having a close relationship. We spent far more time together than I did with my dad, and I developed a wonderful friendship with my mom that remains to this day.

I grew up knowing that I could talk to my parents about anything. No topic was uncomfortable for them, and I felt free to ask them any questions on my young mind. Sex, drugs, religion, you name it. It was all open for discussion and, therefore, was never stigmatized. One of the greatest gifts my parents gave me was not treating me like a child. Subsequently, I became very independent very quickly, and leaving home at barely eighteen to seek my career and fortunes was much more exciting than it was frightening.

2
—

"I WANNA BE FREE"

t is the fall of 1968 and my first day at my new school. I'd love to
now regale you with tales of wreaking havoc at my prior school and
being the unmanageable hooligan forced to leave, but we're talking
kindergarten here. The real story is that after three weeks of their
only child being bullied daily at the local public grammar school,
my parents had had enough and coughed up the dough to send me
to a private school their friend recommended.

My morning ritual was the first thing to change. Instead of
walking out my front door and the thirty yards to the corner of my
street to await the school bus (where three third-grade boys had
immediately singled me out as their target for torment), I waited
inside my Highland Park, Illinois, house until I saw the yellow
equivalent of an airport shuttle pull up in our driveway and hear
the driver beep twice. On the forty-five-minute ride to the North
Shore Country Day School in the affluent suburb of Winnetka, the
bus, which initially carries only me and a female classmate who
lived about five further minutes away, picked up another twenty-
three or so kids ranging in age from five to fifteen. Physical and

verbal bullying is replaced by sleepy kids reading their assignments from the day before or leaning their heads against the window for a last-minute snooze.

On this first day at my new school we are seated on the floor to start the day with Show and Tell. My teacher, Mrs. Goldsmith, is an attractive brunette in her late twenties with thin wire-rimmed glasses, alabaster skin, and her hair tied in a bun. She is soft-spoken and seems to actually like children. At the end of this particular session of Show and Tell, Mrs. Goldsmith rises in front of the group. "Boys and girls, we have a new student joining our class today. His name is Richard Marx. Richard, will you stand up, please?"

I stand and immediately feel all eyes on me. I am met with a conflicting sensation of "specialness" and terror. I like the attention of the immediate moment but fear what will happen in the one that will follow.

"Welcome, Richard. Where do you live?"

"Highland Park."

"Really? That's pretty far. When is your birthday?"

"September sixteenth."

"Ah, so you just had your birthday a few weeks ago."

"Yeah."

Riveting so far, right?

"So tell us, Richard. What kinds of things do you like to do?"

"Umm. I like . . . ummm . . . I like to play with my Matchbox cars. And I like to play baseball. And I'm a singer." (I do not say that I "like to sing" but rather identify myself as a "singer" in a completely matter-of-fact way.)

"Really? Well, would you come up here and sing a song for all of us?"

"Oh . . . SHIT!" I say.

I say this to myself.

I immediately notice a shaking in my legs that's a brand-new sensation, and for some reason all the saliva in my mouth has been replaced with something that feels like sand. But I manage to walk in front of the group of boys and girls sitting cross-legged on the classroom floor, and the first song that comes to my mind is "I Wanna Be Free" by the Monkees.

They were my favorite group, and I loved that song and also had zero doubt about remembering the lyrics, so I figured that was the right call on my part. It's also a pretty short song. Had I tanked it, the kids wouldn't have had to endure as lengthy a shitting of the bed than if I'd chosen "MacArthur Park," a seven-plus-minute opus that was popular at that time.

I began the song and realized that with each next note, my nervousness slightly diminished. I also noticed that all the kids were paying full attention to me, and more important, that within that group, Lynne Harwich, the really pretty little blonde I'd stared at all morning, was looking at me and not looking away.

I guess somewhere in that brief two and a half minutes something inside me clicked because I never lived another single second wondering what I wanted to do with my life. Was it simply being the center of attention? Maybe that was part of it, but even as a little kid I knew the world of music was way more complex than just standing in front of a group of people and singing someone else's song. And I wanted to learn all of it.

It was a matter of months after my classroom debut singing that Monkees song when I was given the opportunity to meet Davy Jones. I was still a mere five years old. My father was friends with a radio promotion man in Chicago who knew I was a massive fan and said he could arrange a private meeting for me with the group when they came through Chicago on tour. My parents even pulled me out of school to make it happen.

The truth is that, yes . . . I was a huge Monkees fan. But I was an even bigger fan of Davy. He was the group's star. He was handsome, and cool, and every boy I knew between five and twenty-five wanted to *be* him. I was no exception. Hearing that I was to meet my favorite group, and my then idol, Davy, I could barely sleep the night before. I was brought to a local Chicago radio station office and led down a few hallways when I looked up and saw Micky Dolenz. I was introduced to him, and I remember him smiling and being nice to me, talking to me for a few minutes despite clearly having little to say to a five-year-old. I was led down another hallway where I briefly passed Mike Nesmith, who smiled and waved in my direction. Peter Tork had recently left the group, so the only one left to see was the only one I truly cared about meeting in the first place: Davy.

The people who brought me to the station walked me into a room that had microphones set up for radio interviews, a small table, and chairs. Within a few minutes I turned around to see Davy enter the room. I think someone had primed him in advance that I was a huge fan. He shook my hand and smiled and asked how old I was. I told him. I clearly recall he said, "No! You're more than five!" The rest of what he said is a blur, but I remember he took time to talk to me and ask about what subjects I liked at school and what my favorite songs were. He also drew a picture for me on a piece of white paper and signed it. Where it is now, God only knows. He was incredibly kind and patient with me, acting as if he had nothing else to do but hang with me. After a few mind-blowing moments for me, Davy gave me a pat on my back as he said good-bye. I couldn't have been happier. There's no way to prove this, but I can't imagine that this encounter didn't further spur my desire to become a musician and songwriter.

Okay, ready for this? Cut to: forty-one years after I sang "I Wanna Be Free" in front of my kindergarten class, I was standing near the baggage claim area of the Harrisburg, Pennsylvania, airport. While my tour manager waited for our suitcases and band gear to drop down the carousel, I noticed a man waiting for his luggage. It was Davy.

Here I was, ten feet from him at the Harrisburg airport. He looked easily fifteen years younger than his age; still had a great head of hair and was very fit. I walked over and said, "Excuse me, Mr. Jones? My name is Ri—"

His eyes widened as he said, "Richard Marx! Hey, man! I'm a fan!"

I looked at him and said, "Okay . . . ummm . . . thank you. But I'm going to need a minute for my head to stop spinning around, and then I have a story to tell you."

As we stood there, I had the amazing opportunity to thank him, all those years later, for being exactly the way I had hoped he would be. He smiled and said, "Well, I'm glad your memory of me is a great one." We then talked about his farm near Harrisburg and how he loved caring for his horses. He showed me the calluses on his hands from tending his farm but also made a point to mention that he still loved performing onstage. "We've gotta just keep doing it. Right, man?" he said. I thanked him once again, and we bid each other a fond good-bye and a hope our paths would cross again someday.

Two years later, I saw in my Google News feed that Davy had died that morning of a massive heart attack. I felt incredibly sad. I certainly didn't "know" the man, but he'd had an impact on my life, and I felt grateful to have met him those two times, decades in between. I was already quite active on social media by this point and decided I wanted to comment on his passing. I wrote a blog telling the story of meeting him at five, and again all those years later. I also felt I wanted to pay tribute to him musically. So I grabbed an acoustic guitar, turned on the camera on my laptop, and sang "I Wanna Be Free" for the first time since that morning in kindergarten. I had my social media team post the video, along with the blog, that afternoon. A week later, Davy's family held a memorial service for him, and during the program, they played my video on a huge screen at the church.

When I think about the events that had to occur to make this a story I can now tell you, I am truly humbled. However, I'm not surprised. For as long as I can remember, I've had the ability to attract certain people onto my path, people who made a particular impact on me from afar. It would happen again and again throughout my life, as you'll come to see.

3

"THE ONE YOU NEED"

I loved my dad very much, but he wasn't around a whole lot when I was a kid. His career in the jingle business was on fire, so he devoted most of his time to writing and recording. We would hang out every so often on a random Sunday afternoon, but it was my uncles who became my regular male presences. Not only were they cool as fuck in my eyes, but also younger than my dad and less likely to discipline me or discourage the silly behavior of youth.

One was my mother's brother, Don. Quiet, cool, and handsome in a Tom Jones style with thick, bushy sideburns and an always tan physique that could easily grace the cover of *Men's Health* magazine, even today at age eighty-one. The other was my aunt Vonda's husband, Bob Coy. Bob looked a bit like a young Elvis with a black pompadour, but unlike Uncle Don, he was very outgoing and always looking for laughs. Though raised in Ohio, as was Don, Bob had a southern twang which to this day I'm not sure was natural or affected. He was scrappy and got into fights frequently, but at the time he and my aunt had no children and Bob doted on me, as did Don.

While both uncles loved music, my uncle Bob was passionate about it. He played a little guitar and taught me my first song when I was nine, Ray Charles's "What'd I Say." I still find myself occasionally absentmindedly playing that electric piano riff on acoustic guitar to this day. A nine-to-five labor man, Bob spent a decent amount of his very hard-earned money on music. Particularly eight-track tapes, which were huge in the early 1970s, as most auto manufacturers had installed players into their newest models, enabling music fans to take their favorite albums mobile. (The very idea that this now completely ubiquitous practice began a mere fifty years ago is a serious mindfuck.) Bob had tapes by the bands and artists whom I not only loved but some of whom would be major influences on me: Creedence Clearwater Revival, the Mamas and the Papas, Simon and Garfunkel, and of course, Elvis.

I had loved and memorized every song Elvis had released since his first album in 1956, but my uncle Bob turned me on to the songs Elvis cut before that, the Sun Records sessions that preceded his releases on RCA. These were mostly blues and old country songs that Elvis reinvented simply by combining rockabilly guitar and his completely unique vocal sound, and it was my introduction to traditional country music.

I wanted to be Elvis and seduce every beautiful girl I knew. One thing that I think was unique about me as a boy was that I never went through a "girls are gross" stage. Even in grade school, I had crushes on girls and wanted to have girlfriends. I romanticized what I saw on TV and in movies. Interestingly, I was sexually a very late bloomer, having developed huge insecurities about my looks from about seventh grade through high school. It was only after I moved to LA at eighteen and became hyper focused on succeeding in my career that I started to have any luck with women. Even then, I was all about romance. I wasn't just looking to get laid. I wanted relationships. This explains why my first real girlfriend, whom I started dating at age twenty-one, became my wife of twenty-five years.

My attraction to the art of romance also informed my songwriting from day one. I wrote songs to get girls' attention. I wrote songs to try to say to a certain girl what I couldn't voice verbally. I wrote songs to vent my deep longing for girls I felt either weren't interested in me at all or had put me in the "friend zone." Love, and all its incarnations, was and is the deepest well of inspiration for songs, and though I've had incredibly happy periods in my life, the songs I like the most (by me or any other writers) are the ones steeped in some melancholy. Unrequited love is in a dead heat with lost love for my favorite basis for a song lyric. Those feelings never fail to offer a path to poetry.

In my sophomore year of high school, one of my best friends was Lynne Harwich. She and I had gone to school together since kindergarten and she was my first crush, back *then*! Even at five years old, she was the most beautiful girl in the world to me. I tried everything to get her to "like" me but to no avail. As years passed, we became friends, though I continued to pine for her silently. By our teenage years, I watched boyfriends come and go, and sometimes I would be her shoulder to cry on: 3:00 a.m. phone calls in which I'd remind her how gorgeous and desirable she was and how those guys were dipshits. Lynne became the muse for the first song I ever wrote, called "The One You Need."

> Here, I've been standing here so long
> Waiting for the opening of your eyes
> Hoping that you'd realize
> That I'm the one you need

It was a simple piano ballad that mimicked the romantic songs of that year, 1979. A mixture of the Commodores' Lionel Richie and some Barry Manilow but drenched in innocence and honesty. A few days after I wrote it, I nervously asked her to meet me in the choir rehearsal room when I knew no one would be there. There was a grand piano, where I sat and played the song for her. It was like those scenes in Elvis movies where he sings to the girl and she falls madly in love with him. Only thing was: it wasn't a movie, I didn't look like Elvis, and while she smiled and told me how "sweet" the song and moment were, she just didn't "like me" like me. Devastated as I was, I owe Lynne Harwich a tremendous debt of gratitude. She was the reason I became a songwriter.

From there, it was like gas on a fire. All I wanted to do was write songs. It was 1979 and I was inspired and influenced by everyone from the Bee Gees and the Doobie Brothers to Elton John and Paul Simon. My biggest songwriting influence in high school was probably Billy Joel, with whom I would become friendly a decade later and even record and perform with onstage.

My writing was all piano based at that time, and luckily, my parents had a beautiful Steinway grand in our basement. I wrote all my early songs on that piano and still have it today. I would spend hours upon hours teaching myself to play the hits of the day, and slowly I found I preferred to spend that time making up my own songs instead of playing others'. My lyrics were mostly about unrequited love, feeling lonely and being a bit of an outcast. Throughout my long career, I've not strayed too far from those concepts. They're timeless, and I believe just about anyone can relate to them.

4

"YOU ARE"

I t was a global superstar and personal hero of mine who encouraged an eighteen-year-old me to move to LA and pursue my career. By then, I had written four songs that I'd recorded into decent-sounding demos, and I'd given a cassette tape of them to a high school friend who was now at college in Boston. I'm not going to use his real name here—for reasons I'll get into a bit later. Let's call him Noah. Noah was one of my first "fans" and would listen to my demo tape in his dorm, cranking it up just as other students were doing with Blondie and REO Speedwagon records. His dorm mate, it turned out, knew a guy . . . who knew a guy . . . who was then working with the group the Commodores, and word got back to me that through this long chain someone would play my songs for the group's lead singer, Lionel Richie.

About three weeks later, I was at my parent's house listening to records when the phone rang. I picked it up. "Hello?"

"Hey, may I speak to Richard?"

"That's me."

"Richard . . . this is Lionel Richie."

For at least thirty seconds, I thought someone was fucking with me. I was debating whether it was my friend Josh disguising his voice or some other guy they'd had call me to prank me. But I was a huge fan of Lionel's and had seen him interviewed on TV and listened to him do radio interviews so I knew his speaking voice, and I was pretty sure it was him.

He carried on telling me that he'd been handed my cassette of four songs and that he'd listened and thought my songs were strong and that he really liked my voice. He was impressed that at only eighteen I was able to write well-structured songs that were also catchy. He asked me about my plans. I was a senior in high school. Was I going to college? He thought that might not be the best move for me. He suggested I finish high school and move to LA. "You can't have a real career in the music business if you stay in Chicago. Move to LA and things will start happening for you." I listened intently and asked him for some advice about what to do, all the while in a bit of a fog, my head spinning that I was actually on the phone with Lionel Richie.

It's important for me to mention here as a side note that throughout the years when I've recounted this story, I would always say, "I couldn't fucking believe Lionel Richie called me!" But the truth is, from the moment my friend's friend of a friend of a friend mentioned the remote possibility of it, I knew Lionel would hear the songs and call me. I just believed it would happen. So the truth of that phone call is that I was blown-away excited but not really surprised at all. I have always had a way of making the things I wanted come to me. Not monetarily, although that has been a by-product. I have willed things to happen with people. It's why I've met, worked with, or become friendly with nearly every musical person who has made a real impact on me.

I graduated from high school in the late spring of 1981, and a few months later moved to LA. My father went with me to help me find an apartment, and the second day there we stopped by the recording studio where Lionel was making his first solo album. He and I had

had a couple of subsequent phone calls and he was kind enough to say, "When you come to LA, give me a call and come by the studio." Though we had spoken a few times, I was nervous to actually meet him. But he was, and still is, such a warm and welcoming guy that he made my father and me feel right at home. He was in the middle of recording background vocals for a song called "You Are," and as we sat on the couch in the control room, the conversations between Lionel and his producer James Carmichael made it clear they had been working on background vocals on that particular song for two days already and hadn't found the right sound. *TWO DAYS????* I thought. Coming from the jingle business, both my dad and I were shocked. It highlighted one of the significant differences between recording jingles and recording albums. In the jingle world, there's an advertising executive, the client, present in the room and watching the clock to make sure budgets are met and no time is wasted. While making albums was very costly, it allowed for a much more relaxed approach to getting work done.

Lionel and two hired session singers, David Cochrane and Deborah Thomas, were out in the large tracking room huddled around a microphone still trying to find the right blend of voices to fit behind Lionel's lead vocal. "You are the sun, you are the rain . . . that makes my life this foolish game."

They sang it over and over and over, and when the music would stop, either Lionel or James would say, "It's just not the sound yet. Try again." Finally, after another unsatisfying attempt, Lionel looked through the glass separating the large recording studio and the control room at me, sitting on the couch facing out to the singers. He stared at me for a couple of seconds and then pointed his finger and mouthed, "You."

I literally did that thing where you get up and look around behind you because you know they can't mean you. No one was behind me.

I turned to Lionel and pointed at my own chest and mouthed, "Me?" He nodded and motioned for me to come out to where he was with the singers.

"I wanna try something. Richard, you sing the part I was singing. Do you know it?"

I had listened to them singing these parts for an hour or more and clearly knew every word.

"Yes," I said.

He then told Deborah and David to remain on the notes they'd been singing and walked into the control room. He sat down at the engineering console and pressed the talk-back button, allowing us to hear him, and said, "Okay, I'm going to play the track. Try it with Richard on my note. Go."

The music I'd been hearing through the control room speakers now filled my headphones, and I was standing shoulder to shoulder with David and Deborah at the mic. I was very nervous but was also silently reminding myself that singing in a studio behind a microphone was something at eighteen that I'd already done for thirteen years of my life. I grew up in a studio. But there was still plenty of adrenaline. I took a quick glance through the glass at my father sitting there watching and saw on his face a combination of immense pride and complete confidence that his son was going to nail this shit.

David waved his hand as a cue for us to start and we sang. "You are the sun, you are the rain . . ." The music stopped, and I turned around to look into the control room at Lionel. He had the biggest smile on his face when he pressed the talk-back and said, "*That's the sound!*"

I was thrilled that he liked the sound because that meant he liked *my* sound. We finished singing all the background vocals on the song within about twenty minutes. When we were finished and had come into the control room, Lionel said, "Hey, come back tomorrow.

I've got another song I want to put you on." He also offered me an invitation that literally changed my professional life. He said, "By the way, man. Just know that if I'm here, you're welcome here. I may not have anything for you to do, but if you want to come by and hang and watch whatever's going on, that's cool."

I don't think I missed a day being in that studio. In fact, in his liner notes on that album, his solo debut, he thanks a few people, including me, who "never missed a day." It was like going to hit record production school. "You Are" peaked at number 4 on the charts. I also sang on two other tracks from that album, "Serves You Right" and "Wandering Stranger."

Lionel had me back to sing on his next few albums. On his second album, *Can't Slow Down*, I sang on "Running with the Night" and "The Only One." On the latter, it's just me and Lionel singing all the vocals. It was very late one night when Lionel called me for "The Only One" session. I was home at my apartment in Westwood, California, and Lionel said, "Doctor!" (Lionel calls people that.) "I need you to stop whatever you're doing and come down to the studio. I need your voice on this track, and we've gotta record everything tonight." When it came to Lionel, there was never any question that I'd drop everything in order to help him out. To this day, I feel a tremendous debt of gratitude to him for believing in the seventeen-year-old me and so graciously inviting me into his world. I jumped in my car and was at Westlake Studio (where many classic records, including Michael Jackson's *Thriller*, were made) in twenty minutes. I loved the song we were working on, and at the very end of the last chorus, Lionel had come up with this extra hook to end the song. He taught me the harmony, and we both stood at the microphone singing, "You stole my heart away . . . you stole my heart away." Then Lionel said, "Okay, we've got that. Now, you sing the melody, and I'll sing the harmony." That's a great trick I've used on my own records when

I have another singer with me in the booth. Switching parts gives everything more of a group sound.

I also sang on a third track on *Can't Slow Down*: the classic party anthem "All Night Long." That's me singing "all niiiight . . . all niiiiight." I distinctly remember the day when Lionel played a cassette of the simple keyboard-vocal demo of that song for some of us a day or two before he brought in a band to record it. Anyone with functioning ears knew it was a smash. So catchy and fun. I was thrilled to get to sing vocals on it, and the session was overall quick and easy, except for one bit: the now famous "Swahili" chant.

> Tom bo li de say de moi ya
> Yeah jambo jumbo
> Way to parti' O we goin'
> Oh jambali
> Tom bo li de say de moi ya
> Yeah jambo jumbo

Lionel taught the three of us singing backing vocals the proper pronunciation as we learned the melody that accompanied it, and just as it would take some time to learn to sing in any other language, this was no different. We must have done thirty-five takes before we finally got "the one." As we took a break, I asked Lionel what the lyrics' literal translation was. He said, "Well, *jambo* is Swahili for 'hello.'" I said, "Okay. What about the rest of it?" Lionel leaned closer to me and said, "The rest, my man . . . is pure gibberish. I just made that shit up."

5

"CRAZY"

Soon after my work with him, Lionel recommended me to Kenny Rogers as a background singer for his album *What About Me?* It was 1983 and Kenny was one of the best-selling artists around. He was coming off a string of massively successful country and pop records including "The Gambler," "Coward of the County," and "Through the Years," and was in the midst of recording a new album. He needed a few guys to sing background on a song called "The Night Goes On." The session was easy. We knocked out the vocal parts quickly, thanks to our studio experience and Kenny having a keen ear and certainty about what he wanted. As they were setting up the next song, I sat inside the control room on a couch in front of the huge engineering console. I had only met Kenny that day. His large frame and iconic silver hair and beard were impossible not to notice. He was nice but all business, very focused on getting things done and not wasting time.

As I sat there, I overheard Kenny say to an associate, "We still need a couple songs for this album. One of them needs to be a really simple ballad that anyone can relate to." Kenny had recently had a massive hit with Lionel Richie's song "Lady," and he's smart enough to know that when people really love something, try to give them more of it.

I heard Kenny's conversation and thought, *I'm coming back here tomorrow for a second day of background vocals. I need to write that song he's looking for.* So, I went home to my little apartment in Encino, a second-floor unit that even after a year had only a bed, a single chair, a kitchen table, and a Yamaha keyboard in it, and wrote a song called "Crazy."

The melody began coming to me in my car, where melodies very often do, on the drive home. I pretended to hear Kenny's voice singing the melody I was creating, and knowing the lyrical subject matter he was after, I focused on phrases that were both romantic and strong. "There's no doubt in my mind, we can make this love go on forever."

The chorus came the way most of my others do. I sing the melody with gibberish words, over and over, trying different vowel sounds until my ears know that, for example, a long *e* sound on a particular note will sound more pleasing than any other. As I sang the chorus melody, my gibberish constantly sang a long *a* and the next thing I knew I was singing "Craaaaaaazy." From there it's a matter of filling in the blanks, telling the story.

I was still pretty new to LA and hadn't made enough money to buy any real recording equipment, so when it came to pitching songs to someone, my only choices were to sing and play it into a handheld cassette machine (which sounded like shit) or sit right in front of them and play and sing the song live. I recorded a decent, hiss-filled version of "Crazy" into my cassette recorder and went to sleep.

The next day, I walked into the studio for my second day of background work, trying to figure out how to finesse telling Kenny Rogers that I, a completely unknown and unproven nineteen-year-old songwriter, had written the song he needed for his album. Now, please hear me when I say that what I was about to do is a really awesome way to get fired. I was hired as a background singer, and I walk in carrying an original song to pitch . . . so not cool. And I knew that even then, but I was brave enough (or stupid enough) to go for it.

Kenny arrived about ten minutes after me, so I had that time to sit in the control room and get a really good sweat going in my armpits and down my back. I'm pretty sure the producers of the film *Broadcast News* took a cue from my flop sweat that day when thinking of how to make Albert Brooks look as nervous as possible as a news anchor.

I looked around the room at Kenny, the engineer, the assistant engineer, the coproducer, and back at Kenny, scanning them for a sign of when I could approach the living legend standing before me, but probably looking like I had either a ticking bomb in my backpack or a steaming dump in my pants. A small sliver of wisdom came over me and told me not to go up to him until after I had sung my parts on whatever songs they needed me on that day. That way, I'd at least have done my work and have to be paid, even if they later launched me out of the building and onto my face.

Vocals done, Kenny came over to me with an extended hand and said, "Great job, Richard. I'm glad Lionel told me about you. I hope to get you back later when we have more songs to work on."

My mouth drier than the Mojave, I said, "Thank you, Mr. Rogers." And, yeah, even in that second I thought of the children's TV show. "I know this is probably frowned upon, but, um, I'm actually a songwriter." Kenny's eyes narrowed and immediately showed a hint of glazing over. Undeterred, I continued, voice shaking: "I overheard you yesterday saying you were still looking for a simple ballad, and so I wrote a song last night I'd, um, really like you to hear."

As he drew a breath to speak, my mind imagined words like "SECURITY!" or "Listen, you Midwestern dipshit" or a variation of a sentence that contained the words "never," "work," "town," and "again."

But what Kenny actually said was, "Well, where is it? Do you have a demo?"

"I just have a cassette I recorded at home." At this point, I thought I was dead in the water. I figured I'd give him that terrible-sounding recording I made using my cheap Yamaha keyboard in an echo-chamber of a studio apartment in Encino, and he'd either never listen to it or get five seconds in, hear the pops and hisses, and stop it right there. My songwriting career would be over before I could even legally drink.

To my great relief, Kenny said, "There's a piano in the next room. Just play it for me."

So, knees shaking just as my voice had been, I walked into the next room and sat down. Kenny sat beside me on the bench, and I played and sang a fairly flawless rendition of "Crazy." Looking back on that three and a half minutes, it was pretty surreal. I was a fan of Kenny's. Not a crazed fan, but I'd bought several of his records and sang along to him in my car hundreds of times. He was one of the biggest artists of that (or any other) time, and here he was sitting next to a kid new to the business, listening to a song I wrote in hopes he'd record it.

He started speaking as I held the last D-flat chord. "I like this, Richard. It's beautiful. But I have a thought. That last line where you say 'You are the dream that finally came true.' Could you say 'For me' after that?"

I added two notes of melody at the end and sang "You are the dream that finally came true . . . for me."

Kenny smiled. "Yep. I like it. Maybe we can cut this next week."

I smiled and said, "That'd be great" and tried to play it fairly cool. Inside my head it was Mardi Gras. Those were the best words I'd heard since I'd moved to LA. I didn't have a cell phone, so when I left the studio, I pulled my car over a block away and called from a gas station payphone with my news. They were elated. My father said, "This is just the beginning, Kiddo."

The next day I stopped into a well-known clothing store on Melrose Avenue called Fred Segal. In the 1980s it was where all the celebs and rock stars shopped. I used to go in and look around, but their inventory was well out of my budget. That day, after twenty minutes of browsing, I spotted a pair of black jeans that I knew I wanted. They were by Big Star and they were $125. Even now I think that's a bit crazy for a pair of jeans. But I made a deal with myself that if Kenny did in fact record "Crazy," I would come back and buy them. And about ten days later, I was wearing them constantly.

But the greatest moment that came out of "Crazy" was when we were recording it. Typically, when you write a song for someone, you're in the studio when they record it in case it needs tweaking or additional work. So, I was in the studio when Kenny was singing his lead vocal, and at one point he took a break, came into the control room, and said, "I'm not sure about the opening of that second verse. The lyrics could be simpler. It needs to say what every woman wants to hear and what every man wishes he could say." He started questioning some of my words. It was nothing specific that he didn't like, but he kept asking "What else can you say here?" or "Is that the best rhyme for the line before?"

Being green and very insecure, I got a bit defensive when I should have had the poise to say, "Let's pick it apart and see if we can improve it." Instead, I said, "Kenny, I disagree with you. I think it's really good the way it is."

He looked across the room at me, and with great deliberation he uttered a phrase that remains my mantra to this day.

"Richard, sometimes you've got to give up good to get great."

I humbly agreed to have a look at the lyrics, and after an hour or so with no good ideas for tweaks or changes, Kenny said, "Okay. I'm satisfied that we at least tried. It's a beautiful song with beautiful words. Let's do it."

The song became a number 1 hit on the *Billboard* Country Singles chart in 1985. It bears both our names as songwriters, despite the fact that Kenny contributed so little to it. He would consistently joke (even on television appearances), "I don't think I wrote much of that song, but I love getting half the money." Truth be told, even if it meant giving up half the money the song generated, I was happier to have my name on a song as a writer with Kenny than on my own. What other nineteen-year-old Midwestern transplant was in the songwriting company of Kenny Rogers? It set up so much of my future career as a performer, a songwriter, and, importantly, a collaborator. And even half of a Kenny Rogers song was going to buy some decent groceries (not to mention a bunch of blank cassettes for new song ideas) for a while.

Kenny recorded two additional songs of mine on the *What About Me?* album. "Somebody Took My Love," which I wrote with David Pomeranz (another deeply gifted songwriter who was a huge influence on me in my teenage years), and a song I cowrote with Kenny and David Foster called "What About Me?" which was not only the album's title track but its first single and would become a Top Fifteen Pop single as well as number 1 on the Adult Contemporary chart, giving me my first number 1 song as a writer.

I remained friendly with Kenny for the rest of his life. He recorded a few more of my songs over the years, and in 2008 we even got to perform together at a charity event in Chicago I hosted for the Ronald McDonald House Charities. We sang "Crazy" as a duet and he joined me on my "Right Here Waiting," but it was being part of his backup band and playing "The Gambler" and "Ruby, Don't Take Your Love to Town" that was a thrill of a lifetime.

In 2010, I visited him at his home in Atlanta. He had recently become the father of twin boys, and he joked that even he couldn't tell them apart. We spent the afternoon catching up and though he complained of some health issues, he was in good spirits. We wandered downstairs to his basement music room, where I started noodling on his electric piano and within a few minutes he was chiming in with melody ideas.

I said, "Wait—are we writing a song?"

He said, "Who knows? I'm just singing to what you're playing. It's nice. Too bad I just released a new album."

We ended up finishing the music before I headed back to the airport to fly home. The next morning, he emailed me a lyrical concept about how it doesn't matter how much money someone has when it comes to love. Rich people and poor people both, if they're lucky, get to have love in their lives. Kenny and I started emailing ideas back and forth and a week or so later "When Love Is All You've Got" was born.

I was about to produce an album for a country artist named George Canyon and I played him the song. He flipped over it and asked if he could have it for the album. It ended up as a duet between George and me, and I'm extremely proud of that song.

Kenny was thrilled with how it came out, and we vowed to write together more often, but his health began to decline and in 2015, he announced his farewell tour. We stayed in regular communication, mostly through email. Kenny always typed in all caps, and I would ask him why he was yelling at me. His emails in the last two years of his life became clear messages that he was in tremendous physical pain and was starting to give up. He'd mention how blessed his life had been but that it was winding down. I'd remind him age is only a number and that I, for one, wanted him to stick around a lot longer. On August 6, 2019, I realized it had been awhile since I'd checked in on him, which I mostly did regularly. I emailed him:

Just saying hi, my friend.

How are you doing? Are you getting some relief from any of the pain issues you've been dealing with?

Hope so.

Let me know how you are.

Your pal
Richard

He quickly responded:

HEY RICHARD

YOU ARE THE BEST OF ALL MY OLD FRIENDS TO KEEP UP WITH ME . . . . . I GUESS I'M AS WELL AS TO BE EXPECTED FOR MY AGE . . . . I'M CONVINCED HAVING PAIN IS PART OF GROWING OLD . . . BUT I DO LIKE KNOWING THERE'S SOMEONE OUT THERE WHO CARES..

THANKS FOR BEING THERE FOR ME..
KENNY

The following January I emailed him again and he didn't respond, which was quite unlike him. Kenny passed away on March 20, 2020, leaving behind a legion of heartbroken fans, including me. I will never forget him.

6

"GUILTY"
(BARBRA, PART I)

Between 1982 and 1986, I primarily made my living as a background singer. Once I had both Lionel Richie and Kenny Rogers on my resumé, word spread quickly about a new young background singer in town, and I began getting steady work.

I have to admit, by that time I desperately wanted to be making my own records and touring, and I was frustrated that every record label was uninterested in signing me. But looking back, the fact that I had a means of making money—*good* money—singing on other people's records and learning about record production, I should have been more grateful. Today, it's somewhere between difficult to impossible to make a living as a background studio singer. I feel lucky to have been in the middle of its heyday. It was a fun job, and I met all kinds of talented and interesting people. I sang background vocals on records by George Benson, Philip Bailey, Chicago, Olivia Newton-John, Paul Anka, James Ingram, the Payolas, Jon Anderson of Yes, and a host of unknown artists. It was like going to record production school. I worked with some of the biggest producers and artists in the business and learned something from every session. I sang on many hit songs, and my name appears in the credits of quite a few massively successful albums.

I sang on Whitney Houston's 1984 debut album, on the track "Hold Me." It's a duet with Teddy Pendergrass that was recorded fewer than two years after the tragic auto accident that left Teddy paralyzed. He was just starting to sing again, and his voice was still pretty weak and fragile. His producer, Michael Masser, had hired me the year before to sing harmony vocals on the Peabo Bryson hits "Tonight, I Celebrate My Love" (a number 1 duet with Roberta Flack) and "If Ever You're in My Arms Again" and asked me to double Teddy's lead vocal to make it sound stronger than it was sounding with just Teddy alone. That required me to adjust the tone of my voice to mimic Teddy's voice, or at least blend in with it seamlessly.

Though I never met Whitney while singing on her album, I did run into her at a studio in LA in 1992. She was recording the soundtrack to *The Bodyguard*, and I was in one of the other studios in the building working on something I don't remotely recall. I took a quick break and was walking down the hall when we literally almost bumped into each other. She smiled that gorgeous smile and immediately gave me a big hug. "Oh my god, Richard. How is it we've never met?" I said, "I don't know, but I'm thrilled to run into you. Congratulations on *everything*."

We spoke for a few minutes, and then she asked, "You have kids, right?"

"Yep," I replied. "Two boys." (Jesse, my third, wasn't even a thought yet.)

She looked around to see if anyone could hear us and said, "I ask you to keep this between you and me but . . . I'm pregnant! And it's a girl!" I hugged her and told her it would be the biggest love she'd ever know. I think about the tragedy that would befall both her and her then unborn Bobbi Kristina and recall that conversation now with great sadness. So fucking tragic.

It became clear to me that one reason I was getting so much work was because my vocal range was wide. I could sing really high for a dude, and even higher in my falsetto voice. I could go toe-to-toe with the Bee Gees any fuckin' day. In fact, one time I actually got to prove it.

Barbra Streisand was mixing her live album *One Voice*, and I was next door in another studio singing background vocals on somebody's record. She popped her head into our studio, looked at me and said, "Hi! Is your name Richard?"

And I kind of freaked out for a millisecond before saying, "Ummm . . . yeah."

While I was always more a rock and roll fan, I knew a bunch of Barbra's records by heart. I had crystal clear memories of one album in particular called *Superman*, but those memories were not just because of the great songs on the album but how ridiculously hot Barbra looked on the cover. It had Barbra in short white shorts, high white socks, sneakers, and a white T-shirt with the Superman logo. The back cover photo was almost the same, but it was of Barbra shot from behind, with just the right amount of derrière peeking out of her shorts. (Insert Beavis and Butt-Head "he-he-he" here.)

"Someone said you're a good singer, and that you can mimic voices pretty well," Barbra said. "True?"

I sort of stammered a "Yeah, sometimes . . . I guess." (So fucking suave.)

"I'm mixing next door and Barry Gibb forgot to sing a line on our duet 'Guilty' when we sang it live. Do you think you could sound like Barry on one line?"

I followed her down the hall into the studio where she was working and took my place at the microphone. Palms a bit damp with nervousness, I heard the track to "Guilty" begin. I had heard the song on the radio countless times, so I knew when to sing my line. Doing my very best Barry Gibb impression, I sang, "It oughta be illeeee–gaa-aa-l," and then heard the track stop. I looked up through the glass to see Barbra smile and say, "Wow. That . . . that was great! Thank you!" My line ended up on the album. No one was any the wiser.

I could blend my voice with many different types of singers in pretty much any genre. So I was getting hired to sing on pop records, rock records, R&B records, and country records. I was even hired to sing on the first English album by Julio Iglesias.

It was 1984, and Julio was already a massive superstar internationally, particularly in Latin America, but was still trying to break through the US music scene. When I arrived at the studio that day, I was surprised to find Julio himself in the control room. I was very briefly introduced to him by his producer, Albert Hammond, before they played me the track I'd be singing on called "Moonlight Lady." Albert then explained what he wanted me to sing and I headed out into the main studio behind the microphone facing the control room window, and within a few takes, Albert pushed the talk-back and said, "I think you nailed it! Come on in and we'll have a listen." By this time, there were at least ten people in the control room in addition to Julio and Albert. Julio always seemed to have a group around him, and these friends/associates/family members/whatever had gathered to hang out and listen to what we were recording. I stood in the doorway looking into the room as the track was played back. Julio sat directly in the middle of the mixing console facing the speakers, occasionally moving volume faders with his fingers to change the balance of the mix.

Within a few seconds of the three-minute song, I noticed that Julio, while listening, was staring at me. Like, really staring. I looked away for a second, but when I looked back, he was still staring directly at me as the music played. I looked away again. It was uncomfortable. I didn't know where to look. As the playback ended, Albert and the rest of the people stood silently looking at Julio for his reaction, as if to say, "All good? Happy? We're done here?" But Julio kept staring at me, expressionless.

Finally, after another ten seconds or so, Julio pointed at me and said, "You. You fuck a lot, don't you?"

I was really not expecting that question. Flummoxed, I said, "Ummmm . . . excuse me?"

Julio said, "Yes, you young people . . . you fuck a lot, but you don't know *how* to fuck."

Everyone cracked up laughing and from that moment, every time I'd run into Julio he would greet me with a huge hug and whisper in my ear, "How many times you fuck today?"

The sad part is, at that time, Julio was in his early forties and I was barely twenty, and I can guarantee Julio was getting laid more often than I was.

I didn't have much time for romance given how crazy my schedule was. I remember during one particular week, I was working at Sunset Sound in Hollywood as a background singer on Lionel's *Can't Slow Down* album in Studio A, on Kenny Rogers and Dolly Parton's Christmas album in Studio B, and on Tubes lead singer Fee Waybill's solo album in Studio C. It was an extremely prolific and lucrative time in the record business. MTV and the invention of CDs had revitalized the industry. The public was devouring new music, and artists were pushing into new territory creatively. I'll always remember the artists I'd pass in the hallway of recording studios. Like David Lee Roth (as his solo career was exploding and he was on MTV every nine seconds) sticking his head in the door of one of Lionel Richie's sessions and saying, "Oooohh . . . some beautiful sounds comin' outta *this room*, ladies and gentlemen!!!"

Or the evening I had just finished singing on a track for Fee Waybill's solo album at Sunset Sound and was walking to my car to head home. Sunset Sound was, and is, a great recording facility, but it is just as famous for hosting some amazing basketball games in its courtyard. Someone many years ago had the good sense to put up a hoop at one end of the outdoor space, and it became a great place to step outside, get some air, and shoot some baskets between recording. This particular night, as I exited the door to Studio C, I saw a small lone figure bouncing a basketball in the shadows of the corner opposite the hoop. At first I thought it was a child. He crouched, raised the ball above his head, and launched it with perfect form at least twenty-five feet right into the basket. All net. As he walked from the shadows to grab the ball, I realized it was Prince.

7

"SHE'S A BEAUTY"

After reading that last chapter, you might be wondering, "Who or what is Fee Waybill?" Fee is best known as the lead singer for the '70s/'80s punk-pop band the Tubes. His given name his John. He got his nickname in his late teens when a band he was in noticed, while leafing through a *National Geographic*, that John looked amazingly like the then king of Fiji. The band started calling him Fee, and it stuck. He is not John. He's Fee. Or as I usually call him, "Fee-man." (I am "Ricky" or "Ricky Boy" to him.)

The Tubes only had one Top Ten hit, 1983's "She's a Beauty," but they enjoyed a passionate cult following since the mid-'70s that continues to this day. They were, at their core, a fusion of new wave and punk rock, but their live show was unlike anything else out there, and "out there" is also an apt description of a lot of their songs and shows. They had elaborate production numbers with girl dancers and backup singers; Fee would dress up in wild costumes and play characters while doing various songs. The music was more sophisticated than most punk stuff because the guys in the band were accomplished players, so while they could rage like the Clash, they could also interject cool chord progressions not unlike Steely Dan, and the hybrid made them unique. Add Fee's always biting, sarcastic, hilarious, irreverent, and poetically brilliant lyrics to his showmanship, and you had a classic case of a band that should have been hugely famous and successful, but instead never sold many records, sank all their money into their stage shows, and ended up barely getting by. The band put out more than a dozen albums over the years, and none of them sold more than a few hundred thousand copies. Today, that would be considered decent sales, but in the '70s and '80s, it got you dropped by your label.

I met Fee in 1983 when the Tubes were in the studio recording "She's a Beauty." I had dropped by the studio that day to meet record producer David Foster in hopes I might work with him on something. This was still fairly early in his career, but I'd been familiar with all the work he'd done at that point.

It just so happened that he was producing the Tubes that day, and I was a fan of theirs, too. David greeted me as I walked into the control room and introduced me to the members of the band. Fee Waybill stands six foot three and though very lean and wiry, he's an imposing figure. As I shook his hand I noticed his was so huge it literally swallowed mine, which is quite normal sized.

He said, "Yeah? You're new to LA from Chicago? Cool. I like Chicago. Good town. But God, it's so fuckin' cold all the time. You must be so fuckin' glad to be out here now and not in that fuckin' Arctic Circle."

First thing anyone realizes about Fee is his fondness for the F word. He also has an extra-large-sized head, which was probably a factor in our early kinship, as my noggin is huge as well. Full of big ideas, I always say.

I told him I was a big fan and then, at David's invitation, sat back down to silently observe. The band went out into the large studio to their instruments and began to work on the basic track of "She's a Beauty" which Fee cowrote with David and Toto guitarist Steve Lukather. Everything was coming together nicely except the main guitar part. The Tubes guitarist at that time, Bill Spooner, had had a pretty rough night of partying and was really struggling with the rhythmic guitar riff that plays throughout the song. Time and time again, David would stop the band mid-recording and say, "Bill, it's just not happening, man. Try again."

Bill, steadily getting more agitated by his inability to get the part right, stood silently with a scowl on his face. Through his black hair hanging down in his face, his eyes peeked through and scanned the room until they fell on me. He'd shaken my hand upon meeting me minutes before, but now, even though I was sitting in the back of a separate room, he looked at me through the soundproof glass as if I were the ultimate interloper.

"You know what? It's already fucking bad enough that I can't hear what I need to hear in my goddamned headphones, but now I also gotta have this fucking stupid kid staring at me while I try to work? Get him the fuck out of the studio!"

I couldn't believe it. I let five seconds of silence pass before I stood up to leave. I knew Bill was just being a prick and that his struggle to get the part right had more to do with a hangover than with me, but I also knew I should take off. I took one step toward the door when Fee said, "Hang on, kid" and walked up to Bill.

"What's your fucking problem?" he said, towering over him.

"Man, we don't need random people in the studio when we're trying to work. He needs to get the fuck out of here."

Fee said, "He's a fucking *kid*! He's here to meet Foster and to learn. He's just sitting there quietly. It's not his fault you can't fucking play your part! Leave him alone." And with that Fee turned to me and said, "Sit down, man. It's cool."

You can imagine what that impression of Fee Waybill made on me.

About a year later, Fee decided to make his first solo album for Capitol Records, and David Foster was producing it. Fee said to David, "I love the songs we've got, but we need a few more, and I'd love to write with someone new." Since meeting him that fateful day with the Tubes, I'd been working as a background singer for some of David's productions, so David said, "Remember that kid you let stay in the studio that day? He's a really good writer. You should try writing a tune with him."

Fee called me the next day. The next evening, he came to my apartment in Westwood Village (where it turned out he also lived, a few blocks away) and filled me in on what he felt was missing from his album. It was a pretty straight-out rock record, but Fee said, "I'm a huge Peter Gabriel fan. It'd be cool if we could come up with something that's rock but that also has a cool dance groove." As Fee lit a joint, I sat at my keyboard and started jamming a riff that would become the bass line of our song. It was slightly reminiscent of the line from the Jacksons' "Shake Your Body (Down to the Ground)" but just different enough that we wouldn't get sued. Over that bass line I started singing a melody with what I thought was simply gibberish when Fee said, "Oh, *nice!! 'Who loves you, baby!!!'* I love that!!!" I stopped and looked at him.

"Huh?"

"That's what you sang."

"I did?"

Listening back to the cassette of us writing the song it sounds like I sang, "Woo . . . muz-doo maybe." But luckily, Fee heard it wrong.

We finished the song in about thirty-five minutes. In addition to recording it on his record, he and David invited me to sing background vocals on nearly the entire album. It was one of the most fun projects I've ever been a part of, and though the album never became a hit, it forged the friendship with Fee that I enjoy to this day. He's the godfather to my sons. And he's still a badass talent.

On paper, we're an odd friendship. The guy who wore platform shoes and Spandex pants with a huge zucchini shoved into the crotch and sang "White Punks on Dope" hanging out with the "Right Here Waiting" dude. Weird, but true. He knows me better than any other guy on earth. He's the big brother I never had, but without any of the meanness, jealousy, pants-ing, or beatings. In fact, I was saying to him very recently, "We've been friends for nearly forty years, and I have never been pissed off at you." He says it's the same for him. But I can tell you that aside from our mutual love of old Westerns, great pasta, George Carlin, Foo Fighters, and the F word, it's Fee's brutal frankness that is my favorite part of having him as my best friend. Here's one of a bazillion examples.

It's 1989 and I'm in the studio recording my second album, *Repeat Offender*. My coproducer David Cole and I are finishing the mix of a track called "Angelia," which went on to be a pretty big hit for me. I had worked especially hard on this track, layering tons of guitar parts, synth parts, and background vocals, and I was so proud of this thing. Nearly six minutes long, the track was, I felt, the closest thing to a perfect representation of my vision of a song. When Fee came by the studio to hang out, I couldn't wait to play it for him.

I sat him front and center in front of the mixing console. The sweet spot for playback. Fee sat listening, eyes closed the entire time, until the last notes of the song slowly faded. He opened his eyes and said, "Wow, Ricky. That . . . was . . . *really* . . . *really* . . . fuckin' long!"

8

"WHITE HEAT"

In 1985, I got a call from a producer I knew named Patrick Leonard. Pat was a keyboard player from Chicago whom my father had been hiring regularly to play on the jingle sessions he was doing in the early 1980s. Around the time I left Chicago, Pat was offered the job as touring keyboard player with Madonna, who was already the biggest female artist in the world. I hadn't seen Pat in a few years and was happily surprised that he was calling to hire *me* to sing background vocals on a new Madonna song. He had begun writing songs with her on the road and named producer of her new album, *True Blue*. Pat rang and said, "Madonna and I wrote a song called 'White Heat' that needs male background vocals in the chorus. It needs to have some grit. It'll just be you and Jackie Jackson [of the Jackson 5], but we'll record several tracks and it'll sound huge."

A few mornings later, as I drove to the studio in the San Fernando Valley, I found myself thinking a fairly random thought: *I sure hope Madonna isn't at the session.* I had never met Madonna, and I realize that was a pretty negative thing to think about a total stranger. But by 1985, Madonna's reputation preceded her. I'd seen several interviews with her on TV and read about her, and she came off as a difficult egomaniac. I just wanted to walk into the studio, learn my part, sing it down, and collect my check. I did not want to have to deal with a temperamental artist who likely fancied herself a "producer" telling me what to do. But artists of her stature are often not present in the studio for sessions like this, so I assumed she'd be absent.

I assumed wrong.

Pat Leonard greeted me as I entered the front door and led me down the hall to the studio where we'd be working. I turned the corner into the small control room and saw Jackie Jackson talking to a woman whose back was to me. When Jackie saw me and stopped his conversation to say hello, the woman turned around to face me. It was Madonna, who smiled and introduced herself, as if she needed to. The first thing I noticed, aside from her warm greeting, was that she was stunningly beautiful. I'd seen Madonna on TV and in magazines hundreds of times, and though I certainly never considered her unattractive, she really wasn't physically my type. But here she was, this *tiny* young woman, wearing a black velour running suit with a white tee-shirt underneath, no makeup, and her short hair tousled and messy. And she was just gorgeous. Between her beauty and her friendly demeanor, I was immediately disarmed.

Jackie and I sat in the control room and listened to the track as Pat demonstrated the background vocal part he and Madonna had in mind (a unison chant-like phrase that went "Get up! Stand tall!") as she sat and watched. But the moment Jackie and I were behind the mic out in the large recording room facing the window into the control room, it was clearly Madonna who was in charge. She would press the talk-back and say things like, "Sounding good, guys. But can you lay back on the 'stand tall' line a bit more? It feels slightly ahead of the beat." She would zero in on every nuance of our performances and make suggestions to make it the best it could be, despite the fact that it was a relatively unimportant part of the song. She was very smart and very professional, and the more we worked on the song, the more relaxed and playful we all became. On one take, she pressed the talk-back and said, "Richard, are you always this pale? I feel as soon as we're done we need to get you to the beach."

To which I replied, "Have you looked in a mirror lately? Hello, Pot? This is Kettle."

When the session was over, we hugged each other good-bye, and I went home and called several of my friends just to say, "I worked with Madonna today, and she's fucking awesome."

9

"SHOULD'VE KNOWN BETTER"

We've all heard the legendary stories of heartbreaks becoming the basis for hit songs. Clapton's "Layla" was really about Pattie Boyd Harrison. Alanis Morissette's "You Oughta Know" was about the dude on *Full House* who was neither John Stamos nor Bob Saget. And nearly every Taylor Swift song seems to be about someone she broke up with or someone who broke up with her.

I've written many songs about several women in my lifetime. But it's never been my way to tell those backstories, especially the ones based in heartache. For one thing, it's not my place, even as the writer, to tell the listener what my songs are about. However people interpret a lyric of mine is fine with me, even if it's nowhere near the meaning I had in mind. The other thing is that I find it extremely distasteful to name names. It's crass and not remotely elegant, and not what I believe a man should do. So, I'm going to tell you the story behind "Should've Known Better," but I certainly won't divulge who it's specifically about. It's a story from my days turning from boy to man, and it's a time in my life that taught me a great lesson about my own integrity.

In my sophomore year of high school, I became good friends with a guy a year ahead of me. This is the "Noah" I mentioned earlier, who led me to Lionel Richie. I don't really recall exactly how we became friends, especially considering that we were in different grades and there wasn't a tremendous amount of hanging out between juniors and sophomores. Noah and I lived about ten minutes from each other and hung out after school a lot. We played a lot of racquetball and tennis. We sat in my parents' basement listening to albums by everyone from the Brothers Johnson to Queen. We spent endless hours driving around in his car listening to tapes of our mutual favorite band, Earth, Wind and Fire. We even went together to see them in concert on their tour supporting the album *Faces* in 1980. And as you would expect, we talked about girls nonstop. I had a huge crush at the time on a girl in Noah's class, and he would sporadically choose a moment to put in a good word for me. It never materialized into me dating her, but thanks to Noah, I was at least on this girl's radar. He, meanwhile, had a thing for a girl in *my* class, so I returned the favor. Neither of us was getting laid, but we were both a bit more of the hopeless romantic type even then, and through the conversations and music, Noah and I became best friends.

He graduated a year before me, of course, and headed to Atlanta to attend college while I finished up my senior year of high school. This was also the year I dedicated myself to writing songs nonstop, much to the detriment of my grades at school. I already knew what I wanted to do with my life and was ferociously hungry to get going. Another fucking chemistry class was nothing but time wasted that I could've spent writing more songs. As I continued writing, I was also recording demos of them occasionally, and when I had what I thought were my best four songs, I mailed a cassette of them to

Noah at his university. He was living in a dorm with a roommate and in addition to the constant stream of REO Speedwagon, the Police, and Blondie that blasted from their speakers was my demo tape. Noah would regularly crank it up, and little by little, students nearby started asking, "Who's that?" Noah's roommate was especially impressed. That roommate turned out to be the guy who started a chain reaction that got my songs heard by Lionel Richie, which essentially launched my career, as I've mentioned.

As Noah dug into college life, and I spent every waking moment writing songs, our friendship began to take a hit that could only be expected. We hardly talked and really never saw each other. There was no rift or anything, but our lives were in different motions. A year later I was out in LA, singing background vocals on Lionel Richie's debut solo album and pursuing my career in any way possible. One day Noah rang me on the phone and said, "I know we've kind of lost touch a bit. Would you be into coming down to Atlanta to hang and catch up? Plus, I really want you to meet Jen."

Jen isn't her real name. She and Noah met at school their first year there. She was twenty-one at the time and from Long Island, New York. She was Noah's first real girlfriend. He'd mentioned her in the smattering of phone calls I'd had with him and seemed to be crazy about her. I remember him highlighting that he found her very bright, and Noah was always a great student and scholastically inclined. He was studying pre-law and planned to become a corporate attorney. Jen was majoring in business but really mostly uncertain as to what career she wanted to pursue. By then, I had abandoned an early thought to study music at Northwestern University in favor of heading to LA and pursuing my music, a decision my parents fully endorsed.

A few weeks later I flew to Atlanta for a weekend visit. I was looking forward to seeing Noah and also just to get out of LA for a minute. He picked me up at the airport on an early Friday evening and we headed to a small apartment just off campus he was sharing with his former dorm mate. (Yeah, *that* guy.) After a quick shower, I jumped into Noah's car and we headed to a local tavern, where we were to meet up with Jen. A few minutes after Noah and I grabbed a corner booth, Jen walked in, and Noah greeted her with a quick kiss on the cheek. "*Finally*, you guys meet!" Noah said, as Jen and I warmly hugged hello. For the next three hours, over beers and pizza and the din of student chatter, we hung out and I quickly saw what Noah liked about Jen. She wasn't a glam/supermodel beauty. She was more like the young, attractive girl you'd expect to see working in a law firm or literary agency. Tall and slender, with shoulder-length hair so dark brown it was nearly black. A thin, longish nose that instead of registering as an imperfection gave her an extra distinct character. And milk-chocolate-colored eyes as big as Bambi's. She was immediately sweet and girlish. And quick with a genuine laugh. She also looked directly into your eyes when she was both speaking to you, and more impressively, listening to you. Or, I should say, me.

Okay. I know what you're already thinking. Yes, I was impressed with Jen. But I was also not attracted to her sexually. There was no particular reason for this, other than she just didn't stoke those feelings in me. It also might have had something to do with the fact that she was Noah's fucking girlfriend.

The next day, Noah and I drove around Atlanta, listening to music in his car loud enough to be heard in Tennessee, and singing along with every song. I had also brought along a cassette of a couple of my own new song demos, which Noah proclaimed would be huge hits in no time. It was a bit like old times. But there was a distance and an unnamed awkwardness between us that wasn't there before.

Our lives had changed a lot since high school, and we hadn't really kept up with each other. He did tell me about the current state of his relationship with Jen, which I found surprising. He said that he definitely loved her, but he had grown a bit bored after a year and a half of dating and wasn't all that riveted by their conversations. He was nearly twenty-two, and this was his first real relationship. It made sense to me that he felt all these things, and while I didn't come right out and encourage him to experience other girls, I was a very understanding ear. That evening, Jen came by the apartment along with a few mutual friends of theirs and we all played music and drank into the wee hours.

The next day was a Sunday and Noah had a pretty big exam the following morning, when I'd be flying back to LA. He needed to spend a few hours studying and suggested I go with Jen to her tennis lesson that afternoon, if only to get outside on a beautiful Atlanta day. Jen picked me up and we headed to the courts, talking nonstop along the way. During her hourlong lesson, I sat in a row of metal bleachers and dove into the paperback novel I'd brought along for the trip to kill time on the plane rides. We stopped at a café on the way back to the apartment and had an iced tea at a table by the street. Conversation with Jen was easy. I liked her. And I particularly remember feeling happy that I liked her, because I wanted to genuinely like my friend's girlfriend and not have to fake it if I found her lame or boring. Noah, Jen, and I went out for dinner that night, and it felt a bit like a Three Musketeers kind of thing. We all laughed a lot together, and I could see Noah was happy that his old pal from high school and his girl had really hit it off.

I flew home the next morning and threw myself immediately back into the pursuit of musical stardom. A few days later, as I was working on a lyric at my apartment, my phone rang.

"Hi, Richard! It's Jen!"

I was happy to hear her voice, if not a little surprised.

"Noah gave me your number. Hope that's okay. It's kinda weird, but I miss you! I loved how much fun we all had together when you were here."

I agreed, and we chatted like the new friends we had now become. From that point on, over the next several weeks, we spoke a few times. Sometimes it would be that Noah called to talk and Jen would be there with him and would jump on the phone and say hi. Through these conversations, the friendship between Jen and me actually blossomed while at the same time the one between Noah and me continued to wane.

It was mid-December when Jen called one night to chat. After several minutes of small talk, she said, "So, Noah has decided instead of coming to New York to spend New Year's with me, he's going skiing with his buddies in Vail. And apparently I'm not invited."

Caught off guard by this, I began to stammer a "Really? Uhh . . . I didn't know . . ." when she said, "Are you free New Year's? Do you want to come to New York? We'd have so much fun. And Noah's totally fine with it."

I wasn't sure how to respond. I really liked talking to Jen and hanging out with her, so the idea appealed to me. But I had hesitations and wanted to talk to Noah. I told Jen I'd have to see what my parents were up to and that I might be going to Chicago to see them. Later that day, I rang Noah, and just as Jen had said, he was on board with me hanging out with her in New York. I asked why he would want to spend New Year's with his pals rather than with his girlfriend. "It's not a big deal. I see her every day. Constantly. I just want to go skiing with my friends. Go to New York and have fun. I think she has a couple hot friends you'd probably meet."

So I flew to Chicago to see my parents for Christmas and went on to New York on December 29. I made my way by train out to the Long Island suburb where Jen's parents lived and was welcomed as if I were part of the family. The next day Jen showed me around her hometown. We walked through the snow-covered streets, stopping for hot chocolate and talking effortlessly. That night after another dinner with her parents at their home, Jen and I drove to a nearby bar for drinks. Almost as soon as we sat down, she started telling me of her unhappiness in her relationship with Noah. By the next evening, New Year's Eve, we were sleeping together.

I knew, of course, that this was the biggest douchebag move anyone could make. No matter what the circumstances, you do not have sex with your friend's girlfriend. And yet I did. Repeatedly. Even worse, I also now found myself with an emotional investment in her, which she claimed was returned. She said she would be going back to school and breaking it off with Noah but assured me that it wasn't because of me. She had just fallen out of love with him. I was already feeling like shit about my own betrayal of him, despite the fact that our current friendship was a shadow of its former self. I decided that if she was breaking up with him, there was no need to come clean to him about what had happened. But I was pretty crazy about Jen by now, and it was all a bit complicated in my twenty-year-old mind and heart.

Two occurrences followed: The first being that Jen went back to school. The second being that she did not break up with Noah.

This is not to say she cut things off with me. She and I would speak on the phone nearly every day when Noah was in class or somewhere studying. She would only explain that he was in a stressful state and she was worried how the breakup would affect him, but that she was falling in love with me and couldn't wait to be with me again. The more I questioned what was really going on, the more her reasons for staying in their relationship varied. And yet somehow I allowed myself to accept it. And over the next ten months, Jen and I carried on a full-fledged affair behind Noah's back. She came to LA to see me under the guise of visiting her family. I met her in New York at least twice. And in the absence of physical contact, there were constant late-night phone calls.

Finally, one morning I woke up in my apartment, went into the bathroom, and began to brush my teeth when I found myself staring into the mirror. *Who the fuck are you?* I thought. I immediately spit out the toothpaste, picked up my phone, and dialed Noah's number. He answered. And I cut right to it. "I've been seeing Jen for almost a year behind your back, and it's time you knew it. I'm sorry." Needless to say, this announcement was anything but well received. He hung up on me. About an hour later, Jen called. Instead of calling to tell me she was relieved and we could now finally see each other openly, she said, "I'm staying with Noah." So by lunchtime, I had been dumped and lost a good friend forever. Rightfully so. Jen's complicity notwithstanding, every choice I'd made in regard to both of them was a bad one, and I knew it.

Still, I was pretty heartbroken about her. That night, I went out with two friends and got as drunk as I ever have. There was a lot of "never again" and "she's such a [fill in the blank]." After my friends dropped me at home, I stumbled into bed where I remained for about thirteen straight hours.

A few days later, driving through Hollywood to a background vocal session where I sang harmonies on Lionel Richie's soon-to-be smash "Running with the Night," I started humming a melody to myself. It was an up-tempo pop-rock vibe in my head, and the melody began with a staccato five-syllable phrase. It began, as my lyrics usually do, as total gibberish. But by the third time repeating it, the words "should've known better" landed perfectly upon those five syllables. Still reeling from the breakup with Jen and feeling like the biggest asshole on earth for my betrayal of Noah's friendship, the song practically wrote itself. I arrived at the studio where Lionel was recording and hurriedly asked the woman at the front desk for a pen and notepad and wrote down:

> Shoulda known better
> Than to fall in love with you
> Now love is just a faded memory
> Shoulda known better
> Something-something-something
> And my heart still aches for you.

The penultimate line, "now I'm a prisoner to this pain," came about four hours later on the drive back to my apartment after the session. As did nearly the rest of the lyrics and melody. I rushed to my keyboard and started working out and refining the chords and melody, and when I felt the song itself was complete, I powered up the Linn drum machine I'd bought about six months before. Drum machines, the new rage in the music business, were not only being commonly used on hit records instead of live drummers but had also become helpful tools for writing and demoing songs. Being able to have a computerized machine keep perfect time and process cool sounds opened new inspiration to me and to many other songwriters, and in the years following, the advancement of this technology has been nothing short of astounding. For many years now, I can closely replicate a full symphony orchestra on my laptop. It's crazy.

I wasn't exactly rolling in dough in those days, and that Linn drum machine cost me about $1,100. But I generally invested the money I made from background vocal work and songwriting into my career. A new keyboard or drum machine was much more appealing to me than clothes or a nicer sofa. I believed in spending money to make money, and I still do.

The actual composition completed, I started imagining in my head what the recording should sound like. I was a fan of Pat Benatar's "Love Is a Battlefield," a massive hit at the time. I thought the drum groove on it would lend itself to my new song, and I programmed a similar beat on the Linn, and added a combination of Fender Rhodes and spacey-sounding strings from my keyboard. Now somewhere in the neighborhood of 4:00 a.m., I listened back to the song and knew it was not only the best song I'd written thus far, but it sounded very commercial to me. I cut a proper studio demo of it a few weeks later with the help of guitarist Michael Landau. Mike was the most in-demand session guitarist in town, and we'd become friendly running into each other at various sessions. I asked him to come and play on two songs, knowing that it was all I could afford to pay him for at the time. Mike was getting double scale for his work (around $600 for a two-hour session), and after he'd played on both songs and was packing up his gear, I sat down and wrote him a personal check. As I handed it to him, he said, "You know what? It's cool, man. I don't need anything for this. Just promise to hire me if you get a record deal from it." This act of generosity was incredibly kind and uncommon, and I'm humbled by it to this day.

The demo was engineered by a Chilean guy named Humberto Gatica. I had met Hum a year or two before on various sessions, when he had befriended the then-teenaged me. We became friends in and out of the studio as we were both big into racquetball, which was very popular in the '80s. Each of us could beat literally anyone else we played, so you can imagine the matches between us were intense. I had youth on my side, but Hum was a great athlete and very competitive. He kicked my ass at least as much if not more than I kicked his. We would both walk out of those courts drenched in sweat. He also invited me a few times to dinner at his house with his family. Humberto was a really gifted sound engineer with incredible ears and was very in-demand when I met him. He was working with everyone from Julio Iglesias to Kenny Rogers to Chicago to Michael Jackson. It was Humberto who Quincy Jones got to engineer "We Are the World." He was also *really* funny. It wasn't just his sense of humor but his accent that made the shit he said even funnier. Hum could look at me and say an otherwise innocuous statement, but his facial expression and accent would put me on the fucking floor. In fact, his accidental catchphrases became as talked about around the session community as his talent for recording. Plus, English being his second language, he would mispronounce words, and it was hysterical. Many of us session guys would invoke one of his phrases at any given time, trying to mimic his accent. I remember in the early '80s when I became aware of the superfood spirulina. I was telling Humberto about it, saying he should start adding it to his protein shakes every morning and he said, "Speedy-Lueena. Okay, compadre."

When it came time to start recording the demos I hoped would get me a deal, I asked Humberto if he could suggest anyone I could afford. He said he'd love to do it himself, as he really liked my writing and singing and wanted to help me. He couldn't do it for free, but if I could throw him half of his usual fee and was okay with him squeezing me into late-night or early-morning sessions here and there, he'd do it. So over the next six weeks or so, Humberto and I would meet at a little studio in North Hollywood called the Lighthouse, where Hum convinced the owner to give me a good deal. We ended up recording the demos to "Should've Known Better" and "Endless Summer Nights" there. Along the way, Humberto said, "If you do get a deal, I'd like to produce these songs for real." Even though I was clearly coproducing with him, I knew what a favor he was doing me and agreed.

"Should've Known Better" would eventually be released as the second single from my debut album and would match the chart success of the first single, "Don't Mean Nothing," peaking at number 3 on the Hot 100. Thirty years later, it's still one of my most played songs on radio. I've mostly forgiven myself for its source material, though I never forget the upset it caused. We were all young, and I'd like to think it was a life lesson that turned into a big hit song.

But that song becoming a hit was still a little ways off. At the time Humberto and I recorded it, "Should've Known Better" was merely the song that led off my then-new four-song demo tape. Suddenly, while not getting an actual deal until 1986, I was getting more positive responses to the songs by some record execs than ever before. And though still as busy as ever with background singing, I'd found myself in an exciting new romance.

10

"MANHUNT"

One night in 1983, a buddy of mine rang me up one night and said, "Let's go to the movies. I want to see this one called *Flashdance*. The girl in it is hot." He was referring to Jennifer Beals, of course, and he was right. But midway through watching the film, it was the girl with short, spikey, blond hair who got my attention.

Her dance routine to the song "Manhunt" was incredibly sexy, and I liked that she seemed to have both a sweet, girl-next-door appeal and a wild side, too. The credits rolled. As we stood up to leave the theater, I turned around to watch them and made a point to catch her name: Cynthia Rhodes. There was no plan to do anything with that information, but I wanted to know. I filed it away in the back of my mind and we left the theater.

Within six months of seeing *Flashdance*, I was hired by Paramount Pictures to be the demo singer on a song for a new film in production called *Staying Alive*. It was the sequel to the classic *Saturday Night Fever* and starred John Travolta, Finola Hughes, and, yep, Cynthia Rhodes. When I arrived at the studio, the only people in the control room were the guy producing the demo, the recording engineer, and Cynthia herself.

The demo we would record, called "Never Gonna Give You Up," was intended as a duet between Cynthia and John Travolta, but John ended up being replaced on the soundtrack by Frank Stallone, whose brother, Sylvester, directed the film. My vocal was used as a guide for John to learn the song.

Cynthia and I spent the afternoon recording our vocals together, and I found myself with a massive crush on her instantly. I was nineteen. She was twenty-six. Six years later, we began a marriage that lasted twenty-five years and gave us three incredible sons.

Once again, I saw something I was attracted to, and within a few months it was within my grasp. Few things changed my life as profoundly as Cynthia did, but it all started when I saw her on film in that black leather getup dancing in front of a painted brick wall.

11

"SOMEBODY LOVES YOU"

One afternoon in the spring of 1985, I received a call from a very nice woman named Mary who said, "Hello, is this Richard Marx?"

"Yes."

"I have Mr. Paul Anka on the line."

Before I could even process that sentence a voice came on the line and said, "Hello, Richard. Paul Anka." His voice was authoritative and becoming of a man who had been a hit songwriter for already thirty years at that point.

I said, "Mr. Anka. What can I do for you?"

"Well, you can start by calling me Paul. I've heard a few songs you've written, and I'm impressed. I'm always looking to write with new, young talent and I'd love us to get together and collaborate."

I said, "Wow. I'm very flattered. I've always had great respect for your songwriting."

I wasn't simply being polite. Although I was obsessed with Peter Gabriel, U2, and the Police in those days, I was well aware of the many songs Paul Anka had composed and I always had an admiration for the era of the Rat Pack of which Paul was a peripheral part.

"Great!" he said. "Come by my place in Century City tonight. Seven o'clock."

I said, "Uh . . . tonight??"

"There's no time like the present, Richard."

Click. Buzz.

I arrived at Paul's condo that evening. He had a tan George Hamilton would envy and was well-dressed and impeccably groomed. He greeted me warmly as we made our way to a living room with a beautiful Yamaha six-foot grand piano. We chatted a few minutes as he asked me about myself. I still recall him at one point asking me, "You have a girlfriend? Boyfriend?" This was 1985, and it kind of shocked me to be asked about my sexual orientation.

"I'm single."

I had just begun dating Cynthia but even then I didn't discuss my personal life with people I didn't really know. That habit has served me well my whole life.

There was a large cassette boombox on the piano. He said, "I just recorded a track with my live band last week that I think could be a good song, but it's not finished. Needs a verse melody and more lyrics." He reached over and pressed Play on the box and sang along with the chorus section. "Somebody loves you . . . somebody loves you . . ." He stopped the tape after the chorus and said, "That's really all I have so far. Should we finish it?"

I had never written this way. I always either composed a song from scratch in my head or began a song with someone else playing a guitar riff or chords on a piano. This already sounded like a finished record but without any melody or vocals, and it was inspiring to write to.

"Can you play it again?"

I began singing a melody over the verse section.

"That's nice!" Paul said. He started suggesting lyrics to fit the melody I was singing. In a matter of about thirty minutes, we had written a complete song to the music track, obviously titling it "Somebody Loves You."

"Richard, I had a feeling we'd be a good team, and I was right. We should write again soon."

A few weeks later my phone rang. "Hello Richard, it's Mary. I have Mr. Paul Anka on the line."

Paul explained he was soon headed to Honolulu for a weeklong residency in the ballroom of the Hilton Hawaiian Village. "Why don't you come to Hawaii that week? I'll fly you there and put you up at the Hilton, and we can write every day before my shows each evening."

A free week in Hawaii. To write songs with a Hall of Fame songwriter. Tough call.

I bought a ticket for Cynthia to go with me and we arrived on a Sunday afternoon. I was scheduled to write with Paul the next day at a house he'd rented on the beach in the Kahala area. When we checked into the hotel, there was a note for me at the front desk saying, as promised, the room was already paid for and that Paul would contact me the next morning to arrange a time to work.

Cynthia and I had a swim and a great dinner. The next morning, Mary called and said, "Richard, Paul has several things to take care of today. He said to just enjoy your day and he'll call you tomorrow morning to arrange a time to write." So, off to the beach we went.

Another fun evening and the next morning, same phone call. Paul is busy. Just hang out and enjoy the island. Call you tomorrow.

This went on for three more days.

Now it's Friday; I'm tan and I'm flying home the next day, and we've not written a note or word. Paul calls me and says, "Sorry I've been so busy, but I hope you've enjoyed yourself. Why don't you and your girl come to my show tonight and, afterwards I'll meet you at my rental house and we can write?"

Paul Anka is a master performer. Even if the music isn't your cup of tea, it's inspiring to see someone on stage who truly knows what they're doing. A bunch of hit songs, a great band backed by a local orchestra, and some pretty funny stage banter. We were really impressed.

I walked Cynthia up to our room and headed downstairs to the Jeep I'd rented and drove to the beach house to meet Paul. Arriving around 11:00 p.m., I thought we'd be lucky to write half a song. Plus, Paul had just finished a week of shows, and I figured he must be a bit fried.

A butler welcomed me and led me to the living room, which contained a grand piano. Paul would be down shortly, I was told. I sat and started noodling around on the keys when Paul entered the room and said, "That's beautiful. Is that something for us?"

"Oh, I don't know. I'm just messing around."

"I'm hearing the words 'No more wine and roses' as an opening line to that melody. Can you try that?"

Within literally twenty minutes, we completed the song "Until the Day We Said Goodbye."

Paul then immediately said, "I've got another music track to show you." It was an up-tempo Latin groove. Just chords and rhythm. No melody or lyrics. I started singing melodies to the track, and Paul began feverishly scribbling down lines of lyrics. About forty minutes later, we had finished a song called "Say It."

We walked to the kitchen where the butler had made coffee and laid out some pastries on a tray. As I leaned against the counter having a bite, I said, "Pretty awesome we nailed two songs. Next time we get together I want to show you something I started the other day called 'One Less Tear.'"

"You're here. Show me now," he said.

Back to the piano. Another song finished within an hour. Me playing chords and singing melodies, and Paul reciting lyrics that fit perfectly.

We then wrote a *fourth* song called "Not Me" before finally calling it a night. Four new songs in about as many hours. I've never had as prolific a writing session since. Now, this would be pretty impressive simply based on energy and output, but literally every song we wrote that night, as well as our earlier collaboration on "Somebody Loves You" was recorded and released.

Paul recorded "Somebody" and "Until the Day You Said Goodbye" on a solo album two years later, "Not Me" was recorded by Glenn Medeiros in 1988, and "Say It" was recorded by Paul and included in the 1985 film *No Way Out*, starring Kevin Costner. Every time that movie is shown, I get a check.

I was and still am impressed by his hunger to constantly write new songs. Much like Burt Bacharach even now, it's cool to see songwriters who've accomplished more than most in our field still filled with mad desire to create. I'm grateful to Paul Anka for writing with me, and for the free Hawaii vacation.

"IF I TURN YOU AWAY"

've written quite a few songs over the years that have wound up in various films. Sometimes it's been a case of the film production company screening a rough cut of their film for me, and me writing a song specifically for it. Other times, a song I'd already written was heard by someone attached to the film and requested to be included.

The first song I ever had used in a film was called "If I Turn You Away" for the movie *St. Elmo's Fire* in 1985. I had only been in LA a couple years, doing a lot of session work as a background singer, when I met a young singer from Edmonton, Alberta, named Vikki Moss. Vikki had been chosen as one of the vocalists on the film's soundtrack, and when she recorded the song, I had been asked to come and sing all the backgrounds.

Vikki was about my age (twenty-two at the time), blond, pretty, incredibly sweet, and fun to be around. I wasn't dating anyone, and upon meeting her at the studio, I immediately turned on the charm and started kidding around with her. As the session neared its end, I was about to ask her to dinner that evening when a young guy strolled into the studio. It was Vikki's boyfriend of two years. She introduced us, and I knew my dinner invitation was a goner. But her boyfriend seemed like a good guy, so instead of bailing altogether, I said, "You guys want to go grab some food?"

We went to a joint near the studio and had some laughs, and the next day when we returned to the studio to finish Vikki's song, her boyfriend came along. He and I had really hit it off and he said, "You need to come visit us in Edmonton soon. I play hockey up there and you should come when we have a game."

About three months later, I took them up on their invitation. They insisted I stay with them at their apartment downtown, which impressed me not only by their kindness but how gorgeous their place was. The next evening, Vikki and I headed over to the local arena to see her boyfriend's hockey team play.

Now, back in 1985 I didn't pay attention to anything except girls and music and not always in that order. I definitely didn't follow sports much and had never in my life been a hockey fan, so this was my first hockey game since my dad took me to a Chicago Blackhawks game when I was seven. I didn't know shit about hockey or the players, but Vikki's boyfriend was now a buddy, and I was psyched to watch him play. He was amazing! Really skilled on the ice. The place was packed with thousands of fans going crazy.

Our team won the game and afterward, we all went to a local bar and I hung out with the team. We all got pretty ripped and there was a band playing. Vikki knew them and got up on the little stage in the corner and did a song as they backed her, and she then, over the microphone, said, "We have a friend in town from LA and he's a great young songwriter but also a *really* good singer. Richard! Come up and do a song!"

I was a few kamikaze shots in and just drunk enough to be dumb enough not to say, "No, thanks!" So I got up onstage and the band just looked at me like, "So, what the fuck are we supposed to do with you?"

I hadn't had any experience singing cover songs, so I was at a loss when the bass player started playing the bass line to Michael Jackson's "Billie Jean," still a massive song on the radio then. I just went with it. But instead of trying to sing it like me, I dove into a full-on MJ impression, with shoulder flips and every "Uh" and "Hoo" from the record. The crowd of hockey players, and especially my new friends, laughed their asses off.

After a few hours' sleep, morning came and I had to head for the airport to fly home to LA. Vikki was hungover and crashed out, so I asked her boyfriend if I could use their phone to call a taxi. He said, "No way, dude. I'll drive you."

We jumped into his very nice Mercedes coupe, and he parked just outside the terminal. This was way before 9/11 and you could still walk someone through security to their gate, but as he did, I started noticing people do a double take and stare.

We got to my gate just as boarding began. I said, "Man, that was such a great couple days. Thanks so much for everything," to which he responded, "Richie"—he had started calling me that from day one—"you're the best. I'm down in LA next month for a game and we've gotta hang."

We hugged and as he turned to leave, I said, "Thanks again, Wayne!"

As Wayne walked back through the terminal, he was mobbed by fans. And even I was surrounded by people at the gate saying, "Are you friends with Gretzky? What's he like?"

That is how out of touch with professional sports I was. I had no idea my new friend Wayne was "the Great One."

Over the next couple of years, I hung out with Wayne, as well as several other members of the Edmonton Oilers, quite a bit. Large amounts of alcohol were always involved, and though I tried hard to keep up, my young, skinny, five-foot-ten self was no match for big, ripped, pro hockey players.

Wayne and I, for no reason I can think of other than "life," lost touch, although we both welcomed sons into the world at the same hospital on the same day in 1992. I was walking down the hallway when behind me I heard, "Richie? Is that you?"

Vikki Moss's song was included in the *St. Elmo's Fire* soundtrack, and the album was nominated that year for a Best Motion Picture Soundtrack Album Grammy, becoming my first Grammy nomination as one of the songwriters. We lost to the *Beverly Hills Cop* soundtrack, which was a huge hit for well over a year.

After the success of my first album in 1987, I was approached with several opportunities to write songs for different films. One of them was an upcoming crime drama called *Tequila Sunrise*, starring Mel Gibson, Kurt Russell, and Michelle Pfeiffer. The producers arranged a private screening of the film for me, and I really liked it. The story involved a former drug dealer (Gibson) trying to go straight while both his former associates are blackmailing him into one more job and an old friend turned cop (Russell) is trying to bust him. And they're both in love with Michelle Pfeiffer. Understandable.

I went home from the screening and quickly wrote a song that I felt not only reflected the Mel Gibson character but felt was a good rock song all on its own. The music was up-tempo and in a minor key, with rock guitar riffs and solos. I titled it "Wait for the Sunrise."

> Friend to fear and loaded gun
> Live life like the owner of a heart of stone
> No one touches, touch no one
> But the road gets weary when you're all alone

I've spent too many nights lookin' over my shoulder
And the ways of the world make a heart grow colder
Got nowhere left to hide
The fight in me has died
So I must wait for the sunrise

I recorded a pretty decent demo of it the next day and sent it to the producers. I heard nothing for over a week. By that point, I felt I had only gained, because whether or not the song was used in the film, I was going to release it. Finally, my manager received a call saying that while they liked my song, they'd been hoping for a romantic ballad to play over the end credits.

They'd never conveyed that to me before, but I probably would've passed on that altogether. I was already getting tagged as a romantic balladeer based on my most recent single, the number 1 "Hold On to the Nights," and felt a need at that time to be defensive of the criticism that I wasn't a real rock artist. I never personally got hung up on labels, but in 1988 being a rock artist who crossed over to pop was cooler than just being a pop singer.

I told my manager to tell them that I understood and wished them my best for success with the movie. When he called to do that, they said, "We found a song Richard wrote a few years ago that we love and think would be great over the credits. It's called 'Surrender to Me.'"

I had written that song in 1984 with my dear friend Ross Vannelli. Ross is the brother of the great singer, Gino. In fact, Ross wrote Gino's big hit of 1978, "I Just Wanna Stop." Ross and I met in 1983 and hit it off as fast friends, as well as cowriters. We had done a demo of "Surrender to Me," which we conceived as a duet, with me singing the male lead and a local LA demo singer singing the girl's part.

The film folks wondered if I'd do the song as a duet with a well-known female artist, but I really did not want another big ballad to be my next song on the radio after "Hold On to the Nights" so I politely passed on singing it. "Surrender to Me" was recorded by Ann Wilson of Heart and Robin Zander of Cheap Trick as the film soundtrack's single and became a Top Ten single in March of 1989, peaking at number 6 on *Billboard*'s Hot 100.

I've run into Robin Zander a few times over the years, and he's laughingly thanked me for not singing it so he could have his only Top Ten single under his own name. He and Ann, one of the greatest voices of all time, did a superb job. And I released "Wait for the Sunrise" on my *Repeat Offender* album.

Another song I wrote for a film was "Love Is Alive" from the 1985 film *The Goonies*. My cowriter? Philip Bailey.

When I was in high school, no other band's music affected me the way Earth, Wind and Fire's did. I lived and breathed their records "September," "Fantasy," "That's the Way of the World," and "After the Love Has Gone." While there are other albums of theirs I loved and wore out, their 1979 release *I Am* is my favorite album by anyone—ever.

Founder Maurice White was a master producer, arranger, writer and musician. From Chicago himself, he had known and worked a bit with my father back in the days before EWF was formed. He was, in my humble opinion, the most underrated singer ever. In the summer of '96, I was recording what would be my last album for Capitol, *Flesh and Bone*, and had written a song for it called, "You Never Take Me Dancing." I had produced the track as a modern tribute to the R&B records I had loved my whole life, and as we worked on it, my mind envisioned background vocals that could only be sung by Maurice. I threw up a Hail Mary and called him. He liked the song and agreed to do it the following week. When he arrived at the studio, he suggested that he and I sing all the parts together on the same mic, to make it all sound bigger and fatter. Imagine how it felt for me to stand there, next to *MAURICE FREAKIN' WHITE* and sing. He even agreed to sing some ad libs at the end of the track, complete with his signature "Yee-owww." It certainly ranks among my most cherished experiences in the studio.

Philip Bailey, EWF's other lead singer, got most of the praise for his voice, and understandably so because his vocal acrobatics were mind boggling. At the time of *The Goonies* song, Philip was on a big chart run with his duet with Phil Collins, "Easy Lover." I was recommended as a cowriter to Philip by a mutual friend, and we wrote "Love Is Alive" quickly and effortlessly. Philip asked me to sing all the background vocals with him, which was another surreal experience in my young life. After writing with me and hearing my voice, Philip asked me to travel to Paris with him and his band to perform on a big television show there. I sang Phil Collins's part, as Phil was busy touring with Eric Clapton at that time.

My other movie songs include "Now and Forever," a Top Ten single that I recorded as the end-title song to the 1994 Alec Baldwin–Kim Basinger film *The Getaway*, "One More Time," recorded by Laura Pausini in the 1999 Kevin Costner, Robin Wright, and Paul Newman film *Message in a Bottle*, and, in what is quite possibly my most esteemed career credit, I cowrote a song featured in the 1986 critically acclaimed blockbuster *Hardbodies 2*. The most stunning thing about it was that someone felt the need to actually *make* a *Hardbodies 2*.

13

"ENDLESS SUMMER NIGHTS"

Between 1984 and early 1986, I shopped my demo tape of four songs to every label in the music industry. Every label passed. The rejections came mostly in the form of letters ("Your music is not something Warner Bros. is interested in pursuing at this time") and sometimes phone calls from A&R guys who told me everything from "I don't hear any hits" to "You don't have the right look" (I think I was considered both not "pretty" enough to be a pop star and not "tough"-looking enough to be a rock star) to "Have you considered another profession?"

It didn't take me long to figure out that nearly every single person making the decisions as to who got signed at labels were as musically clueless and inept as they could be. (It's important to note that of the four songs on my tape at the time, two of them were "Should've Known Better" and "Endless Summer Nights," both destined to hit Top Three on the *Billboard* Hot 100.) But somehow these folks had a way of staying around despite not making money for their label bosses. It seemed to me that usually, if a guy actually did get fired from Epic Records, for example, he'd get hired by Atlantic within a month. So the swamp would never drain. (Excuse the Trump-ism.) Despite knowing that the opinions of these bozos were consistently void of taste, and that every artist has their own personal history with rejection, it was difficult at times not to question whether or not my dream of being an artist was realistic.

By the dawn of 1986, I was contemplating the idea of simply focusing on trying to write and produce songs for other artists and no longer seeking a deal of my own. I really believed I had the goods, and that I was writing potential hit songs for myself, but no one in a position to help make that happen agreed with me. Then one morning I got a call from my friend Bobby Colomby.

Bobby was the former drummer of Blood, Sweat and Tears and had gone on to a successful career as a record company executive and television contributor for *Entertainment Tonight*. We'd been friends for a couple years. He had championed my talents as a songwriter and singer but wasn't working for a label at the time and so not able to just grab a pen and sign me. He had recently, however, agreed to consult his dear friend Bruce Lundvall, who had recently launched a subsidiary of EMI called Manhattan Records.

Bruce Lundvall was a veteran record executive with a stellar history of signing well-known artists, mostly in the jazz world. He was looking for a couple of pop artists to sign to Manhattan and asked Bobby to be on the lookout.

"I'm going to introduce you to Bruce tomorrow night," said Bobby on the phone. "He's in town from New York for a few days. We'll meet at my house and you can play him your demos and we'll see what happens."

While I was grateful and excited, I was also nervous as fuck. I realized that this would be the complete antithesis of what I'd experienced trying to get a deal. There would be no dropping off my tape with the security guard. No leaving multiple messages with the secretaries of A&R guys. This was the president of Manhattan Records. I would never again get an opportunity like this to go straight to the man with the power. He would hear my stuff and either sign me or reject me. Period. When I arrived at Bobby's Westwood, California, house the next evening around nine, I kept driving around the block in circles until my nerves settled slightly.

It was just Bruce, Bobby, and me. Bruce greeted me warmly and said, "Bobby says great things about you. I'm anxious to hear your songs." Tall, with white hair and beard, wearing a perfectly tailored suit, and at that time fifty years of age, Bruce had a booming speaking voice and was easy with a laugh. He made me feel very comfortable. In midsentence his eyebrows raised and he said, "Hang on a second! Marx with an *x*, right?" I nodded.

"Are you any relation to Dick Marx the jazz pianist?"

"He's my father."

"Oh my *god*! Richard, I saw your dad play at a club in Chicago years ago! He's incredible!"

I took this as a very encouraging twist of fate.

Bobby had a room on the upstairs level of his home that he'd designed for listening to music and watching TV. As large a TV screen as anyone made back in the mid-'80s, gigantic speakers, and every piece of gear you could imagine, from reel-to-reel tape machines to laser disc players. It may sound archaic now, but trust me: back then, it was the shit.

We climbed the stairs and settled into this sonic spaceship of a room. I held a copy of my four-song demo in my hand, which was still a little shaky with anticipation. Bruce said, "Okay, Richard. What song do you want to play first?" As I opened the hard plastic cassette case to retrieve the tape, Bobby said, "You know, I was thinking. We can certainly listen to Richard's demos, but I think an even better idea would be to have him play a couple of songs for you live. Let's go back downstairs to the piano."

I stared daggers at Bobby as Bruce headed back to the stairs. I thought, *What the FUUUUCK are you thinking???!!! My tape is made up of pop-rock songs with full band production. Have you ever heard a guy play an up-tempo rock song alone at the piano? It's hideous!!! Even Elton John uses a band!!! Are you trying to fucking SABOTAGE ME???!!!!*

Since that diatribe was all internal, Bobby could only go with my facial expression, which he could see was full of alarm. He winked at me and said, "It's gonna be great."

I trailed Bruce and Bobby down the stairs and considered tripping Bobby so that he'd tumble headfirst to the bottom. That way we'd have to call for an ambulance and then eventually I could say to Bruce, "So, here's the tape." Instead, I took a seat at the bench in front of Bobby's gorgeous six-foot Bösendorfer. (I ended up writing several songs on that piano over the years, including coming up with the intro to "Hold On to the Nights" one 3:00 a.m.)

Bruce and Bobby sat on the living room sofa next to the piano, and I launched into a solo piano-vocal rendition of "Should've Known Better." I had never played that song on the piano, and my already frayed nerves almost went right to full-puke mode as I made my way through it. Bruce smiled and clapped at the end and said, "Wow! Good song! *Love* your voice, man! Play another!"

Feeling slightly less nauseous, I gave "Endless Summer Nights" a try. Again, I'd never played it on the piano this way, and though I could see Bruce was enjoying it, I was still trying to concentrate on the chords while thinking of all the ways I wanted to murder Bobby.

"That's a hit song! Really, really good!" Bruce exclaimed. We talked a few more minutes at the piano about different musicians I would love to get to play on the songs, and finally Bobby said, "Okay,

Bruce. I just wanted you to hear that Richard's the real deal. Let's go back upstairs and listen to his tape." When the four songs were over, Bruce looked over at me and said, "Young man, you should be making records. And I'd love you to make them for me at Manhattan."

For what felt like two hours but was probably five full seconds, I just stared at him. I couldn't believe my ears. Years of writing, hoping, practicing, wishing, and paying dues had led to this moment. I drove home on a cloud of excitement and anticipation. I remember that a few days later, when a person from Manhattan's legal department called me, I had the momentary thought that he was about to say, "Sorry, but we've changed our minds." In fact, he was calling to set the terms of my record deal.

14

"DON'T MEAN NOTHING"

B ruce Lundvall not only signed me, but he did so on the basis of the exact same songs every other label had rejected. He also inexplicably offered me the opportunity to produce my own album. "I love your demos and I love your instincts. Why would I want to dilute that?"

I had previously agreed to let Humberto Gatica, the engineer who recorded the demo for "Endless Summer Nights," produce two songs if I ever got a deal. True to my word, I hired Humberto to produce "Should've Known Better" along with "Endless Summer Nights." We ended up basically using the demo of "Endless" because it was so magical, and even when we tried recutting it with a killer band of players, it just didn't have the same vibe. We added some live percussion by the great Brazilian Paulinho Da Costa, some live bass by Nathan East in place of the synth bass on the demo, and a sax solo by Dave Boruff.

Humberto mixed both songs and then went off to other projects while I and an engineer-coproducer named David Cole recorded the rest of my album. I loved what Humberto did with "Endless Summer Nights" but had real concerns about his mix on "Should've

Known Better." I had even mentioned some things to Hum during the recording. Like, "I'm not sure this vocal of mine is hard enough. Rock enough. This was written as a rock song, but it's all sounding a bit poppy." Humberto disagreed and loved what we had, and he was my producer.

Ultimately, my label demanded that "Should've" be remixed or not be included on the album. Humberto said he was too busy to remix it, plus he felt strongly it didn't need to be remixed. So I went in with David Cole, rerecorded my vocal, and remixed it to sound more in keeping with the rest of the album.

Humberto was very angry with me over that. So much so we almost got into a physical altercation one night soon thereafter. I didn't see him again for many years until running into him at a hotel in Beverly Hills one afternoon. All the animosity was long gone and we greeted each other with a hug, chatted a few minutes, and went on our way. Hum continued to have a very successful Grammy-winning career, working with Céline Dion and Michael Bublé, to name a few.

The ink still wet on my record contract, I decided to write as many new songs as I could instead of using songs I'd written and stock-piled over the last few years. I was twenty-two and very prolific, and I knew my songwriting was improving constantly. Keeping "Endless Summer Nights" and "Should've Known Better" onboard because I still believed them to be hits, I went into full-on writing mode to complete the album, sequestering myself in the very first home I owned, in the Los Feliz neighborhood of LA.

Royalties from the couple of number 1 singles I'd written for Kenny Rogers had paid for the three-bedroom house in the hills beneath the Griffith Park Observatory. It was contemporary, with mostly black and gray moldings and accents, and had a small pool in the backyard. I lived there for about two years, and I loved it. The only real drag about it was that the house was about a quarter of a mile below the entrance to the Greek Theatre, and Vermont Avenue is a divided street, so leaving my driveway, one must turn right and head *up* the hill for about forty feet until you can turn left in a space in the median, then another left to head down to the main street of Los Feliz Boulevard and go wherever you need to.

This was not at all an inconvenience *unless* there was a concert at the Greek. When there was, the traffic on Vermont was a virtual parking lot for hours before showtime on my side of the street, and hours again after the gig on the other side of the street. So the usual seventeen seconds it took pulling out of my driveway and turning around to head down the hill could easily turn into forty-five minutes on a show night. More than a few times I'd made dinner plans somewhere not realizing the Greek had a show, and I'd look outside, call whoever I was supposed to be meeting, and say, "Gig up the street. I'm fucked. Not coming." (It was sweet irony in 1988 when, while still living in that house, I headlined the Greek myself. Lucky I made it to the gig on time.)

I wrote quite a few songs in that house on Vermont. It had an inspiring energy, which is something I look for in a home. One afternoon, while I was writing furiously for that first album, I took a break to run some errands. I was driving home and, as has happened during several thousand car rides, I had a melody start revealing itself to my brain. By the time I pulled into my driveway, the chorus to what would become my breakthrough hit song "Don't Mean Nothing" was written.

It began as a guitar riff in my head, and then lyrics started to join the melody of the riff. I've always been a pretty rudimentary guitar player at best, but I have amassed a stellar collection of acquaintances and friends who are brilliant guitarists, so in their hands, my stupid guitar ideas sound pretty badass.

One such friend is Bruce Gaitsch. I met Bruce in Chicago when I was fourteen. He was in his midtwenties. Bruce played guitar on many of the jingles my father wrote and produced, and I'd see him at my dad's studio all the time. I had just begun writing songs, and though it was mostly a self-contained activity, I knew I had much to learn from collaborating with other writers. I wasn't sure if Bruce could write songs, but I knew he was a great guitar player and seemed like a good guy, so one day (as Bruce recalls) he was leaving a session when I stopped him at the elevator. "Hey, would you be interested in writing a song with me sometime?" He looked at me, this ninth-grade student with a Jew-fro and slight acne, and said, "Sure. When?"

A week or so later we got together and wrote two songs. It was easy. And fun. And we liked hanging out together. It began a friendship and professional relationship that endures to this day. Bruce has played on a huge percentage of my records, and we've written many songs together over the years. He followed me out to LA about a year after I headed there, and when I pulled into my driveway with the chorus to "Don't Mean Nothing" blasting in my brain, I called Bruce and said, "I've got a cool idea. Come over."

We finished the music in less than an hour. I started singing a melody that Bruce mimicked on his electric guitar, and we realized it was a really catchy riff, as well as a good chorus melody. The rest of the melody and chords came very easily. We knew it needed to be a loose, swampy groove, and something about the feel and the tone of the music inspired me to sing the words, "Oh, it don't mean nuthin'." I wasn't sure what those words meant in the moment, but when Bruce went home, I sat on my living room couch with a notepad and started writing down scenarios and characters.

The director smiles as you walk in the door.
He says "I love your work, babe, but you're just not what we're
    lookin' for."

I knew that verse had to be about the bullshit struggling actors have
to endure. In the last verse I chose to focus on the inner workings
of the music business. I thought of Kenny Rogers changing a single
word on my song "Crazy" and asking for 50 percent, which I gladly
gave him to ensure getting him to record it. I remember thinking,
Shit, man. One hundred percent of nothing equals nothing.

Aside from not wanting to attack Kenny in the song directly, I also
knew this kind of thing was commonplace in my industry. So I wrote,

The producer says, "Lemme change a line or two,"
And a little bit of somethin' can look awfully good to you.

In a couple hours, I had finished the lyrics to "Don't Mean Nothing."
A biting, cynical look at Hollywood written by a twenty-two-year-old
kid about to release his first album. Yep.

Bruce came back the next day, and we recorded a basic demo of
the song with drum machine, electric piano, and guitars patched
through what was called a Rockman, which was a piece of gear that
you could use if you didn't actually have a guitar amp. I banged down
a rough mix onto a cassette tape and drove to my then-manager
Allen Kovac's office.

I had interviewed several managers before deciding on Allen. You
see, the normal progression is that you get a manager, and then,
hopefully, he or she gets you a record deal. But I already *had* a deal. I
just needed a manager who would work with me to break my career.

Here's what I remember about the first couple managers I met with. The first guy had me come to his house in Beverly Hills to meet him. It was on about four acres, and the house was at least 10,000 square feet. The next guy I met at his office in Century City. It was this massive space with gorgeous views from every window, and a shit ton of platinum plaques all over the walls from the different artists he'd represented. They both talked a very big game and how this artist and that artist would be nothing without them. All I kept thinking was, *This guy is gonna work his ass off for me? I don't think so.*

I then met with Kovac. He had been recommended to me by a friend who said, "This business is all about radio and concerts, and Allen used to be in concert and radio promotion."

His offices were in a very modest house near the Hollywood Hills. He had no secretary at the time. I sat and played him a few tracks I'd recorded for the album. At the end of "Should've Known Better," he said, "That's a hit song. No question." Then I played him the demo of "Don't Mean Nothing." I honestly figured it might be a fun rocking album track but certainly not a single.

Allen flipped out.

"Richard, this is a hit song! This should be your first single!" We listened again and he said, "It kinda has an Eagles vibe about it, right?"

I said, "Yeah, I guess so. I've always loved them and know every album by heart, so it probably creeped in there."

Allen said, "I've known Randy Meisner for a few years. We should see if he'd be into singing backup vocals on it."

I said, "Wow! That'd be amazing!"

Sure enough, a few days later Allen called with the great news that Randy loved the song and would be happy to come to the studio and sing on it. And then I remembered that Bruce Gaitsch had recently been working with Timothy B. Schmit. I asked Bruce to reach out to Timothy about joining Randy and me on background vocals, and we got a yes from him, too. I was like a kid. I could barely believe it.

We recorded the basic track to "Don't Mean Nothing" at Capitol Studios with a great rhythm section of Bruce on guitar, John Keane on drums, Nathan East on bass, and Michael Omartian on piano. Michael was and is not only a brilliant pianist, but he was also a hugely successful writer and producer in the '80s and '90s for everyone from Christopher Cross and Donna Summer to Rod Stewart and Jermaine Jackson. I knew Michael a little bit and greatly admired his musicianship, and I was also a bit insecure about my piano playing and felt Michael would be better suited to the track. I was right. His performance is fucking killer.

I recorded my lead vocal later that evening, and a few days later, Randy Meisner and Timothy Schmit arrived at the studio to do the background vocals. They'd both been members of the Eagles (and the band Poco), but at different times, as they both played bass in the band. They'd met briefly before but had never worked together until my session. The three of us worked out harmonies, deciding that because we all had a similar range, we would get a great take and then switch parts on the second and third passes, resulting in all our voices singing each part. When we listened to the playback I had chills all over my body. *That* feeling . . . *that* sensation: it's like heroin. I've felt it so many times, and I still can't get enough. It's really the ultimate motivation for me to create.

I thanked Randy and Timothy profusely. Neither of them would accept any payment. Here I was, an unknown singer making his first album, and two of the Eagles were onboard for free. As Randy was leaving the studio, he said, "I noticed you haven't cut a guitar solo on this yet."

"Yeah," I said. "We still have some more overdubs to do."

Randy said, "I'm still buddies with Joe Walsh. I bet he'd love to play on this."

I just stared at Randy.

"Don't fuck with me, man."

He laughed. "I can't promise he'll do it, but I'll ask him if you want."

"Are you kidding? I *want*!"

A few days later my manager called me. "Dude. Walsh loves the song and wants to play the solo. We just need to figure out a time in his schedule."

The inside of my head spun around. I had had a good feeling that this was going to happen, but the reality of it was pretty mind-blowing.

It was about a week later that my engineer-coproducer David Cole and I sat anxiously inside Studio C at Capitol and waited for Joe to arrive. I invited Randy Meisner to be there, and when Joe walked in and saw him, his eyes lit up and he threw his arms around Randy. They hadn't seen each other in quite a while, and Joe's affection for Randy was obvious. Joe was warm, friendly, and immediately complimentary to me about the song. We fired up the track, and Joe spent a few minutes dialing in his sound before we started recording takes. His second attempt is what's on the record. It was inspired and perfect. And now, this little song that Bruce and I had made up in my house on Vermont was not only my debut single on EMI Manhattan Records, it was a mini-Eagles reunion. We were all very excited about the song and the launch of my artist career.

Well, not exactly all.

Several weeks before the release of the single, I flew to New York to meet the team at my record label. I knew that company president

Bruce Lundvall was in my corner. He'd signed me and was very vocal about how much he liked the album I'd delivered. But among the executives who my manager, Allen, and I met in their offices that day was the head of pop radio promotion, Jack Satter. In his late thirties and already a radio promotion veteran, Jack was a pretty stone-faced guy. Stocky, clean-shaven, and not very chatty, Jack cut right to the chase. "Richard, there are several songs on your album I think might do well at radio. But 'Don't Mean Nothing' isn't one of them. It's just not a hit song."

Stunned, I looked at Allen, who said, "Well, Jack . . . it's the single we're going with, and hopefully, you can bring it home for us."

Ten steps out of Satter's office, I turned to Allen. "What the fuck! The head of pop radio at my own label hates my single?"

"Don't sweat it, Richard. Lundvall loves it and it's already becoming a monster smash at rock radio. Jack will come around."

And that he did, within a week or so. Jack and I went on to have some very successful singles together over the years, and our initial conversation became a funny anecdote.

It was the spring of 1987, and there hadn't been a new Eagles record since 1980's *The Long Run*. Eagles fans had all but given up on the band. All humility aside, I know "Don't Mean Nothing" is a well-written song and a solidly crafted record. But having three of the Eagles on it certainly gave my single more attention than a typical debut single from an unknown artist would expect. Rock radio immediately embraced it, and in its first week of release, 117 rock stations across the country added it to their playlists. It was (and still is, I believe) the most radio station adds for a debut artist in rock history.

The video we made to support it was directed by Dominic Sena, who went on to direct several major motion pictures. The video was much more like a short film, featuring actor G. W. Bailey (famous for his roles in the *Police Academy* movies), Fee Waybill, *Playboy*

Playmate and actress Ava Fabian, and starring my girlfriend Cynthia Rhodes. Radio had plenty to talk about with the Eagles members on the record, and the MTV VJs talked about the cast when playing the video.

I distinctly remember having been to a grocery store completely and, as usual, unnoticed the day MTV first played the video, and the next day being recognized within five minutes of walking into a mall in Sherman Oaks, California. Everyone and their mothers had MTV on all day and all night. And for the next decade and then some, that cable channel (and its sister channel VH1) kept my face and voice regularly in front of the public.

Helped by the success of the video and word of mouth, along with me immediately going on a club tour with my band to promote it, "Don't Mean Nothing" hit number 1 on *Billboard*'s Rock chart and soon crossed over to the Hot 100 where it reached number 3.

I've been asked by so many interviewers over the past thirty years, "What's your favorite song you've written?" It's a question that's always irritated me, not solely because I find it so unimaginative, but because it's pretty impossible to answer. All my songs are different and mean different things to me. I have a unique relationship with each of them. Some I've grown fonder of with passing time, and others I'd be happy to never hear again. (Though only a few of the latter!)

Lately, however, as I have continued to tour throughout the world and enjoy it more than ever, I think I have a "favorite." And it's "Don't Mean Nothing." Not because I think it's a better song than many others I've written, but because it's the song that introduced me to the people who have supported my career all these years.

"HOLD ON TO
THE NIGHTS"

"Should've Known Better" isn't the only song from my debut album that caused a disagreement between me and EMI (which I ultimately named "Every Mistake Imaginable").

"Hold On to the Nights" was one of those new songs I wrote in that feverish writing stretch in the Los Feliz house. As is usually the case, the music came to me first. I wrote the verse and chorus quickly, followed by the now instantly identifiable piano intro. The bridge that follows the second chorus came a day or so later and employed a tool I started using around that time and continue to rely on today: I let the melody note dominate the process and find a chord underneath it that you wouldn't expect. It creates great opportunities for key changes and unique chord progressions. I actually use it twice in the bridge, starting with the first chord and at the end underneath the line "right theeeeeeere . . ." It sets up a great guitar solo and then a modulation, which pushes the song to a huge crescendo.

My original intent, however, was to produce the song with an ethereal and spacious atmosphere throughout. It was late 1986, and earlier that year I had purchased and subsequently memorized the entire Peter Gabriel album *So*. It was and is an iconic record featuring classics like "Sledgehammer" and "Big Time." But it was tracks like "Mercy Street" and "Don't Give Up" that moved me the most. I was really taken by Peter's production restraint. Those tracks are so minimally produced, leaving so much space for the vocal and the expression of the lyrics. I believed I could apply this to a more straight-ahead pop love song and create something fresh.

I recorded the entire song with just me playing piano to a click-tempo track. I then sang a scratch vocal, which I would later replace after the track had been built out. Little by little, my engineer and coproducer David Cole and I would add elements to enhance the song, always mindful to leave space around my voice to tell the story. I brought in Michael Landau, the brilliant session guitarist, who played lines and notes that were thematic and not typical guitar parts. I had envisioned a fretless bass on the song and was lucky enough to have Patrick O'Hearn from the band Missing Persons come in and play after a friend of a friend made our introduction.

I added a few light synthesizer pads and then brought in drummer Tris Imboden (whom I'd known through Kenny Loggins) to play some very sparse and tasteful percussion parts.

But as we got toward the end of the drum session, I realized we had an opportunity to create a real "moment" in the record. Not unlike the thrilling drum fill on Phil Collins's "In the Air Tonight," we could make a sudden and powerful transition from the calm, ethereal pace of the song into a big, arena-rock record. It took only two takes for Tris to deliver that "moment" and I knew we'd made a unique, artistic, and yet commercial record.

Months later, after my entire debut album was delivered to my label, several members of the radio promotion team came to me saying, "You need to go back in the studio and work on 'Hold On to the Nights.' Radio loves it and thinks it's a smash, but the drums take too long to kick in."

This was code for "Make your song sound like every other song." Though I'd not yet sold a single record, I dug in my heels and said no.

"Look, just because I could easily turn this into a big, arena-rock ballad doesn't mean I want to. This is a really personal lyric that people can relate to, and I want space around the words I'm singing so the listener can engage with them. Plus, I just don't want to make a record that sounds like everybody else's record. The record ends up pretty much where you guys are describing. I just want to take a more elegant journey getting there."

My manager warned me that resisting would likely create friction with the label and affect their support, but I knew I would forever feel shitty compromising. I also knew the suits were wrong.

"Hold On to the Nights" was my fourth single and became my first number 1 single on *Billboard*'s Hot 100. To this day, I can't sing the first line of the chorus—"Hold on to the nights"—without the audience in front of me immediately taking over on "Hold on to the memories." More than a number 1 single, it was also a song that really connected emotionally with millions of people. I have the letters to prove it.

RIDING THE SPEEDWAGON

About three months into my artist career, as my first single "Don't Mean Nothing" was nearing the top of the charts, I got an offer to be the opening act for REO Speedwagon on their upcoming summer tour. My band and I were playing clubs and small theaters and selling out, but opening for REO would put us in bigger outdoor venues. Their popularity on the charts was starting to decline a bit, but they were still selling concert tickets, and I wanted to have their audiences hear me.

Our first show together was in Cape Girardeau, Missouri, on a July night in 1987. When I was in my senior year of high school, REO was the biggest band in America. "Time for Me to Fly" was in constant rotation on the radio and their album *Hi-Infidelity* was massively popular. I had a copy myself. Now, a mere six years later, here I was, opening on their tour.

I had been told that being the opening act on a big tour is humbling and a mostly miserable experience. You get no sound checks because the headlining band uses up all the time, you only get to play for your allotted time (mine was forty-five minutes), if you go a second over, you'll likely have your lights and sound turned off, mid-song, and there's a good chance you'll at least start your set to a small number of people because most fans come later to see the main act on the bill.

On that summer afternoon in Cape G, the guys in REO had been delayed a bit, so I had been told early on my band and I would not be getting a sound check. *Figures*, I thought. So imagine my surprise when REO's lead singer, Kevin Cronin, comes knocking on the door of the shitty, dilapidated trailer my band and I were sharing behind the stage, and says, "Hey, Richard! Welcome to the tour! Listen, man, I'm so sorry you didn't get a sound check today. It was beyond our control. But please know we'll do everything we can in the future to avoid this problem."

And for the next twenty-five or so shows we did with them, we always got a sound check. We also had the members of the band routinely stand in the wings and not only watch our show but also give us thumbs-ups and high fives. Not only did we never have the lights and sound turned off, about five shows in, I was told to go ahead and play an extra song at the end of my set as an encore because the crowds were getting bigger and getting there earlier. Once, on my way to a radio interview, I heard Kevin on the same station saying, "Hey, if you're planning to see us tonight, do yourself a favor and get there early to see Richard Marx and his band. They're great." His is the kind of generosity that only comes from artists who are either very kind, or very secure, or both. The guys in REO were both.

At one point, about a month in, REO took a week off. I couldn't afford not to work, and I was offered the same situation, opening for Night Ranger, who were pretty big at the time. My band and I flew to Oregon for the first of three shows. The Night Ranger guys weren't late at all, but we still didn't get a sound check. I closed my forty-five-minute set that night with "Don't Mean Nothing," which had a chant/singalong with the audience at the end of it. The crowd was going nuts, so I did one more round of the chant, which would have put the end of my set at forty-five minutes and about thirty-eight seconds. At exactly the forty-five-minute mark, the Night Ranger crew shut off our sound and turned off the lights. The crowd erupted in boos and gave a very chilly reception to the "headlining" band as they took the stage.

When we saw the REO guys a few days later to reconvene that tour, every member of my band and I walked up to the members of the REO band and crew and hugged them. And when I became a headlining act, I made sure that every opening act on my tour was either given a sound check or an apology and explanation for not getting one. I'm proud to say that thirty-four years later, Kevin Cronin and I are still good friends.

"EDGE OF A BROKEN HEART"

By the time 1987 became 1988, my career was what anyone would consider hot. I was releasing my third single, "Endless Summer Nights" from my debut album, after seeing the first two ("Don't Mean Nothing" and "Should've Known Better") both reach number 3 on the charts. I was also beginning my first headlining tour in large clubs and theaters that would last till the fall of '88.

By the time the first tour wound down, I'd been on the road for fifteen months straight and had played over two hundred shows. There were many times when I did two shows in one night, and I recall at least one masochistic day when I played an afternoon show at a high school in Milwaukee, then drove immediately to open for REO at 8:00 p.m. in Madison, and then jumped right back into the bus and hauled ass to Green Bay, where I played a late-night club show. I also remembered that I did *not* have the next night off.

I was exhausted but exhilarated by the heady experience of having my records rising up the charts and the venues we played getting bigger and bigger. Each day was pretty much straight out of the movie *Groundhog Day*. Wake up around 6:30 a.m., guzzle some iced coffee, and go to the biggest radio station in whatever town I was in for their drive-time morning show, where I'd endure the hosts' "zany" on-air "antics" with a smile, then be driven across town to the second-biggest station for some more predictable questions the jocks thought were insanely clever like, "Any relation to the Marx Brothers? Aaaah-hahahaha!!!!!" Next, lunch with either the local sales or promotion person from my label, then *maybe* (on a lucky day) a quick one-hour power nap before heading off to the venue for sound check, followed by another radio interview backstage before the show. Hit the stage and finally play my set, then a quick bite in my dressing room and either onto the tour bus or back to my hotel room to sleep as many hours as possible (although it takes so long to wind down after a show for screaming fans that "sleep" was often elusive) only to wake up and do it all again.

Let me be crystal clear: I'm not complaining. I was always, even when bitching to my manager or friends, very aware that I not only had an incredibly fun job, but I was doing exactly what I'd dreamed of doing. That said, it required great stamina. It also left extremely little time for my great love: creating new songs. I did write on the road, but only in small windows of moments between all the other activities and commitments. So when, in early '88, my then-manager Allen Kovac called me about writing and producing a song for a new all-girl hard-rock band, I was both completely psyched about it and incredulous that I could physically pull it off.

The band Vixen had just been signed by the same label I recorded for, EMI. They were also being managed by Allen, and they were nearly finished recording their debut album. Allen called me in some town somewhere in the world and told me about this four-piece group, saying he felt they had a real shot to be huge. "They could be the female Bon Jovi!" said Allen, with his typical over-the-top hyperbole. "But we don't have a first single. We've got good songs but need that no-brainer, one-listen smash. And I want you to write and produce it."

Allen knew my background was in writing songs for and with other artists; he knew I was prolific and knew how to write a hit chorus. They needed to have this song mixed and delivered to the label within two weeks, and I only had one forty-eight-hour window between Allen's phone call and the delivery due date. I wrote the melody and music that night after my show, and when the chorus melody revealed itself, I instinctively sang "I've been livin' on the edge of a broken heart."

Lyrics have always been much more difficult for me to write than music. I mean, I can always write lyrics, but I'm talking about *great* lyrics. Historically, I've tended to write my songs by myself. But in my years of collaborating, it's almost always lyrics with which I've gotten help. In the case of this song, I not only needed great lyrics, I needed them fast. So I rang up the best lyricist I know: Fee Waybill.

With me in a St. Louis hotel after my concert and Fee at his home in Westwood Village, we wrote the lyrics over the phone the night before I flew to LA to produce the track, with Fee having written a great first draft on his own. Any changes I want to make on lyrics Fee writes are never based on quality or content, but rather only on whether or not the words he's written *sing* as well as they could. There are many words that just don't sound pleasing to the ear when sung. Fee is, at heart, a poet and doesn't concern himself with how a word sounds when it's sung. But I think that's a crucial component of a great song, and certainly of a hit song. I can't recall the handful of words in Fee's original draft of "Edge of a Broken Heart" that I wanted to change, but there's no ego between us, so we jumped on the phone and modified them easily.

The next day I went to a rehearsal space in Burbank to meet the girls in Vixen for the first time. Roxy Petrucci was the drummer, Share Pederson on bass, Jan Kuehnemund on guitar, and on lead vocal was Janet Gardner. The main reason I wanted to work with the band, aside from my manager's request, was Janet's voice. I loved her sound. Very powerful but clearly versatile. I was really looking forward to producing her vocal. The girls were all sprawled across two large couches at one end of the large rehearsal room, each wearing the epitome of classic '80s hair-metal garb. Leather jackets with studs and fringe; skin-tight jeans with patches and strategic holes in the knees, as well as frayed at the bottom; depending on the girl, either big, clunky biker boots or snakeskin cowboy boots; and all covered in scarves, chains, and tons of bracelets. Like a million other people in the late '80s, none of these ladies could ever possibly sneak up behind you without creating a cacophony of noise from all the silver, gold, and beaded shit they were wearing.

They all stood up and greeted me warmly. While they were all certainly attractive, Janet was particularly striking, and through the process of making the record and several interactions thereafter, she and I developed a harmless crush on one another.

After a few minutes of small talk during which the girls outed Jan as having a poster of me on her wall for the past several months (which flattered me greatly), I grabbed a guitar and started teaching them "Edge of a Broken Heart." We were going into the studio the following day, and I had a concert out of town the night after that, so it meant we had to fully record the song, including lead and background vocals, in one day. That was not a common practice at that time, and though I felt pressure, I actually thrived on it. I had hoped that spending a few hours with them the day before to learn and rehearse the song would facilitate our time in the studio.

The girls really loved the song (looking back, I still can't believe everybody just took the leap of faith that I'd not only write the *right* song but be able to produce it in a matter of hours), and we started working out the parts. I felt very quickly that it was going to go well. The only concern I had at that rehearsal was the guitar player, Jan. There was no doubt she was an accomplished player, but she seemed quite slow to learn the parts and play them correctly. Since we recorded the rehearsal on a cassette, I figured she'd have a night to hone her parts and all would be fine the next day.

I was wrong.

We started the session at A&M Studios in Hollywood (now Jim Henson Studios) in studio A at 10:00 a.m. Since we had to cut *everything* in one day, there was no luxury of starting at a rock and roll–preferred hour later in the afternoon. The recording engineer, Brian Foraker, and the studio staff had been there setting up since 8:00, and I arrived around 9:30 to make sure we could be ready to get cracking when the girls showed up. Everyone was prompt, and so we dove into recording, with Roxy, Share, and Jan out in the large live recording room, and Janet in a nearby isolated vocal booth.

After about an hour of tweaking sounds and playing the song several times, two things were clear to me. One being that the main rhythm track of bass and drums would be easily done in no time. The other being that getting great guitar tracks from Jan would be extremely difficult, if not impossible. I kept trying again and again to be encouraging as I would stop the takes at various points in the song, explaining that Jan wasn't playing her part right. It wasn't even that it was wrong notes. It was just completely lacking in tone and style. It was rhythmically all over the place and just sounded so amateurish.

I could see she was getting frustrated, and she could see the same in me. Normally, I'd have taken all the time needed to work with her and get a killer performance, even if it meant doing it line by line. But the clock was ticking fast, and I knew that if I didn't make a judgment call, the whole record could easily be a casualty.

After at least another ninety minutes of trying to get even a marginally good "full band" take, I pushed the talk-back button and said, "Okay, let's go again." Only this time, in the control room where only myself and the engineer could hear, I muted Jan's guitar tracks and listened only to the bass and drums. Roxy and Share were in a great zone, and after a couple minor tweaks, I had a perfect take.

I said, "NICE, ladies! We've got the take!"

As the girls walked into the control room, I knew they'd want to hear a playback, and Jan's guitar performance was still far from any good. I said, "You guys, I just need you to trust me. Time is running out and I still have all of Janet's vocals and backgrounds to do, as well as any keyboards I'm going to add. But it's going to be killer."

They weren't thrilled about it, but they each reluctantly hugged me and left the studio so I could zero in on the other work. I already felt a bit of a connection with Janet, so when the other girls left, I said to her, "Can you give me a couple hours to put this track together in a better way so you'll really enjoy singing to it?"

She gave me a somewhat suspect look but agreed and went to a nearby restaurant for a bite. The door behind her hadn't even closed when I grabbed the studio phone and called Mike Landau.

All through the '80s and into the '90s, Mike was the busiest and most sought-after session guitarist. He played on nearly everyone's records, from Rod Stewart and Steve Perry to Stevie Nicks and Kenny

Loggins, plus hundreds more. Having worked with him on my own album, I knew Mike was not only an amazing musician, but also a really quick study. By some fluke, I caught him at home where he'd just returned after a long morning session. I explained that I had an emergency, and he arrived at the studio about forty-five minutes later, accompanied by a van carrying his extensive guitar-god gear. As expected, within an hour, the guitar parts were not only done but magnificent. It suddenly sounded like a big hit rock record.

Janet returned to the studio just as Mike was leaving and stared at me with an icy glare.

"What's going on?"

I said, "Please sit down. I need to explain."

I told her I'd had to mute Jan's tracks because I couldn't get a decent rhythm take, and that I had decided hours before I would need to bring in another guitarist. Janet was livid.

"Who the fuck do you think you are? We're a BAND! We don't use studio musicians! This is bullshit!"

I said, "Look, I get it. But these are peculiar circumstances, and if I didn't do this, the whole thing would be fucked. So before you yell at me some more, all I ask is that you listen to the track."

She graciously took a deep breath and turned her chair toward the big speakers in the control room. The engineer hit Play. And when the song faded and the Stop button was pushed, she just sat there, staring straight ahead. Finally, after what seemed an hour, she quietly said, "Jan could never have played like that. It's . . . amazing. Holy shit."

I knew I needed to be the one to try to explain things to Jan, but Janet insisted that it should come from her. Regardless, all that had to happen later. I needed to get Janet's vocals recorded, which turned out to be a fun and effortless task. She sang the song as if she'd written it herself, and I loved that no matter what I suggested she try, she nailed it immediately every time.

By the time her lead vocal and all of her background vocals were complete, and I had added some simple synthesizer pads I played myself, it was past midnight. I had a 6:00 a.m. pick-up for a 7:30 flight to my next gig.

Fast asleep while my plane was in the air, Janet made the call to Jan to tell her the good news/bad news. The bad news was I'd had to use a session guitarist on the song. The good news was that he didn't care if he was credited, so no one other than those in the studio would know it wasn't her. To Jan, there was absolutely no good news whatsoever, and she went ape-shit. I totally understood her anger. I felt horrible. But I didn't see another alternative under the circumstances. It wasn't at all that Jan wasn't a good player. It was that she couldn't do what was needed at that high a level within those time restrictions. A couple days later, I got a call from my (and Vixen's) manager, Allen Kovac, saying that everyone was raving about the track and that it would be the band's first single.

About six weeks later, a video was filmed for the song in LA, and I happened to be playing a show in town the next day, so I was asked to come by the filming and make a brief cameo. It would be the first time I'd see the members of Vixen since the recording session, and I had heard from Janet that Jan, if anything, had only grown more angry and bitter about my replacing her guitar parts. In fact, she told me that Jan had now taken to regularly using the poster she had of me on her wall as a dartboard.

My cameo in their video was simply me greeting them with kisses on a street in Hollywood. Janet, Share, and Roxy were genuinely happy to see me. Jan smiled for the camera but was pretty icy to me when we saw each other. In retrospect, I should have said to her, "Look, I know you're very angry with me, but let's go somewhere and talk and see if we can put this behind us." But there were crew people everywhere shooting the video, and it just wasn't the time or place.

"Edge of a Broken Heart" became a hit at both rock and pop radio and the video got heavy play on MTV. The band's debut album went gold, and they did some pretty big tours with major rock bands. They were never able to follow that success on the charts and ultimately broke up within a few years, a very common fate for bands in the '80s.

Although Janet and I stayed in touch now and then (she sang background vocals on "Hands in Your Pocket" on my 1991 *Rush Street* album), I never saw the other girls again. Jan had left the music industry and was living in Colorado when she passed away from cancer in 2013 at the age of fifty-nine. Although I'm sure our studio incident had faded from her mind long ago, it saddened me greatly that we never got the chance to talk and put it behind us.

While it wasn't one of the biggest hits I was involved with, it's a song that people clearly remember from that time. A couple years ago at one of my solo acoustic shows, in between songs, I heard a woman's voice yell out "Edge of a Broken Heart!" So, I sang a chorus from it, and the whole audience cheered.

"BURNING OF THE HEART" (THE RICHARD MARX AMENDMENT)

"Don't Mean Nothing" launched my career quickly and decidedly. As soon as the song began to peak on the charts, we readied my follow-up single, "Should've Known Better" by shooting a video in downtown LA and within a few weeks, the new single was climbing the charts and passing "Don't Mean Nothing" on its way down. The same thing happened with the next two singles, "Endless Summer Nights" and "Hold On to the Nights." Each single did progressively better on the charts, with "Hold On" reaching number 1 in the summer of 1988.

In addition to the success of the album and its singles, I toured exhaustively for fifteen months, starting in small clubs while promoting "Don't Mean Nothing," graduating to larger clubs (with dressing rooms!) and opening for bands like REO Speedwagon and Night Ranger at outdoor amphitheaters, to playing smaller theaters and eventually headlining the same amphitheaters I'd played the summer before as an opener. It was a slow and steady build, and I worked my ass off, sometimes doing as many as thirteen and fourteen nights in a row with many of those days having two shows in a day. I was twenty-three, healthy, hungry, and laser-beam focused.

I appeared on as many television shows as would allow me. I was usually up at 6:00 a.m. on tour to do live morning in-studio radio interviews and performances in whatever town we were playing that night and doing phone interviews with music journalists around the world. I barely had the time or energy to eat. But I was seizing the moment, and, in retrospect, I'd have done nothing differently.

All that hard work paid off: a Top Ten double platinum album (it would eventually sell over four million), with four Top Three singles. By the time my third single, "Endless Summer Nights" was climbing the chart, it was that time of year when Grammy nominations came out. People around me were saying, "There's no way you don't win Best New Artist." It was true that no other debut artist had had close to a better year than I had, but I don't like to overthink those things. I just kept working.

So, one morning soon after, the Grammy nominations were announced, and I was nominated. For Best Rock Vocal Performance. I wasn't even nominated for Best New Artist. While I was thrilled to be nominated in the rock category for "Don't Mean Nothing" (I was nominated against Bob Seger, Sting, Tina Turner, and Bruce Springsteen, who won), I was puzzled, as were my label and manager. Well, my label and I were puzzled. My manager, Allen, was livid. After some irate phone calls, he got the story from someone at the academy who awards the Grammys. "There's no question Richard was the most successful new artist of the year, and the stellar quality of his work speaks for itself. He was simply disqualified for Best New Artist because he released a record two years ago. So this album and its singles are not eligible."

What? What the fuck are they talking about?

Oooohhhhhhh.

In 1986, I was a few months away from meeting Bruce Lundvall and getting signed to EMI. I was writing songs for various artists but mostly making my living as a background singer and would occasionally sing demos for songwriters and producers. One day I received a call from Pat Leonard, who had co-produced the Madonna record I had sung on the year prior.

"I've been hired to score the new Tom Hanks movie and write songs for the soundtrack," Pat said. "I've got a song I need a young male voice on to pitch to the movie people. Are you free to sing the demo tomorrow?"

I arrived at the studio the next day and Pat taught me the song quickly. It was a very "movie-soundtrack"-ish, up-tempo pop-rock tune called "Burning of the Heart," and I loved singing it because it had me using most of my vocal range. Pat was thrilled with my vocal on the demo and said, "Shit, man. Too bad *you* can't sing it in the movie. But the soundtrack is on Arista and [then–Arista president] Clive Davis has some new young male singer he's putting on the soundtrack." I was just happy to make my $250 session fee. I thanked Pat for calling me and went home.

About a week later Pat called and said, "We recut that song with the guy on Arista, but when the movie execs heard it they said, 'What is this? This isn't what we heard last week.'"

Pat had sold them on the song by playing my demo version, and now they were disappointed in this new one. Even the film's director, the late Garry Marshall of *Pretty Woman* fame called Clive Davis and said, "This song is featured very prominently in a key scene in the film and I don't like this new guy's voice. I like the demo, and that's what I want in the film." So some lawyer from Arista contacted me, and I made a deal to be the artist on that one song on their soundtrack. I was not signed to Arista. It was a one-off.

The film *Nothing in Common* starred Tom Hanks and Jackie Gleason as father and son. It was mildly successful, but the soundtrack (which featured Christopher Cross and Carly Simon, among others) was anything but. No hit singles and no album sales. My track on the album wasn't ever released as a single, and the whole project came and went very quickly.

Cut to 1988 and Grammy nominations time. We thought I was a shoo-in for a Best New Artist nod, and apparently, the Grammy voting committee was about to make that a reality. Until they received a call from Clive Davis, I was told by several people in the know. Clive was still angry because a similar situation had occurred with his artist, Whitney Houston, a year or two prior. She was disqualified for Best New Artist for having sung a duet on a Teddy Pendergrass album. "You can't nominate Richard Marx," Clive said. "He sang on an Arista soundtrack. Technically, his debut album isn't his first release."

And the committee had to agree.

Well, not really. They didn't *have* to agree. They could have said, "You know, this is ridiculous. We need to rethink this category's requirements. We're basically penalizing artists who've had massive breakouts if they recorded something years ago that no one ever heard." But instead, they walked the "committee line," and that was that.

Someone told me that in addition to others, Gladys Knight voiced her displeasure at my disqualification, just as she had when it happened to Whitney. That criticism led the committee to change the parameters the following year, and at the time, the written changes were titled "The Richard Marx Amendment."

19

"RIGHT HERE WAITING"
(BARBRA, PART II)

Having your first album spawn four, big hit singles sounds like a dream to anyone, but I have to say, the pressure that comes with that is not something one would gladly invite into their creative life.

The label had me touring incessantly and doing all the crazy shit one has to do to desperately try to not let the train slow down. I couldn't keep track of the cities and towns I was in unless I'd glance at my hotel room key or ask the driver where we were on my way back from the show. It got so bad that more than I'd like to admit I called an audience by the name of a different town. Big mistake. A little like moaning the wrong name to the woman you're making love to. Not. Cool. I finally started writing the name of the town where I was performing on the set list at my feet onstage every night. Since that first whirlwind tour, and making that mistake a couple times, I've never made it again, I'm proud to say, because I eye that set list a few times throughout the show. The point is that I was in the midst of a career tornado that had only just begun.

One day before a sound check in some town, my manager called me.

"Barbra Streisand's office called and Barbra wants to speak to you."

"Wow. Really? Did they say what it was about?" I asked.

"Nope, just asked that you call."

I called the number and Barbra's longtime manager, Marty Erlichman, answered.

He said that Barbra was a fan of my records and songwriting and was about to start a new project and would like to meet with me about writing something for her.

I was due back in LA in about two weeks, so we set up a meeting at Lion Share Studios, a studio in which I'd recorded many times. As I drove to the meeting I couldn't help but be a bit nervous. While I was always more a rock and roll fan, I knew a bunch of Barbra's records by heart, and was always profoundly impressed by career longevity. In 1988, she was still an icon and she still is today.

I walked down the long mirrored hallway of Lion Share into Studio C and there she sat, with an assistant who immediately left us alone to talk. I decided not to mention that we had met a few years before, in that very same studio, as there was no way she'd have remembered. She was beautiful, wearing a long, black sweater. Her hair was just the right amount of perfectly messy. And I distinctly remember how great she smelled. It wasn't particularly "perfume-y" but rather Barbra's own intoxicating scent. To put it simply, she was sexy. Very sexy. Her demeanor put me quickly at ease, and we just sat and talked as if we'd known each other for years.

We talked about some of the songs she'd recorded, and I mentioned one that was very obscure and never a hit single called "Lullaby for Myself," written by Rupert Holmes (who had a massive hit himself in 1979 with "Escape [The Pina Colada Song]").

She said, "Oh, yeah! I love that one, too. I liked that whole album." She was referring to the album *Superman*, which came out when I was fourteen years old.

I said, "Yes, great album. But, and I hope this doesn't embarrass you, the only thing better than the music was the back cover. That back cover helped me through puberty."

She stared at me for a second as I realized I had just really fucking overshared with a complete stranger, but then she reared back in her chair laughing.

"Oh my god! Really? That's so sweet!"

We still talk about that exchange over dinner sometimes.

"Look," I said, "one thing I know about you, Barbra, is that I need some direction from you because I know you're very specific about what you want."

She smiled and said, "The truth is I'm never really sure what I want. But I'm very specific about what I don't want. I don't want to sing songs from the perspective of a woman who has been victim-ized. I don't want to sing weak songs. I want to sing and write from a place of strength. And pride."

I wanted nothing more than to come up with the perfect song for her, but I was headed back on the road the next day for a slew of more concerts. Then I thought about this little song I'd written only a few weeks prior. I felt it was a really good song but way too personal for me to record on my next album.

Right around this time, I couldn't see Cynthia because she was away in Africa making a film, and I was on the road doing a tour. I had made arrangements with my agent and manager to give me two weeks off in the middle of Cynthia's three-month shoot. She was filming in Johannesburg, and I planned to fly there to be with her.

This was during the peak of apartheid when many Americans, particularly celebrities, were trying to bring as much press attention, and inspire as much outrage about it, as possible. The South African government was equally combative and often made entry into the country anywhere from difficult to impossible. Two days before my scheduled flight, the South African government, assuming that I was on my way to protest apartheid, denied my visa, forbidding me entry.

Now not only was I not going to see my girlfriend for three solid months (a lifetime in the early days of a relationship before cell phones or the internet), but I had two weeks off the road with nothing to do. I didn't greet this development with a sense of joy. It never dawned on me that I could use a vacation back then. I was just totally bummed. And when I get sad or depressed, the best thing for me to do is to make music.

I called my friend, Bruce Gaitsch, with whom I'd cowritten "Don't Mean Nothing," and said, "I'm coming over, and we need to write the angriest rock song ever. I'm bummed and pissed off and I need to purge."

Within half an hour of arriving at Bruce's garage studio, which he named Frantic, we had almost finished this blistering tune of angst surrounded by huge arena-rock guitar riffs. I called it "Arrow Through My Heart."

We were finishing lyrics when Bruce's phone rang and he stepped into his house to take the call. I walked over to the electronic keyboard he had set up and started to play a piano melody. Before I was even aware of what I was doing, the whole melody practically wrote itself. I was sure it had to be someone else's existing song. It was too memorable.

Then, very atypical of my writing process—where the music comes fast but the lyrics need a decent gestation period, thought, and plenty of time to reveal themselves—words I wanted to say to Cynthia in the moment came flooding from my lips. I guess I missed her so terribly that this whole song just fell out of me in a heap of angst and loneliness.

Bruce popped his head into the garage and said, "Dude! What the fuck is that? That's gorgeous."

We recorded a quick piano-vocal demo within about twenty minutes, and the song was fully born. I had no intention of including it on an actual album, as it felt much too personal. Almost like publishing a love letter in the newspaper.

Weeks later, after my meeting with Barbra Streisand, I thought it might be a great song for her. I sent it to her house via messenger. The very next day she left me a voicemail, which I have kept to this day.

"Hi Richard, it's Barbra. I got your song and I think it's an interesting melody. But, I need you to rewrite the lyrics because I'm not going to be 'Right Here Waiting' for anybody."

It would take many years before Barbra did, in fact, record one of my songs. (The first was the 1998 duet with Vince Gill, "If You Ever Leave Me.") Her turning down of "Right Here Waiting" didn't make me rewrite the lyrics for her, because the song was written from such a personal place, it would've felt wrong.

Soon after, I was recording my second album, *Repeat Offender*, and was diligent about filling the album with up-tempo rock songs that would also serve my live show. I decided that aside from the mid-tempo anthem "Children of the Night," which I'd written about a homeless shelter, I wanted only one ballad, and had already recorded a song I'd written with my dear friend Fee Waybill called "No Sleepless Nights." It was a huge power ballad that got a great reaction from people wandering in and out of the studio sessions. But the simple piano demo I'd recorded of "Right Here Waiting" had been played for a number of people, and the reaction to that song was on another level.

I decided I would spend a full day recording it and then see which ballad got the best reception from the ears I allowed to hear it. The track was recorded in a matter of a few hours at Lion Share Studios on a November day in 1988. Just keyboards and Spanish guitar. No drums. No power. No fanfare. I walked out to the microphone to sing the vocal and placed the typewritten lyrics on the music stand, put on the headphones that were hanging on a hook to the side of the stand, and heard the track come through into my ears. My mouth opened and out came, "Oceans apart . . . day after day . . . and I slowly go insane . . ."

Not really needing to refer to the lyrics, I sang the whole song down top to bottom with my eyes closed, and as the last chord rang, I looked through the glass into the control room where my engineer and coproducer David Cole, the studio's assistant engineer Peter Doell, and Fee were sitting, listening. Fee had just dropped by the studio to say hi and asked what we were doing. I told him about the simple ballad I was attempting to record. He hadn't heard it and was already depositing mental royalty checks in his head from our "No Sleepless Nights" that he was sure would be *the* ballad on my new album.

There was a long silence as David and Peter just stared at me with a look that said, "We just witnessed something really fucking magical happen." The silence was broken by Fee, who stood up, pressed the talk-back button, and loudly said, *"Goddamn it! My fucking song is off the record!"*

He was right. "Right Here Waiting" became *the* ballad on the new album, and the biggest song of my life.

20

"ANGELIA"

Historically, the act of making a new album has always been a deliberate and intentioned decision. Back in the heyday, that decision was often made for me by the standards of the music industry. Back in the 1980s, to go more than two years without releasing a new album was considered anathema. You were risking your fan base forgetting about you and moving on to other artists, and more concerning, you had your record label constantly up your ass for new product. It was the era of "album-tour-album-tour," a treadmill on which you either stayed or got thrown off.

I would come back from a yearlong tour, exhausted and wanting to just hang out with family and friends and watch *NYPD Blue*, and ten minutes after hanging the clothes from my suitcase back into my closet, my label would be asking, "So, when can we expect some new tracks?" They wanted to strike while the iron was hot and breed more profit ASAP, and the fans wanted new earworms. The pressure to feed the beast was not inconsequential, and the only thing that could sate the hunger was new songs.

I've heard many artists say they are unable to write songs while on the road. That the mind-set of being a touring performer handcuffs the mind-set of the songwriter. I have never experienced this. I released my first album in the summer of 1987 and started touring immediately, not stopping for fifteen months. I knew that, unlike my first, my second album would not only be highly anticipated but also scrutinized in a way none of my work had been before—by my label, the critics, and the fans. That's a lot of pressure for any artist, let alone someone in their midtwenties still newly navigating life and career.

There's a term, the "sophomore jinx," that's been applied to authors, film directors, and screenwriters, but mainly it's a potential albatross around the necks of young singers and songwriters. The idea being that you had your whole life to create your debut but only a limited time to come up with the goods a second time. Many creative people cave to this pressure and end up being "one-hit wonders."

I was aware of these pitfalls early on, and I knew that as tiring and mentally draining as touring can be, I needed to be writing my second album while on the road. It never really became a challenge for me. I would be so amped up after a show that I couldn't sleep for hours, and I wasn't into partying, so I would head back to my hotel room or into the back lounge of my tour bus and write songs. It also helped that although I did occasionally collaborate, I mostly wrote songs by myself. I would often work on songs well into the early hours of daylight and then sleep until sound-check time. It was a vampire-esque existence, but I was determined to have better songs ready for my second album than had been on my debut.

When I look at the track listing for *Repeat Offender*, almost every title evokes a memory of me writing it in some town on the road.

The opening track, "Nothin' You Can Do About It," was written on a jog through the campus of the University of Colorado a few hours before my show in Denver. This was well before cell phones, so I'd always carry a small handheld cassette recorder with me everywhere I went. I remember coming up with the entire melody and the opening lines, "Have you heard the news? I'm doin' what I said I would." Those lines came from my subconscious and inspired the rest of the song to be a huge "fuck you" to all the people who had told me I'd never make it in the music business, including one person in particular who knows who he is.

"Children of the Night" was written in the guest room of a friend's house in Nashville at 3:00 a.m. after an outdoor show at the city's Riverfront for what local police estimated to be 100,000 people.

I wrote "Real World" in the first few weeks of my first tour while being driven the sixty miles from my home in Los Feliz to Riverside, where I opened for the Fabulous Thunderbirds. My band and I had been playing forty-five-minute sets consisting mostly of songs from my debut album, but also a couple cover songs like "Chain of Fools" by Aretha Franklin and "Stay with Me" by the Faces. I very much wanted to have only my original songs in my show, and that meant coming up with new material while touring. I also wanted another fun, up-tempo rocker in the set, and that's how "Real World" was born.

It's a very simple rockabilly vibe, and the melody came to me entirely within about twenty minutes. As the lyrics began to reveal themselves during the car ride (which was fortunately on a Friday afternoon and took two hours instead of the average fifty minutes, giving me more time to write), I decided I would teach the song to my band at sound check, and we would perform it that night.

I arrived with about 75 percent of the lyrics done, taught the song to the band during sound check, and finished the lyrics backstage about an hour before showtime. I knew I couldn't memorize all the words that quickly, so I placed the handwritten lyrics on a large sheet of paper taped to the stage floor, next to my microphone stand, and we debuted "Real World" at that Riverside show. The fans were up dancing to it immediately, and I remember by the last chorus seeing some of the faces in the crowd actually singing the words "real world" along with me. It was surreal.

(Quick side note: during that car ride I wrote the lines, "I'm gonna live with a lady on a quiet beach / I'm gonna have me three kids, maybe one of each." At the time, I was dating Cynthia, who would two years later become my first wife. We would end up spending most of our marriage in a house on Lake Michigan, on a property with our own private beach. We would also eventually have three sons, with three entirely different personalities. So I kind of consider myself quite the prophet.)

The melody for "Angelia" arrived in my brain during a lunch with executives from the Australian branch of my label. We were at a popular restaurant in Sydney called Doyles, which offers beautiful views of the harbor. I knew it was special and that I needed to record it so I wouldn't forget it. I didn't have my trusty handheld recorder with me, so I decided to find a payphone, call my answering machine at home, and sing the melody onto the voicemail. I'd done this successfully many times on tour in the States when I was out and about and without a means of recording, and people always got a kick out the fact that I'd figured out a unique and crafty way of keeping good ideas from disappearing into the mental ether.

I stopped a busboy and asked where I might find a phone, and he said, "In the men's room." So, there I was, singing the melody to what would become a Top Five *Billboard* pop single into the receiver while several men relieved themselves a mere few feet away. I should also mention that the ninety-second phone call from Sydney to Los Angeles in 1988 cost me about twenty-five bucks.

Though I knew it was wise to have a recording of the melody, I never actually needed it. It was etched in my brain in the hours and days that followed the lunch at Doyles, and all I needed to do was write lyrics to it. The music felt a bit sorrowful to me, and I began to assemble a lyrical story of lost love. My long-distance voice message even contained vowel sounds which appeared to say, "Where you runnin' to now?" I decided the song title would be a girl's name, and my melody required it to be a name with four syllables. But I wanted it to be an uncommon and beautiful name, and I was having trouble finding one I loved.

A few weeks later, back on tour and flying with my band from Houston to Dallas, I was settled groggily in my seat when the flight attendant started rolling a beverage cart down the aisle. I was in an aisle seat and as she got to my row, I noticed two things. First, that she was extremely beautiful, and second, that her name tag read "Angelia." She offered me a drink and I said, "I'll have a tomato juice, thanks. By the way, that's a beautiful name. Angelia." I pronounced it as I assumed it should be, with the first A sounding like "and" or "bad." She smiled and said, "Oh, thank you. Actually, I pronounce it 'Angelia.'" (With the A sounding like the letter A.) My eyes flew open wide and I said, "Holy shit! That's it! THAT'S IT!!!" Before she could call for an Air Marshall, I explained about needing a name for my song. She said she was extremely flattered and that she hoped it would be a hit.

It never fails to truly amaze me how songs are sometimes so randomly and inexplicably created.

21

THE ELVIS INCIDENT

E ver since I can remember, I've been an Elvis fan. I can't recall the first time I became aware of him, but I must have been about two or three, and that was that. I became one of "those" Elvis fans, the ones who collected his records and memorabilia (minus the hair strands or toenail clippings) and tragically knew more about Elvis's life and career than anything I ever studied in school. I've seen every one of his movies at least eight or nine times. I have every original record and movie poster. For years, I even used Elvis movie character names as aliases on tour in hotels. I can't belabor the point enough that I was "Elvis-ed" out of my mind.

My adoration for the King became something my own fans were aware of, and very sweetly they started bringing Elvis-themed gifts to me at concerts. I'd go backstage and there would be Elvis posters, Elvis books, Elvis wallets, Elvis-shaped cookies—you name it. The one thing I made a point to keep were Elvis tee-shirts, because starting near the end of my first long tour, I got in the habit of changing into an Elvis tee for the encore sections of the show, and I liked to have a variety to choose from.

By the second tour, for *Repeat Offender*, I had amassed quite a collection, which I kept in the bottom drawer of a road case. The road case was always put in my dressing room each night, and I would lay out whichever Elvis shirt I wanted to wear that night, and my then wardrobe assistant, Rosie, would bring it to the wings on the side of the stage for me to change into for the encore.

In the later months of that fifteen-month tour, we played the Greek Theatre in Los Angeles, and had several celebs attend the two-night run: Rick Springfield was there, David Coverdale from Whitesnake, Kelsey Grammer. And the first night, I got word that Priscilla Presley wanted to see the show. I was so excited. The King's *wife*! (Okay, ex-wife, but *still!*)

Priscilla was accompanied by our mutual friend and ex-Memphis Mafia member, Jerry Schilling, and I arranged to put them in the front row. I played to her several times throughout the show, all the while anxious to meet her afterward backstage. She looked beautiful and was smiling all night.

Because it was LA and I had not only VIPs to see but lots of label execs and radio people, I had forgotten to pick out an Elvis shirt from the now huge pile in the bottom of my road case and lay it out for Rosie. As we hit the last notes of the main set, I ran into the wings and said, "Rosie! I forgot to lay out a shirt. Just grab one from the drawer right now. Hurry!"

Within seconds, Rosie had the shirt and in the darkness of the wings I changed into it and walked back onto the stage for "Hold On to the Nights," the first of three songs in the encore. I sat at the piano in the dark and began playing the song's intro as the lights dramatically came up. As I began the song I started thinking: *Here I am, playing two sold-out nights at the Greek Theatre, a venue where I have seen so many of my favorite artists play. And the audience has been amazing! And holy* SHIT! *Priscilla Presley is* front row! *This is like a dream. I can't even wrap my brain arou—*

And then it hit me. And the facts before me were these:

I was playing my number 1 single in front of thousands of people, Priscilla Presley is front row watching my every move, I'm wearing a shirt with a photo of her ex-husband, the King of Rock and Roll on it. And just below his photo are the words: "ELVIS HAD A STINKY BUTT."

It was a shirt a fan had given me that I thought was funny. And of the forty or fifty shirts in that road case drawer, Rosie had somehow randomly chosen that one.

My heart sank and my mouth went dry. I don't know how I even kept singing. I immediately looked down to see how much of the phrase (mercifully written at the bottom of the shirt) was visible, and I chose to sabotage my piano playing in order to try to somehow tuck that fucking shirt in. I used my left hand, abandoning any bass notes for a bar or two, and tucked it in enough that it would be hard to read.

But then I remembered that I always dramatically leave the piano and walk to the front of the stage for the last chorus. I did that, but I must have looked like Quasimodo, all hunched over to ensure I wouldn't pull the offensive phrase into view right in front of Priscilla. I finished the set and took the fastest bow in history and ran off the stage.

Priscilla came back afterward, raved about the show, and was as sweet as I could have imagined. She either didn't see what the shirt said or saw it and ignored it. Either way, I dodged a bullet.

2 2

"YOU'RE THE VOICE"

Very soon after my first taste of mainstream success in 1987, as my second single, "Should've Known Better" was climbing into the Top Five and my debut album was nearing the Top Ten, I made it known to my manager and my record company that I wanted more. Yes, I wanted more success and hits overall, but this was a specific "more." I wanted my music known all over the world.

You must remember that in 1987 there was no internet. Moreover, most countries didn't even have access to MTV or American radio stations. Whereas now the second an artist releases a new song, it's available literally everywhere in the world, back then it was necessary to show up in these countries, or at least have a division of a label release and promote your record for anyone in that territory to be aware of it. I made it clear that it was of vital importance to me to have hits in as many parts of the globe as possible, and I was ready to get on a plane to make it happen.

The process started slowly, mainly due to the enormous success I was having at home in America, which meant an almost nonstop touring schedule across the US. There just wasn't much time to go to other countries, and we also didn't want to lose the momentum we were experiencing. Still, I persisted, and a few months later I had an opportunity to go to the UK, Germany, and Japan.

I was unknown in these territories, so bringing my band and doing gigs wasn't an option. Instead, the divisions of my label arranged radio and press interviews, as well as a TV show in Tokyo where I would sing live to the track of "Don't Mean Nothing" backed by four Japanese musicians pretending to play the parts on the record. I hated every second of it because despite my singing live, it all looked ridiculous and fake. The TV show had a large audience, however, and within a week or so, I and my debut album started to get some attention. Same thing happened in the UK and Germany, even without any TV appearances. I wasn't exactly an overnight hit singer like I'd been in the US, but it was a beginning.

While my focus was to break my career internationally, I also selfishly just wanted to travel. I'd been to London briefly when I was twenty-one, and to Australia with my parents when I was thirteen, but I wanted to see it all. That wanderlust, or curiosity, or whatever it was that existed in me is still in my soul today. I've been all over the world, but there are still many places I haven't seen, and I want to cross every one of them off my list.

Thanks to that brief promotional trip to just three countries, word started to spread and the following year, by the end of the fifteen-month tour supporting my debut album, I had done a club tour of about twelve cities throughout Europe and played in theaters in several cities in Japan.

In 1989, *Repeat Offender* was an instant smash and became the album that broke me internationally in a big way. "Right Here Waiting" became a worldwide hit and reached number 1 in dozens of countries. I was thrilled to be able to say I was headed back out on my first world tour. While the bulk of concerts on that 1989–1990 tour were in the States, I also played all throughout Canada and Europe, including a few shows opening for Stevie Nicks and a tour of massive stadiums in Germany with the amazing Tina Turner. I remember standing on the side of the stage every night watching Tina. She was like a panther on that stage. She worked her audiences (crowds of thirty or so thousand) into a frenzy. Her energy was inexhaustible. She was and is an absolutely gorgeous woman and my favorite female rock singer ever.

I also made it back to Australia, where I met one of my heroes.

While dial switching the TV in my early twenties, I randomly stumbled upon a video by an Australian artist named John Farnham. The song was "You're the Voice," and aside from the song itself grabbing my attention, it was John's voice that amazed me. His tone and phrasing were matched only by his power and range. I thought, *Jesus Christ! This is my favorite singer of all time!*

John's albums weren't carried in any US record stores, so I had to have them specially ordered and shipped from Australia, where John was a megastar unparalleled. During his heyday in the late '80s and early '90s, literally one out of three Aussies owned a John Farnham album. As I'd done with several other artists before, I dove into John's recorded catalog and had every note, nuance, and vocal lick memorized in no time. I told anyone and everyone who would listen about him, though no one I knew had ever heard of him.

On that first tour of Australia, the gigs were all sold out and the last show was in Melbourne, where John and his family lived. Finishing my encore, I retreated to my dressing room to towel off when my tour manager knocked, poked his head in, and said, "There's a guy named John Farnham outside. He'd like to meet you."

John and I would become friends, perform onstage together, and cowrite several songs he recorded in the early '90s.

THE TALE OF TAIPEI

Near the end of the *Repeat Offender* tour, I did a run of shows in Southeast Asia. My success in Japan had opened the door to other Asian territories, and "Right Here Waiting" quickly became a song known by nearly everyone in that part of the world. In just about every country in Asia, my albums were selling like hotcakes. (Is that still a thing? Probably not, but I still say it because I'm old.) The tour there took place in July and began in Japan. From there we played in Hong Kong, Malaysia, Bangkok, Singapore, Indonesia, and Taiwan.

The venues were all huge outdoor stadiums with the biggest crowds I'd ever played as a headliner. The fans were incredible. Many times I looked out and saw faces with tears streaming down their faces. At that time, American artists performing in Asian countries was not so common, and the fans really seemed caught up in how special these shows were. I was having a blast and though the tour schedule—which always also included full days of television and radio interviews and press conferences—wasn't allowing me to actually see much of where I was, I was grateful to know my music had become international.

There were, however, a few things that happened on that tour that were anything but fun.

Upon arriving in Kuala Lumpur, Malaysia, I knew I would be going right from the airport to a press conference at the hotel. There was a crowd of about a hundred fans at the arrival gates as we deplaned, and airport security was pretty flustered about how to deal with them. As we made our way through the terminal, I waved to everyone as flashbulbs went off like lightning. I was worried about people tripping and falling over each other, but nothing got out of hand. I was whisked into a waiting limo outside and driven to our hotel. I remember thinking, *Here I am in MALAYSIA! And there are fans going crazy at the AIRPORT! This gig is going to be a blast.*

We arrived at the hotel, where the press conference was set up in a section of the big main lobby. It was a long table with several Malaysian dignitaries sitting next to each other, and behind them on the wall was a sign that read "Salem." A few weeks earlier, I had spotted that name on a faxed memo of various details about the upcoming tour and called my manager.

"Why am I just now seeing that Salem is sponsoring my show in Kuala Lumpur? Everyone who knows me knows how against smoking I am. I just did a PSA for the American Cancer Society, for fuck's sake."

He assured me that he'd already looked into it and that the company sponsoring the show was Salem Tourism. Not the cigarette company.

Now, as I approached the long table to take my middle seat and begin the press conference, I saw packages of Salem cigarettes placed in front of each microphone, including mine. My blood started boiling. There were about twenty-five members of the press waiting to ask questions about the tour. As I took my seat, I leaned into my microphone and said, "Thank you all for coming today. I'm thrilled to be here in Malaysia for the first time. But before we talk about anything else, I need to express my displeasure at being lied to about the company sponsoring the show. I could not be more against the tobacco industry, and I would never have agreed to this sponsorship had I known the truth. Before we go any further, I need all these cigarette packages removed and preferably tossed in the trash where they belong."

Several of the press folks gasped and started whispering to each other as my tour manager ran up and got rid of the cigarettes. As the press conference began, questions about my album, my show, and me were quickly replaced with questions about why I felt so strongly about this subject. I explained that the science was irrefutable and that smoking was a horrific habit that not only stupidly risked the health of those who smoke but also selfishly risks the health of those around them.

We did our show the next evening, and the crowd that packed the stadium was incredible, all up and dancing and singing along. About six songs into the set, during a guitar solo, I ran offstage and returned a minute later holding a huge banner above my head which read, in very bold letters, "SALEM SUCKS!" The audience went wild and I made my point. Win-win.

The promoters weren't happy with my stunt because Salem executives who'd come to the gig got in their faces and demanded I apologize before the end of the show. That was never going to happen, and it didn't.

Our next stop was Jakarta, Indonesia. We played two nights at this gigantic stadium. It was a sea of people both nights and again a lively and loving crowd. But for the first time in my life, I witnessed something at a concert I never had before. Large venues almost always have a barrier between the stage and where the audience begins. It's where security stays during the show to prevent fans from jumping up onstage. (One thing I love about playing theaters is that there is no barrier and fans can come right up close. Makes for a much more exciting experience for me.) As I paced the edge of the Jakarta stage, singing and waving to the audience, I looked down into the barrier and saw something that really took me aback. Every member of security was pointing a rifle at the crowd. It would've been unnerving enough had they simply been *carrying* rifles. But they were *pointing them at the fans*. I couldn't get it out of my mind. I don't think anyone noticed, but I performed those shows pretty distracted by what I felt was a sad function of a fascist culture I simply couldn't comprehend. Nothing says, "Let's party!" like an assault rifle pointed at your face.

Those experiences in Malaysia and Indonesia, however, were nothing compared to what happened in Taiwan.

Taipei was the last destination on the Asian tour. The band, crew, and I were on a high from the amazing, huge crowds we'd played to in the days before, so we were excited to both close out the run with two more stadium shows and to head home to our families and take a breath. Cynthia was six months pregnant with our first child, Brandon, and though she was supportive of my international touring, she was also looking forward to me being back home.

When we arrived the evening before the first show, my tour manager, Bob, mentioned to me that the only concern was that there was a chance of heavy rain and storms the next day. Our shows were obviously outdoors and weather like that threatened the chances of us being able to safely play. I woke up and looked out my hotel room window the next morning to see heavy clouds but no rain. My crew was already at the stadium setting up the stage for the show along with members of a local sound and light company when around noon, it began to rain. And rain hard. Within an hour, there were three inches of rain on the stage, and my guys had to remove all the amps and anything electrical.

The rain kept up like that for several more hours when Bob called me in my hotel room, minutes before I was to be driven to the venue for a sound check. "Boss, you need to sit tight. The rain is starting to let up a little, but the stage is covered in water. We can't plug anything in. I've told the local crew that they need to figure out how to sweep it off the stage or else we cannot play. So far, they're just ignoring me and not doing anything."

By five o'clock, the situation was the same. Bob called again and said, "We can't do a show tonight. It's impossible. Hopefully, it won't rain again and the stage will be dry enough to do the show tomorrow night, but there's no way tonight can happen."

Disappointed for the fans *and* for me, I told Bob I understood but that he needed to have the promoters get the word out to the fans on local radio right away. I didn't want thousands of people showing up for no performance.

A few minutes later, one of my two band guitarists, Paul Warren, rang my room. "Hey, Richard. I just heard about the gig. That sucks! Hopefully tomorrow will be okay." Paul asked if I wanted to join him for a bite in the hotel restaurant, and I met him downstairs soon after. We had drinks, ordered some food, and chatted about the tour and my pending fatherhood. At this moment, to our obliviousness, chaos was ensuing all around us.

Apparently the local promoters tasked with getting the word out to fans that tonight's show was off went first to the person who'd put up the money for my concerts in Taipei. His name was Mr. Chen, one of the leaders of the Chinese mafia. My agents and manager had only dealt with the concert promoters and had no way of knowing who had actually financed the shows.

To put it extremely mildly, Mr. Chen was not understanding of our situation.

Our hotel was gigantic with several lobbies and common areas. As Paul and I sat in the restaurant, a group of a dozen armed men with machine guns arrived and approached the clerks at the front desk, demanding to know where I and my entourage were. A moment later, my other guitar player, Don Kirkpatrick, walked past the front desk and was immediately grabbed by two of the armed men and dragged into a hallway off the lobby. Accomplices of those men then spotted two of my crew members, Neil and Mike, and marched them at gunpoint to the spot where Don was being held.

Under threat of being shot, the front desk clerk gave several other men my room number and the room number of my agent, Randy Garelick, who had accompanied us on the tour. While I was luckily not in my room but with Paul in the restaurant, Randy was relaxing in his room when his door was suddenly kicked in. He was told at gunpoint to sit in a chair and stay silent. All of this was happening as Paul and I were finishing our dinner, completely unaware of what was transpiring.

As we left the table and started to exit the restaurant, we saw my tour manager, Bob, running toward us.

"Thank fucking God I found you guys! You've gotta come with me now!! No questions. Just *move*!"

My heart was pounding with fear that something horrible had happened. Bob ran us down a back corridor and into a service elevator, frantically pushing the Door Close button over and over. As we ascended, he said, "The hotel is under siege. The guy who put up our shows is a mafia guy and he's after all of us. He not only didn't let the promoters get the word out, but he also let thousands of fans into the stadium where they stood in mud for almost two hours before somebody with a microphone announced that you just don't feel like playing. The crowd went nuts and started tearing up the stage and rioting. We need to get you somewhere safe."

My head was spinning. I thought this had to be an elaborate practical joke. I'd have been very impressed.

We ran down the hallway of the seventh floor to Bob's room, locked the door, and pushed any piece of furniture we could move against it. I grabbed the phone and called an operator.

"I need you to connect me to the American Consulate right away!"

In broken English, she responded, "Consulate? No. There no consulate in Taipei."

She was right. This was 1990, and the United States did not have diplomatic relations with Taiwan.

As Bob called my manager back home to ask what the hell we should do, I looked out his window and realized we were too high up to climb out using sheets, and definitely too high up to jump to safety. I had my first flash of a real fear of being shot by these crazy fuckers. Of never seeing my family again and never holding my first child. I knew I needed to stay calm and focus on figuring out a plan.

Minutes after hanging up with my manager back in LA (who immediately started making calls to our booking agents and some private security firms in Asia to ask for guidance), the phone in Bob's room rang. It was Randy Garelick calling from his room. Bob answered and Randy, very quietly, said, "Bob, I need you to put Richard on the phone right away."

Handing me the phone, Randy spoke these words I still find hard to fathom.

"Richard, I need you to listen very carefully. I'm in my room, and Mr. Chen and some of his men are with me. They found my room and forced their way in. I'm sitting in a chair and one of his men is holding a gun to my head. I'm now going to hand the phone to Mr. Chen, but he's made things very clear. Either you agree right now to do two shows tomorrow, no matter what the weather may be, or he will instruct this man to shoot me right now."

My brain could barely comprehend the reality of what was happening.

Mr. Chen's voice came on the line.

"Hello?" I began, "Mr. Chen, please . . . I beg you not to—"

"YOU NO TALK! YOU NO TALK!" he immediately started screaming at the top of his lungs. "YOU NO PLAY! YOU COST ME! WHY YOU NO PLAY? YOU WANT ME KILL YOUR FRIEND?"

I tried to stay calm and hoped to somehow calm him.

"Mr. Chen, I'm very sorry. The stage was flooded. It would have been very dangerous for everyone if we had—"

"YOU SHUT UP! YOU NO PLAY! YOU COST ME!"

Slightly reducing his volume if not his intensity, Mr. Chen explained that either the band and I play an afternoon show as well as an evening show the following day, or he would put a bullet into Randy's head. He would keep Randy with him and his men until our arrival at the venue. Of course, I agreed, telling him I would do whatever he said as long as he didn't harm Randy.

I hung up the phone, my face white as a sheet, and told the guys what was happening. We all stared at each other in disbelief for a moment, as if we were in some strange and disturbing dream, waiting and hoping for something to awaken us.

My manager was able to contact a private security firm in Taipei made up of ex-military guys. They knew very well about Mr. Chen and advised that he was not to be taken lightly; he had a history of violent and deadly actions. They suggested a plan to not only save

Randy's life, but also to get all of us safely out of the country, but it would require us playing the two concerts as ordered.

After an hour or so, and feeling that the worst of the night was over, the guys walked me back to my hotel room only to find the door kicked in and the room ransacked. Apparently, Mr. Chen's men made a point to tell a few of the fans who had stood for hours in the mud at the stadium waiting for my show which room was mine. Nothing of real value was taken, but it was just another in a stream of incomprehensible events.

None of us slept a wink all night, and around noon the next day, the head of the security team arrived to go over the details of our plan. We got to the stadium about an hour before the first show, my crew arriving earlier to make sure everything was ready. The weather had cleared, so we could at least cross "death by electrocution while rocking out" off our worry list.

Shortly before showtime, several cars pulled up, and out came Mr. Chen along with Randy, who had a man standing close on each side of him. Randy's face was that of a man who didn't know if this would be his last day alive. They stood on the side of the stage for the entire performance.

As the show began and I took the stage, I looked out to a much smaller crowd than had been standing in the same spot the previous evening. The fans who'd bought tickets were never informed why I had not appeared and therefore the assumption was that I simply bailed on the gig, so many of them were very angry. Though this afternoon audience numbered in the thousands, a good chunk of the stadium was empty.

I began the first song, which always prompts a huge wave of screams and cheering, but instead heard nothing. Instead of the smiling faces with which I'm always greeted, this crowd was a collective mob wearing their disappointment in me on their faces. I looked to my right and saw a large, spray-painted sign held above the heads of about twenty "fans." Instead of the usual, "I love you, Richard!!" or "Taipei Loves Richard Marx," this sign read, "WE DON'T LOVE YOU ANYMORE."

My heart sank. I understood their anger but knew I'd have no opportunity to explain the truth about what happened. Glancing occasionally over at Randy and his "escorts." in the wings, I just carried on singing for nearly ninety minutes to mostly tepid applause, my usual fun banter with the crowd replaced by simple introductions to the next song or merely "Let's keep it moving, guys."

We finished the show and exited on the opposite side of the stage as Chen and his men with our new security team waiting to walk us to our dressing room. The leader of our team, a Chinese man around thirty who spoke nearly perfect English, explained to us what needed to happen next.

"We've made an agreement that once the next performance begins, your agent will be free to join your crew. However, if you guys walk offstage at the end of the show into the arms of Chen and his men, there's no telling what he will do. We have cars waiting, and we are as heavily armed as Chen's men are. You will end the show, run to our side of the stage, and get right into the cars, and we will escort you immediately to the airport. Leave your equipment. We'll have a few of my guys gather it and bring it to you as soon as they can. We just need to get you out of here."

The evening show began with much fuller attendance and a more welcoming audience. I guess since I had played already that day, this crowd decided to forego their anger, trust I was absolutely there to play, and just rock out with us. Though the band and I made no noticeable errors, our minds were really on nothing but our escape.

As I finished the last song, my adrenaline, fueled by fear and no idea of what would happen, was almost too much. I glanced at one side of the stage to see Mr. Chen, scowling, along with about seven of his men, before yelling, "Thank you, Taipei! Good night!" as I turned and began running to the other side of the stage. Our security team immediately surrounded me and the band as we bolted down the back stairs of the building and into the waiting cars.

I was in the backseat of one along with my guitarist, Paul. "GO! GO!" I heard someone yell and our heads snapped back as the car peeled out of the parking area onto a highway. Next to our driver was one of "our" guys with a Glock in his hand, ready for whatever might occur. Our caravan of cars headed toward the airport and immediately we saw that Chen's men were in pursuit. It was only after reaching speeds of about 100 miles per hour and outpacing them that we saw them finally give up and turn around.

Thirty minutes later, we pulled up to the curb of the Taipei airport and were met by airport security, who ushered us to a lounge to await the next available flight out. There was one in two hours, which would connect in Tokyo before flying right to Los Angeles. True to his word, our security chief arranged to get our gear to us and the band, crew, and I finally settled into our seats in the lounge. For at least five full minutes, no one said a word. We all just looked at each other. The insanity of what we'd just experienced needed a minute to sink in. We boarded the plane and only when I was in my seat and the wheels left the Taiwanese ground did I truly exhale.

We exited the plane in Tokyo and descended the stairs to the tarmac. I stopped at the bottom and immediately kissed the ground. Our connection was mercifully short, and before I knew it, I was headed home.

I had deliberately not told Cynthia what was happening. When I spoke to her the night before, I said everything was going great and that I was really looking forward to being home. She was six months pregnant, and I feared that if she knew the danger I was in she could freak out and something might happen to the baby. As I curled up in my seat, I thought about how I would tell her this fantastical story.

Hours passed as we flew through the night sky. Though everyone in the plane looked to be asleep, I was wide awake. My thoughts recalling the past two days would not let me rest. I stared out the window into the night sky, forty thousand feet above the earth, and replayed the insane events in my head as if watching a suspense movie.

Then, in the silence and tranquility, I saw a light. Not so much a light as a spark. A shooting star? A reflection in my seat's window? Then, there was another. About seven seconds passed before I realized that a flame had been ignited in one of the engines hanging just below the right wing. Yes, ladies and gentlemen: the plane was on fire.

As my muscles clenched and I turned to bolt from my seat, I saw several flight attendants literally running past me to the cockpit. Other passengers were awakened by the commotion as the sound of *ding* echoed through the cabin and the "Fasten Seat Belt" sign illuminated. I turned back to check the wing, and now the engine was engulfed with flames. But as my heart began beating through my chest, in a single second, the fire disappeared. I felt the plane descend slightly before the captain's voice appeared on the PA system.

"Ladies and gentlemen, this is your captain speaking. It appears we had a small fire break out in the engine which sits under the nearest section of the right wing. I have shut that engine down and the fire seems to be out. Now, I want you all to stay calm. This aircraft has four engines and, if necessary, I could land with only one. But we want to be as safe as possible so I've radioed ahead and we will be making an emergency landing in Honolulu in approximately two hours."

I know. This is the part of my story where you finally call "bullshit." There's *no way* this actually happened, right?

Wrong.

Everyone on board remained relatively calm and, sure enough, two hours later we safely and uneventfully touched down in Honolulu. A few hours after that, I boarded yet another plane for LA and managed to make it home for dinner. My parents came over, and as I sat at our dining room table and regaled them and Cynthia with the "Tale of Taipei," I lost count of how many times I saw their mouths drop open in stunned disbelief. I vowed to never return to Taiwan. Ever. No matter what.

I kept that promise until 2010, when my agent called me with a lucrative offer to play an arena show there. I explained why I had decided to never return, and he said, "I totally get it. But that was twenty years ago. Much has changed including our diplomatic relations with Taiwan. Let me do some investigating and come back to you before you absolutely rule it out."

A few days later, he called back and said he'd found out that a few years after my nightmare experience there, Mr. Chen had been killed in a hail of bullets. The victim of a mob hit. The entertainment industry in Taiwan had become legitimate, and many artists were performing there with no issues.

I reluctantly agreed to the gig and was greeted by one of the most amazing audiences to which I've ever played. I've since returned two more times and have (almost) permanently erased the horrific memory of that fateful trip in 1990. I'm simply grateful to have lived to tell the story to you now.

24

IT'S A BOY, IT'S A BOY, IT'S A BOY

On September 11, 1990, Cynthia gave birth to our first son, Brandon. We were both convinced this baby would be a girl. We just knew it. Her name would be Jesse, with the traditionally male spelling and without the *i*. I even wrote a piece of music soon after Cynthia got pregnant called, "Jesse's Song." Given Cynthia's age of nearly thirty-four, it was strongly advised she have an amniocentesis to detect any potential issues or concerns (which, thankfully, were absent) and in doing so, the sex of the baby would be known. We were shocked and then immediately thrilled to know our daughter would actually be a son.

Lucas arrived almost exactly two years later, on September 14, 1992, and our third son made his debut fifteen months later on January 4, 1994. We named him Jesse.

Three boys. Holy shit, right? I was once on a plane flying to a gig when my kids were in their teens. The guy sitting next to me struck up conversation and mentioned his kids. I asked how many he had. "Three girls," he said. "By the way, I know who you are and I'm a fan. You have three boys, right?"

"Yep. Three boys."

He said, "Well, look at it my way. You have to worry about three penises. I have to worry about three thousand."

When Brandon was born, I was about to turn twenty-seven and my career was at full speed. I never really gave much thought to having children, as success in music was always my primary focus. By the time we got married, Cynthia wanted to be a mother and her biological clock was ticking. It's not that I was against it, but at that time, my head was totally into my career and building it bigger and bigger. The success I'd always dreamed of had just arrived, and I wanted to enjoy it. I loved the idea of having a family but was also concerned about the juggle of fatherhood and my work. As my kids grew up, I felt I did a pretty good job at that juggle. I instituted a "two-week rule" that meant I'd never go longer than that without seeing the boys. Sometimes that meant taking breaks in a tour, which was quite costly, and sometimes the family would join me on the road. In their early years, I wrote a lot of songs and changed a lot of diapers. I never missed a birthday and hardly ever missed any school events, even if it required me to charter a jet to make it.

By no means is this a complaint, but it was far from easy for me to feel I was both serving myself as an artist and individual and also serving my wife and kids. It was always somewhat stressful. I was a husband and young father but also the breadwinner and, at that time, a rock star. I had grown up a child who never caused problems. I was well behaved and very responsible. Now, still in my twenties as my fame was just being ignited, I needed to be more responsible than ever.

I did concerts all over the world, wrote my own songs, and produced my own records. But I was also expected to be an attentive and focused father to three kids. Cynthia and I never employed nannies. Her sister, though never a mother herself, had experience as a nanny and moved in with us when Brandon was born and helped out Cynthia mostly when I was away, living with us until the boys were in high school.

As school years approached, I suggested we leave Los Angeles and move back to Chicago near the suburb in which I grew up. I felt that raising our boys away from a town consumed with show business would provide a better upbringing, and I still feel it was the right decision at the time. But I was also leaving behind my closest friends, who lived in LA, as well as the true pulse of the music business at a time when my career was still thriving. I believed those personal sacrifices were needed for the benefit of my kids. Now, I'm not so sure it was the best move. It was a pretty isolating existence being in Chicago, and every time I would visit LA for work I would remember how much I missed living there.

Parenting is the hardest job and the most important. Cynthia was and is a great mom. I did my best to balance being a hands-on, present father and a guy who needed solitude to write songs and be creative. As the boys got a bit older, they would take turns accompanying me on tour for a few days at a time. I believe it was those trips that most bonded me to each of them. Except for sharing me with fans for two hours a night as I performed, each had me all to himself. We'd have amazing conversations and be stupid and silly together. I'd put them to work, helping with guitars and gear or helping at the merchandise table. They saw me doing my thing on the road. It not only helped them understand when I had to be away, but it also lit a fuse in all of them to pursue music as a career.

In their middle-school years, the recording and touring parts of my career slowed to near nonexistence as my songwriting and producing career flourished. That meant that I was home a lot more but also busier than ever juggling projects with an array of artists. I had a state-of-the-art recording studio built on our property, with floor-to-ceiling windows looking out onto Lake Michigan and bedrooms for visiting artists and musicians to stay during projects. My boys were able to watch the creation of songs and records that became hits and got to know all the people with whom I would collaborate. Not every kid can say that J. C. Chasez of NSYNC picked them up from day camp and Keith Urban watched one of their local rec-center basketball games.

Like me, all three of the boys' musical talents were evident at a very early age. They all had great singing voices and sang very well in tune. They constantly and obsessively listened to music, and I encouraged them as children to make up their own songs, which I would record in my home studio and make into pretty elaborate productions, which was great fun for all of us. Jesse named his first song "Benji" after seeing that film. Its first verse being:

> Benji goes in his cage
> And then he comes out
> And then a guy shoots him.

Though Jesse wrote it at only five years old, I think any songwriter can appreciate his sense of lyrical economy. He just spells that shit right out.

As evidenced by everyone from the Everly Brothers and the Carpenters to the Bee Gees and the Jonas Brothers, there is a uniquely amazing sound to musical sibling harmony. In the mid-2000s, I started an annual tradition of recording classic Christmas songs with my sons, trading solo verses and singing three-part harmony together. I would film the sessions and create homemade videos in iMovie and email the clips to friends as our family holiday card. Some of these are still on YouTube, actually. People not only looked forward to each year's new track, but many would say, "They *have* to become a real group and make records!" I was all for that idea, but all the boys said no. They each wanted to pursue their own individual careers.

Jesse became a huge fan of metal and hard rock, and though clean-cut and lacking any tattoos or piercings, he has written and produced some incredible rock songs that he hopes to release very soon. His voice possesses great range and power, and his layering of beautiful melodies on top of thrashing guitar-dominated tracks is uniquely wonderful. Lucas is steeped in modern pop and though a really great singer with multiple credits as a top-line vocalist, he has become focused on writing and producing other artists, with some exciting collaborations happening as I write this. Brandon's passion has been in hip-hop and electronic music, and he continues to both produce tracks for various artists and release his own solo work. Again, it's his incredible singing voice and melodic sense that make his creations special. I only wish the music industry weren't a shadow of its former self. The opportunities for real and sustaining success are few and far between since streaming has replaced the sale of music, and therefore drastically reduced the earning potential for songwriters and artists everywhere. But I know my sons love what they do, and they'll figure out their path.

Though certainly not perfect, I feel I have exceptional relationships with each of them and consider them among my closest friends. At this stage of their lives, I appreciate the friendship part but also really love the occasional times they come to me for help with something and simply need me to be Dad. I will never tire of that.

At age eighteen, Brandon and his high-school girlfriend, Jessica, had a baby. A girl. It was an emotionally trying time back then for everyone involved, and that story has had its share of complexities ever since. But my granddaughter, Madison, is a lovely, wise, and soulful young lady, and I cherish having her in my life. Living across the country from each other, we haven't spent a tremendous amount of time together, but my hope is that we develop a close and loving bond as she grows up and time turns the page.

25

"KEEP COMING BACK"

Luther Vandross and I met in 1990 at an American Music Awards show. I remember that on that particular night, he had won the award for Favorite R&B Male Artist, and I had lost the Pop/Rock Male Artist Award to Bobby Brown. (Billy Joel was the third nominee.) What I recall most vividly, aside from the brief collapse of spirit upon not winning, was that Alice Cooper was presenting the award. I was never what you'd call a "devoted fan" of Alice's music, but his persona is very charismatic. I'd seen him in some interviews where he came off quite wise and soulful. That wasn't what I expected from him, so I thought he was cool. I'd wished he'd read my name as the winner but was well aware he had no control over that at all.

Whether you win or lose an award at those TV shows, if you are nominated, or really if you are anyone who is recognizable, you are expected to greet reporters and photographers backstage in what's called the "press room." So, a bit down after not winning, I headed backstage to fulfill my press responsibility. As I walk into the press room, I'm greeted by a wall of music journalists and photographers; cameras snapping, flashes flashing, and microphones right in my face.

"Richard, how does it feel to lose to Bobby Brown?" I hear some-one ask. "I'm happy for him," I said, before mumbling a few sentences about my current tour as I started to make my way back to my seat in the audience.

As I turned to leave the room, kind of spaced out given the press experience, I smacked right into what only can be described as the widest set of black tuxedo lapels I'd ever seen. I looked up to see the one and only Luther Vandross. A man whose exceptional talent had always greatly impressed me, he was wearing a very flashy tux with what looked like a Keith Haring pattern emblazoned all over it and, yes, the widest set of lapels I'd ever seen. He was also, at that time, in one of his "skinny phases," as he used to call them.

He didn't seem upset that I wasn't paying attention and bumped into him, but I immediately apologized and told him what a fan of his I was. And that's when I first saw it. He flashed me that wide, pearly white smile that lit up whatever already bright room he was standing in. We stood and talked for a few "mutual admiration society" min-utes before he said, "Here's my number. We should hang out. I know you're touring a lot, as I am, but maybe when we're both back in LA."

Our hanging out together took several months to actually occur, but in the interim we started talking on the phone now and then from our respective hotel rooms while both on tour. Through those phone calls, a friendship had already begun that was solidified when we were both back home in the same town.

My son Brandon was born in September of 1990, and the first time Luther met Cynthia and me for dinner (at a cool, now defunct Studio City Italian eatery named Spumanti), he gifted us with a gorgeous sterling silver rattle from Tiffany & Co. Luther was a very generous gift giver and loved to embrace the extravagance of any situation. He routinely took his friends and business associates to Hawaii or the Bahamas for all-expenses-paid vacations, and his homes in LA and

Connecticut were filled to the ceiling with beautiful furniture and rare pieces by Lalique, Lladró, and Baccarat. He drove a series of Rolls-Royce Silver Shadows. He would have friends over and screen new films in his home theater, accompanied by all kinds of gourmet snacks and desserts. He loved embracing the spoils of his labor and was more confident in (and unapologetic for) his lavish lifestyle than anyone I've ever known. He'd come from nothing, been handed nothing, and earned this lifestyle all on his own. Why wouldn't he celebrate that?

Though I'm never one to judge what someone wants to spend their hard-earned money on, there was one purchase of Luther's that I'll never forget.

At one point Luther bought a mansion in Greenwich, Connecticut. It was the late '90s, and the first time I visited, he gave me the grand tour of the nearly 20,000-square-foot, seven-bedroom, seven-bathroom behemoth. Driving up, I was greeted by a red driveway complete with a working fountain at the center of it and a garage bigger than most normal people's homes.

I parked and walked through the front door to be smacked in the face with some of the most magnificent black and white marble tile work I'd ever seen in my life. He must have had someone polish it every single day. There wasn't a smudge anywhere. I was taken through the massive state-of-the art kitchen that put some Michelin-starred restaurants to shame, through a library lined with solid oak walls and rare books, and all of the rooms were wide open and full of windows overlooking a meticulously manicured back lawn with a marble terrace, pool, and tennis courts.

When we entered the formal living room, I was mesmerized by the cream-colored walls that seemed to be made of fabric. I pointed to a wall without saying a word and Luther smiled and said, "Cashmere."

Now, I don't know about you, but if someone tells me a wall is made of cashmere, what's the first thing you're going to do? Touch it, right? So I move my hand toward the wall until I was startled away.

"Richard Marx! Don't you even think of putting your nasty hands on my cashmere walls!"

I turned to him and said, "Oh, yeah? Guess what? I'll tell you what I'm going to do. I'm going to drive my kids over to this house and on the way, I'm going to give them a bunch of M&Ms. Then I'm turning them loose in here."

As he turned to continue the tour, I heard him say out of the corner of his mouth, "Yeah, well, that'll be the last muthafuckin' thing you do."

Prior to my knowing Luther's taste in wall fabric, he and I cemented our friendship one winter when we were both off the road for a bit. We started hanging out somewhat regularly. I was never the most social person in LA, so "regularly" means something different to me than it might mean to you. But I made a point to spend time with Luther because he was both a gracious host and a really fun guest.

I think at least 83 percent of my time in Luther's company, we were laughing. He was wickedly funny, with an infectious laugh that came from the soles of his Bruno Maglis up through the top of his Jheri curl. And nothing could beat him regaling you with a story in which he'd given someone a piece of his mind. He had several about Anita Baker, with whom he'd toured and truly detested. Sometimes just to get his blood going, I'd say, "Hey, tell me more about your lovefest with Anita."

During one of our first dinners together, Luther very casually said, "So, you're starting your new album soon, right?"

"I am," I said. (Is the Neil Diamond song in your head right now? Because it's in mine.)

"Well, if at any point you need any background singers, let me know."

I stared at him.

"Dude. Are you fucking with me? You know what that's like? That'd be like me having dinner with Michael Jordan, and saying, 'You know, Michael, on the weekends I like to play pick-up basketball with a few of my buddies at the park.' And Michael Jordan replying, 'Really? Well, if you ever need someone for your team, let me know.'"

He laughed and said, "Well, just know I'll be there anytime you want."

I'm not a stupid man, so I immediately began plotting how to get Luther to sing on my album. A few weeks later, with car keys in hand, I started to leave my house for a session at the studio where we were scheduled to cut two rock songs, when a melody crept into my head. It stopped me at my front door. It was really memorable, I thought.

So, I threw my keys down and ran to the piano in our living room and the chorus to "Keep Coming Back" spilled out of my mouth and through my fingers on the keys. I could hear the whole record in my head, and it was reminiscent of the classic '70s R&B records I worshipped growing up. Records like "Just to Be Close to You" by the Commodores, "Love's Holiday" by Earth, Wind and Fire, and pretty much anything by Donny Hathaway. I sat and wrote the rest of the music within about twenty minutes and was already singing the chorus: "I don't know why . . . I . . . keep coming back to you, baby."

I was really excited about this tune, but then it hit me. I was in the midst of recording the hardest-rocking album I had ever attempted. This was partly because I was listening to mostly that kind of rock stuff by other bands and artists for enjoyment, but also to silence critics who had labeled me a mellow ballad singer. It didn't matter that 90 percent of my recorded work at that point was up-tempo rock, my label had released five ballads over three years. They realized early on that these ballads were an easy sell to radio, which then sold more albums.

After the massive success of "Right Here Waiting" off *Repeat Offender*, I had begged the label to next release a track called "Nothin' You Can Do About It." I felt it was a really solid song and would cross over between the Top Forty charts and the rock charts. It would also be a harder, guitar-based rocker that would show my diversity and also better represent the album overall. Instead, they released "Angelia," which became my seventh straight Top Five single but also pigeonholed me as simply a balladeer in many people's eyes. That's a perception I still battle today, and it kind of pisses me off.

I had already written and recorded a few songs for album number three that were edgier, musically, lyrically, and sonically, than anything I'd ever recorded, so I felt I could branch out a bit on some other songs to give the album variety. "Keep Coming Back" would simply fill a slot that was currently vacant.

The track was cut in about three takes. Effortless. Nathan East played bass, Jonathan Moffett on drums, Bruce Gaitsch on guitar, and, feeling the Fender Rhodes part needed much more proficiency on this song than I possessed, I asked the crazy talented Greg Phill-inganes to play. Though I almost never used my band members on my albums, I thought my then–sax player, Steve Grove, would be great on this track, and he was. I recorded my lead vocal in lightning-fast time. The only thing left were the background vocals.

I called Luther and stopped by his house, where we sat in my car in his driveway and I played him the track. He loved it. A few days later, he arrived to sing at A&M Studios in Hollywood at around 6:00 p.m. By 7:30, he and I were sitting in a nearby restaurant ordering dinner. If only every recording experience could be that easy. Few people know that before Luther started having massive success as an artist, he was a very successful jingle singer and background vocalist on many artists' records. His experience behind the microphone and my knowing exactly what I wanted him to sing made it possible for our session to be fun, quick, and musically killer.

A few months later, I completed the album, which I named *Rush Street* (after the famous street in my hometown of Chicago), and delivered it to my label. They were a bit perplexed by how much heavy guitar rock was present but were placated by the more commercial tracks that rounded it out. We all agreed to go with "Keep Coming Back" as the first single. I was thrilled because I knew it would be an unexpected new sound and, hopefully, broaden my fan base.

The single went to number 12 on the Pop chart, gave me my first appearance on the R&B chart, and spent six weeks at number 1 on the AC chart. While I'm very proud of writing that song, I have no doubt that Luther's presence on the track contributed greatly to its success.

26

"HAZARD"

I was well into the *Repeat Offender* tour and fast asleep in the back lounge of my tour bus. It was around 4:00 a.m., and we were somewhere between Illinois and Indiana when this piece of music woke me from my slumber. A bit groggy from the previous evening's concert and post-show tequila shots, I had the presence of mind to immediately reach for my trusty Panasonic handheld cassette recorder. Because it was 19-fucking-90, and iPhone apps weren't an idea, let alone a thing.

I started singing the melody and chord progression into the tape machine and realized this wasn't just a snippet of a future song. It was the *entire* song. No lyrics. But I had written the verse, chorus, and bridge melodies in my sleep. There was a vibe to this music that was haunting. Almost ominous. Sad. Suspenseful. I could hear the whole production in my head. What the drum pattern sounded like, what the finger-picked guitar part should be, and even the sound of the synthesizer pad. But I had *zero* clue what the lyrics should be.

For weeks, I listened to the tape recording of this melody until it was simply etched in my brain. Then, one rare evening off with no gig, it occurred to me that this music could lend itself to a proper story. I had always loved great mysteries. I didn't read much as a kid, but when I did, it was usually mystery fiction. Sherlock Holmes was a favorite, and I loved the old black-and-white films starring Basil Rathbone. I thought it could be really fun to try to create a murder mystery to this melody. I pictured a small rural town in the Midwest and immediately knew that my voice needed to not only tell the story but be a key character in it. The first line arrived.

My mother came to _____ when I was just seven

I had no idea where my fictional mother had come to other than, based on my melody, it was a town with a two-syllable name. Within a few hours, I had constructed a story that took place in the state of Nebraska. Again, the melody dictated the lyrics. As I sang, "and leave this old ba-bup-ba town" I knew I needed a state with three syllables. It could've been New Hampshire. It could've been Ohio. It would not have been Florida because that word sings so awkwardly against the notes of that melody.

You songwriters understand.

When I sang "Nebraska" to those notes, it just felt like magic. I finished the entire lyric that evening. A beautiful young woman meets a young man and they strike up a relationship, sharing their mutual dream of getting out of this small Nebraska town. Suddenly one evening the girl goes missing and is later found dead, drowned in the river that runs through the town. The young man, always viewed as strange by the townspeople, is assumed to be her killer and arrested. He proclaims his innocence but is resigned to a fate of misunderstanding.

There's no escape for me this time
All of my rescues are gone, long gone

There were a few moments in the writing process where I nearly abandoned the song. It started sounding like a really stupid episode of *Twin Peaks*. But self-doubt is an often unwelcome guest in creativity, and one needs to overcome it. So I carried on.

The song was complete except for one single and extremely vital piece of information: the name of the town. This would also be the song's title, so I kinda needed to figure it out. I had a few days off from the tour at home and it being the pre-internet age, I called the state of Nebraska's Chamber of Commerce and asked if they would fax me a list of every town in the state. (You under-twenty-fivers can Google "fax" now, too.) About an hour later, my fax machine began spitting out page after page of a two-column list of names. I gathered the eight or nine pages and shuffled them like cards. I then laid them out on my home-office desk, closed my eyes, and dropped the end my index finger to the desk.

My finger landed on the name Ogallala, which clearly wouldn't work and not only because of having more than two syllables. I closed my eyes and dropped my finger again, and I honestly don't recall what it landed on, but in the column directly to the left I saw the name Hazard. I immediately knew it was right.

My mother came to Hazard when I was just seven.

I couldn't wait to record this song. But I had several more months of concerts ahead so that day didn't arrive until early the following year.

Whereas I almost always prefer to record with a live band, I chose to record "Hazard" with synthesizers and a drum machine. The keyboard player in my touring band, Mike Egizi, had been teaching himself drum and synth programming, so we got together one afternoon and I painstakingly attempted to verbally convey the sounds I was hearing in my head to Mike's fingers on his keyboard. Eventually, the track came together except for the guitar parts, which I wanted to be played by my friend and master acoustic guitarist Bruce Gaitsch. I had written a very intricate arpeggiated guitar part for the chorus, which Mike had programmed on synthesizer just as a guide. Bruce learned the part note for note.

But upon hearing it played by a real acoustic guitar, I found I preferred the sound of the synthesized "fake" guitar. Even Bruce agreed. I asked him to play a nylon string solo, the melody of which he and I constructed together. I recorded my lead and background vocals later that evening, and "Hazard" was fully realized.

Much as I personally liked it, I honestly expected the song to be one of those tracks known as an "album cut." It certainly didn't sound like anything pop radio was playing. But as I began to play the song for people, everyone from my manager to various friends, I was aware of a uniquely strong reaction. People were fascinated by it. And much to my surprise, my record company not only liked it, but they wanted to release it as a single.

The first single from *Rush Street* was "Keep Coming Back." When that song peaked on the charts, "Hazard" was released, so it was time to make a video to promote it. I met with several music video directors, including Michael Bay and Dominic Sena, both of whom I'd worked with before. Their concepts for the video were okay but not anything I felt was deepening the existing story.

I then took a meeting with a young indie filmmaker named Michael Haussman. Michael hadn't done much yet, but what he had done was impressive in its look. I saw this video in black and white, and Michael agreed. We storyboarded ideas together and fleshed out the plot to include additional characters. In doing so, we chose to abandon the idea of being faithful to my song lyrics literally.

My character is arrested for the murder of Mary but is ultimately released due to lack of evidence. Upon returning home to the small trailer he calls home, he finds it engulfed in a fire set by the towns-people who wanted him gone. We included the character of the town sheriff (a role my longtime friend actor Robert Conrad of the classic '60s TV series *Wild, Wild West* fame graciously agreed to portray) which created a plot twist. Did my character kill Mary? Or was it the sheriff? Or did she drown accidentally? The video, just like the song itself, never answered those questions.

As the song became a hit back in 1992, people began to ask me, "So, who killed Mary?" Journalists would ask me in interviews. Fans from the audience would yell it to me onstage. Waiters serving me breakfast would softly whisper to me. "Dude. Who killed the girl in your song?" It was terribly fascinating to me that anyone cared. I wrote the story deliberately as an unsolved mystery and never even formed an opinion myself on what really happened to Mary.

The song became a Top Ten single on America's *Billboard* Hot 100 and a huge hit around the world, hitting the Top Ten in the UK and going to number 1 in Australia and several other countries. The song drove sales of the *Rush Street* album past three million, and I won an ARIA Award (the Australian equivalent of a Grammy) for Best International Single.

Writing that song was a great experience for me all around. But I'll let you in on something I've found pretty perplexing. From the time "Hazard" became a hit in 1992, right up to literally nine days ago as of this writing, I've had person after person after person come up to me, to my face, and ask me if this song is autobiographical.

I just stare at them.

I think, "You actually believe I killed a girl in Nebraska years ago, and wrote a song about it?"

27

"SUDDENLY"

In the early 1990s, I was asked to sing a couple of songs at a charity event in Malibu. I agreed and was thrilled to arrive at the sound check that afternoon and find that Olivia Newton-John was there and would also be singing.

In my teen years, I, along with the rest of the world, had a mad crush on Olivia. In 1980, her film *Xanadu* was released, along with the soundtrack. For reasons I can't recall now, I didn't see the film but bought the soundtrack the week it came out. "Magic" was the big hit single, but it was her duet with Sir Cliff Richard, "Suddenly," that I was crazy for. Still in high school, I spent countless days in my parents' basement, cranking my father's stereo to that song. I had learned Cliff's part perfectly, and would imagine myself looking into Olivia's beautiful eyes, singing this gorgeous love song with her.

By my nineteenth birthday, I was singing background vocals on her *Two of a Kind* soundtrack album and writing songs with her. One night when I was around twenty, she invited me to her home in Malibu and cooked me dinner. We hung out and talked and laughed, and somehow the conversation turned to her film career.

I said, "You know, I'm embarrassed to tell you but I've never seen *Xanadu.*"

She laughed and said, "You're not alone, love."

I said, "No, I'd like to. I just haven't remembered to rent it." (This was back when renting a movie on VHS tape from a video store was the barbaric equivalent of Netflix now.)

Olivia said, "I have a copy here if you're really that keen on seeing it."

So we popped some popcorn, poured a couple glasses of wine, and sat in her living room in front of a big-screen TV and Olivia Newton-John showed me one of her movies. Personally.

Now, I realize I set the scene for what you readers might've thought would be a different kind of story that night. And I won't sit here and lie and tell you that I wasn't mad for Olivia and full of all kinds of fantasies. I was twenty and single, but she was in a relationship at the time, and though her boyfriend was out of town that night, she never led me to think she was open to outside advances. And therefore, I felt making a move on her would have been disrespectful on multiple levels. I just sat next to her and watched her film, breathing in her beauty, kindness, and perfume.

The benefit in Malibu was the first time I'd seen Olivia in years. She looked so beautiful. Olivia has this radiance that is like a constant glow of moonlight. She's had a tough go of it throughout her life, battling multiple cancer diagnoses, and remains nothing but the epitome of grace and elegance.

We were in the midst of catching up with each other when her musical director said, "Hey, why don't you two do something together tonight. How about 'You're the One That I Want?'"

I said, "I don't think that one's for me. But how about 'Suddenly'?"

With a big smile, Olivia said, "Ohhhh, I *love* that one! Haven't sung it in a while."

So the house band worked up the arrangement from the original record and we performed it as a duet that evening. Imagine how I felt. I'd sung this song in my parents' basement as a teenager, and now here I was, on a stage, singing those words to Olivia, who was singing and looking back into my eyes.

Just a few years ago Olivia and her husband, John, came to my show in Jupiter, Florida, where she was living at the time. She came up onstage that night and sang "Right Here Waiting" with me as a duet. And the circle was complete.

1967. Age four.

1970. Singing a jingle.

1982. First year away from home outside the Motown Studios where Lionel Richie was recording his first solo album.

1984. With Lionel Richie after singing background vocals on his classic "All Night Long."

1984. My first live gig
ever at a long-gone club
in Studio City, California,
called Sasch.

1984. In the studio with Kenny Loggins.

1986. Making my first album. Recording background vocals on "Don't Mean Nothing" with Randy Meisner and Timothy B. Schmit at Capitol Studios.

1987. Backstage with REO Speedwagon on the last date of the summer tour as their opening act. (Left to right: Dave Koz, Paul Warren, Jim Cliff, Gary Richrath, Mike Derosier, Alan Gratzer, Neal Doughty, Kevin Cronin, me, Jon Walmsley)

1988. Backstage after a concert with my grandfather Duane celebrating the news of my first number one pop single, "Hold On to the Nights."

1988. With my parents, Dick and Ruth. Photo by Nels Israelson

1988. In the studio with (left to right) engineer Brian Foraker and Vixen band members Share Pedersen and Janet Gardner recording "Edge of a Broken Heart."

1988. With David Cole (left) and Bobby Colomby.

1990. Backstage with Olivia Newton-John after my performance at the Greek Theatre in Los Angeles.

1990. Onstage at Miami Arena singing "You May Be Right" with one of my songwriting heroes, Billy Joel.

1991. With Bruce Lundvall (who gave me my first record deal) during my record-setting *Rush In, Rush Out, Rush Street* tour.

1991. Undertaking photographer Nels Isrealson's experiment in the making of the *Rush Street* album cover.

1998. Rehearsing with Luther Vandross for the Music for Life benefit in Chicago.

1998. Backstage at The Vic Theatre in Chicago before the Music for Life benefit concert.
(Left to right: Michael Bolton, me, Fee Waybill, Kenny G, Luther Vandross, Kevin Cronin)

1999. In an Orlando studio recording "This I Promise You" with NSYNC. (Left to right: Justin Timberlake, Lance Bass, Chris Kirkpatrick, JC Chasez, me, Joey Fatone)

2000. With Kenny Rogers and engineer David Cole.

2000. With Cynthia and our boys outside our home in Lake Bluff, Illinois.

2004. Onstage in
New York City.

2010. Onstage with Matt Scannell during our *Duo* tour.

2011. Backstage with Hugh Jackman after filming my PBS special, *A Night Out With Friends*.

2012. Backstage with Joe Walsh at a benefit for Senator Tammy Duckworth.

2014. Finally learning to play as hard as I work.

2014. With Ringo Starr at his home in Los Angeles after writing "Not Looking Back."

2017. With Fee Waybill.

2018. Valentine's Day at our home in Malibu with James Brolin and Barbra Streisand.

2018. Backstage with Keith Urban in Sydney at the Aria Awards.

2018. Outside Woodshed Studio in Malibu, California, with the legend known as Burt Bacharach (left) and Greg Phillinganes.

2019. With my sons Jesse, Brandon, and Lucas.

On a plane going somewhere with my partner in everything, Daisy Fuentes.

28

ELTON AND THE DISAPPEARING TOOTH

made lots of mistakes in my early days as live performer. One of them was handling the microphone properly. It's a learning curve. (Trust me, Steven Tyler didn't do his first gig with perfect rock-star moves and those awesome scarves wrapped around the mic stand. That developed over time.) And my learning curve included a few shows where I misjudged the distance from mic to mouth and banged the ball of the mic into my teeth.

On the first tour, I chipped one of my front teeth (at an outdoor show at Knott's Berry Farm to be precise), and during the second tour I chipped the other one at the Detroit venue then known as Pine Knob. I remember it being a euphorically great audience, and at one point I stood on top of my grand piano, mic in hand, and leapt about eleven feet down to the stage and—*bang!*—right in the teeth with the fuckin' mic. (Those jumps off my piano were also the reason I had both my hips replaced in 2015. Which didn't bother me as much as it could have because I was finally able to hear the words *Richard Marx* and *hip* in the same sentence.) So at the end of the second world tour, I went to my dentist, who supplied me with two veneers over my then shorter and tour-ravaged front teeth.

About a year and a half later, in 1992, I was in London doing concerts and a few television appearances. "Hazard" had become a bona fide smash in the UK. I was invited to perform the song on Britain's biggest music show, *Top of the Pops*. The show could prove a huge catalyst in either turning a song into a hit on the charts or taking a song already on the way up and rocket-lifting it higher.

Having done the show previously a couple times, I was aware of both the benefit it could provide and the mind-numbing boredom doing the show ensured. You see, the show is shot out in the middle of Bum-fuck, England, and you have to be there really early in the morning for the first sound check. You then wait about an hour and a half, and then go back onstage and sound check again. Another ninety minutes and they have you stand in place in front of cameras. Ninety minutes later, another camera block. Same freakin' thing! Then you come back two hours later and have a dress rehearsal. Then after dinner, they bring in an audience and tape the show. It's a very long, very boring day, and you're stuck there. You can't leave in between. Part of the deal.

But this show was different. Instead of the usual six to eight performers on the hourlong show, this show was dedicated to Sir Elton John (not yet a Sir at this point), and I was the only other guest. Elton had a new album that he was promoting, *Made in England*. The first single, "Believe," was headed up the charts, and I really loved it.

Having never met him, and being a true lifelong fan, I was just thrilled that I might at least get to shake his hand. But after we had settled in to our dressing room that morning, Elton's assistant came over and said, "Elton would love to meet you and said if you'd like to come and hang out in his dressing room with him and his band, please come on over."

As you can imagine, unlike my six-foot-by-six-foot mirrored closet of a dressing room, Elton's was much larger. Still Kremlin gray and ugly, but bigger. And he had his staff put up curtains on rolling stands, and they had candles lit.

I walked in and Elton greeted me like an old friend. Warm and charming, he immediately engaged me with questions about my travels and shocked me by complimenting me on specific songs of mine he had heard and said he liked. He put me so at ease, as did his band, and in between each tedious rerun of sound and camera blocking, he'd have me back to his room and we'd pick up the conversation where we left off. We laughed a lot, and he told truly entertaining stories while never clearly dominating the discussion. A true gentleman. More than once I found myself thinking, *I'm sitting here hanging with Elton Fucking John.*

It was a few minutes before the actual performance taping, and I was in my dressing room making sure that each chest hair—visible because I was wearing only jeans and a black vest with no shirt (and, yeah, thinking this was a cool look, by the way)—was strategically in place, when my tour manager walked in and said, "Dude, have you eaten *anything* today?" I was, and occasionally still am, pretty bad at looking after my metabolism, especially when I'm on the road and busy. I've also been either vegetarian or pescatarian since I was eighteen, and strictly vegan since 2014, which can make eating while traveling extra precarious in meat-heavy parts of the world. I was getting pretty scrawny, and my TM was concerned.

Looking like an ashamed twelve-year-old, I said, "Nope." So he bolted next door and came back with a small tuna sandwich wrapped in plastic wrap. As I tweaked my lion's mane of a coif (the mullet long gone but still huge hair), I wolfed down a few bites of the sandwich. And as I did one last quick mirror check, I noticed that one of my veneers from a front tooth was gone. I had just swallowed it along with a mouthful of tuna, lettuce, and wheat bread. And as this sickening realization hit my brain, a British voice over a loudspeaker yelled, "Places!"

All I could do was walk to the stage, mouth closed, and strategize on the way. I decided I could get away with this. "Hazard" is a song about a murder in a small town. Not something I'd be smiling while singing anyway, thank god. And though I usually kidded around with studio audiences and posed for photos, this time I'd play it completely "serious musician." This was the only option. If I smiled at all, I looked like someone named Gomer.

Somehow I got through the performance without opening my mouth any wider than to let the lyrics sink into the microphone, and I waved to the crowd without a smile and left the stage. When we got backstage, my band, noticing my unusually stern demeanor, asked if everything was okay. I looked up from my chair and cracked open a big smile, and you'd have thought these guys were seeing the last scene in a snuff film. *"Oh, god!" "Dude!" "What the fuck?" "Holy shit!"*

Needless to say, it didn't help make me feel any better about my appearance. But the show was over, and, mercifully, I was headed home to LA the next morning, so I could get immediate dental reconstruction. The only problem now was I hadn't said good-bye to Elton John.

It would have seemed really odd, after hanging out all day, for me to leave without at least saying good-bye. He was packing up his bag as I walked into his dressing room and gave him a quick hug and said, lips covering my front teeth so that I now sounded like I had taken a crash course in mumbling that very afternoon, "Really great meeting you. Travel safely." And before he could say anything but "Bye," I was down the hall, into a car, and gone.

To this day, I can't help but wonder if he thought, *Wow, is that guy moody.*

29

"I'LL NEVER FALL
IN LOVE AGAIN"

When I was about seven years old, the only singer who came close to Elvis in my hero worship was Tom Jones. He was a huge star and had a television variety series that was on every Friday night. On every episode, Tom would have celebrity guests, do comedy routines, and then close the show with a two-song live concert. He always came out for those two songs in a tuxedo with a bow tie, and between the first and second song, he would untie the tie and throw it to a woman in the audience.

Thanks to being the ring boy, at age six, in my uncle's wedding, I had a tux that still fit me, and every Friday night my mom and grandmother (and usually a visiting aunt or two) would join me in front of the TV for Tom's show. I would dress in the tux and wait for the concert segment, and knowing all of Tom's songs, I would get up and sing along with him. And when he threw his tie to the adoring lady in the TV studio audience, I took *my* tie off and threw it to my aunt. Looking back now, this was easily one of the geekiest things I ever did, but hey, I was *seven*.

Flash forward twenty-three years. I'm in my house in LA and I get a call from a guy named Mark Woodward, who is not only Tom

Jones's manager, but also his son. Mark tells me he's trying to get his old man into the studio to record some new material, and they're both fans of my writing and would like to see if I have any songs for Tom. I say I'm honored and interested in seeing if I can help, and the next day I'm invited over to Tom's house for a meeting.

As I pull into the gates of Tom's mansion (previously owned by Dean Martin), I'm filled with memories of my childhood admiration of him. Not so much the tie throwing, but the countless hours in my basement listening over and over to "Delilah" and "Daughter of Darkness" and my absolute favorite, "I'll Never Fall in Love Again." I hoped he'd be a cool guy, and I was far from disappointed.

Warm and friendly, Tom greeted me out by his pool looking about twenty years younger than his actual fifty-three. He showed me around his home, which included a room full of photos of Tom with a dizzying array of superstars, and then we sat at a piano and talked before I played him an idea or two. He loved one song of mine I'd just written, and we went into my demo studio in the San Fernando Valley the following week to record it.

We spent most of our time in the studio laughing. I'm a huge fan of the old comedy routines of Derek and Clive, the fictional team of Dudley Moore and Peter Cook. Their recordings were as foulmouthed and inappropriate as it gets, and possibly the funniest material I've ever heard. I knew much of it by heart and, it turned out, so did Tom Jones. We laughed ourselves stupid doing Derek and Clive routines for each other, finishing each other's sentences and punch lines.

Tom was due to play a concert a few nights later at the Universal Amphitheatre and invited me. I went backstage to say hello before the show, and after we caught up and talked about the music we'd been working on together, I said, "You're going to sing 'I'll Never Fall in Love,' right?" (Actually, the official title is "Looks Like I'll Never Fall in Love Again," but nobody's going to say that title in a casual conversation.) He said, "No, we haven't done that one in a long time." I was mortified. I said, "Are you fuckin' *kidding* me? How can you not do that song? It's my *favorite* song you've ever done!"

Just then, his musical director walked by and Tom said, "Hey, do you guys even have a chart for 'Never Gonna Fall'?" (See? Even Tom wouldn't waste all that oxygen on the whole title.)

The MD said, "Yeah, we have a chart. But we've never rehearsed it. We could probably just wing it, though."

So Tom, being the über-cool dude he is, grabs a set list and decides to slot the song in as the second song of Act Two after intermission, just as a favor to me.

The show starts and by thirty minutes in, two things are evident. One, Tom Jones is singing his *ass* off and has never sounded better. He's singing "Hard to Handle," the old Otis Redding song, but with the newer Black Crowes arrangement. And he's blowing me completely away. But two, it seems I might be the *only* one he's blowing away.

The audience of middle-aged and up women are just sitting there, and aside from the few who are at least bouncing up and down in their seats, the crowd is pretty dead. By intermission it's the same, and as the house lights go up I'm thinking to myself, *What the hell? He's killing it up there, and these people are lame. I don't get it.*

Twenty minutes later, Act Two begins with "Thunderball," the old James Bond theme Tom sang in the film of the same name, and though he thoroughly slays the song, it does little to rile up this apathetic audience. Tom then says, "This next song is one we haven't done in a long time, but a friend of mine in the audience asked me to sing it, so here goes."

The band kicks in, and Tom sings, "I've been in loooove so many tiiiiimes . . ." and proceeds to use the song as if it's a master class in singing and performance, nailing that brutally high last "in looooooove" better than ever. The song ends and the audience goes mental. Everybody's out of their seat for an extended standing ovation and remain up and dancing and screaming (and yeah, throwing their underwear, although at that point it was more like a bunch of flying pairs of Depends).

After the show, we went backstage and Tom looked at me and before he could say anything, I said, "Dude, fire that manager son of yours and hire ME!!!"

30

"THE WAY SHE LOVES ME"

M y tour supporting the *Rush Street* album was an eighteen-month journey around the world, and I knew that soon after the last show, I'd have to start recording another album to feed the beast that was my record label. In order to do this, writing songs on the road became a natural routine. I was never much of a partier and was always concerned about preserving my voice for shows. Instead of staying out with the band and crew, I was usually in my hotel suite within an hour of that night's last song, trying to decompress. The adrenaline rush of a show stays with you for a while, so sleep never came very quickly. I often used that alone time to write songs, using the buzz I was feeling from the show as inspiration to make the next album, and therefore the next tour, better.

On that particular tour we ended the European leg in London with two shows at the Hammersmith Odeon. Although my first ever show in London, in 1987 at a famous club called Ronnie Scott's, had been a pretty lame experience (the mostly journalist audience was not the most adoring crowd), I had developed a great fan base in the UK, and the Hammersmith shows were always a blast.

I wolfed down a quick sandwich in the dressing room after the last show and headed to my hotel in Kensington. Pacing around my large suite, I started absentmindedly singing a melody and lyrics. "Lemme tell ya 'bout the way she loves me . . . oooh, na-na-na-ne-na . . . I'm crazy 'bout the way she loves me . . . oooh, la-da-da-de-da . . ."

It sounded like it could've been some old Everly Brothers song, but I knew it wasn't anything previously written. By the time I fell asleep, I had written most of the song, which came to be titled "The Way She Loves Me," singing the bits and pieces into one of several handheld cassette recorders I carried with me everywhere. It was catchy and retro. But I knew I could cut a great pop-rock record of it and that it would be a fun song to play live. I also knew immediately that the chorus melody was ripe for a great three-part harmony. I could hear it all in my head.

I had already procured some great singers to grace my previous albums with their voices. Timothy B. Schmit and Randy Meisner from the Eagles, Bill Champlin from Chicago, Bobby Kimball from Toto, and the aforementioned Luther Vandross, whose vocals on my *Rush Street* album still wow me to this day. For the vocals on this new song, I felt confident I could not only come up with perfect vocalist choices but also probably get them on the phone as well.

I started cutting the album that would become *Paid Vacation* in the summer of 1993, and "The Way She Loves Me" was one of the first tracks recorded. The rhythm section was made up of three guys I had recorded with many times: Madonna's drummer Jonathan "Sugarfoot" Moffett, Leland Sklar on bass, and my old friend Bruce Gaitsch on guitar. A few weeks later I had Bill Champlin in to play Hammond B-3 organ on several songs, including "The Way She Loves Me," and the track was then ready for my lead vocal and the backgrounds.

I had decided to ask Luther to again honor me with his talent, and once he agreed, I thought about who might be the ultimate "get" to sing with him. The answer was Lionel Richie. The question was, however, would he do it?

As I wrote earlier, it was my work as a background singer that put me in a room with Kenny Rogers (on Lionel's recommendation for Kenny to hire me), which resulted in Kenny recording three of my songs and jumpstarting my successful songwriting career. So, my session that day with Lionel singing "You Are" was an enormous catalyst in my life. I often think about all the circumstances of timing and destiny that could've prevented it and altered my professional life completely. I'm just grateful as fuck it happened as it did.

So yes, Lionel and I go way back. But by 1993, given how hectic touring and recording can be, I hadn't seen or spoken to him in about five years. It was nothing personal, just our two lives moving in different directions.

I still had his number and finally reached him one night around midnight.

"Lonnie B!" I said. This was Lionel's longtime nickname.

"My brother, how the hell are you? It's been too long. I see you out there on TV and tearing up the charts. I'm so proud of you."

"Well, thanks to you for getting the ball rolling and believing in me. Listen, I've written a song for my new album, and I have Luther Vandross coming in to sing background vocals on it, and I would be so honored if you'd come sing with us."

"Doctor [Lionel calls people "Doctor" a lot], you got a deal! I love Luther and I'd do anything for you, you know that. When and where?"

We made arrangements to meet up the following week.

On the day of the recording session, I arrived at the studio around ten minutes prior to our agreed start time of 3:00 p.m. Luther was already there, sitting in the control room and wearing a colorful, checked sweater. He gave me a big hug and we sat down to chat while the engineer began setting up the microphones.

"I really like this song," he said, "but I'm also really looking forward to singing with Lionel."

Three o'clock came and went. We crept past 3:30, with no sign of Lionel. Cell phones were uncommon at this point, so aside from calling his assistant, there was really no way of checking on Lionel's arrival or safety. By 3:45, Luther was starting to get a little edgy. Deep sighs. Pacing.

Finally, a little after four o'clock, with still no Lionel, Luther said, "You know what? This is bullshit. I'm not going to sit around and wait for anyone, including Lionel Richie."

I started to say something to ease the situation when I heard a sound around the corner. I got up and as I stood in the studio lounge doorway, I saw Lionel headed toward me.

Despite the tension with Luther, I was happy to see my old friend and reached out to hug him. He literally pushed me aside without a word and walked directly to Luther and said, "Hey, man, I'm Lionel. It's so great to meet you, and I'm so sorry I'm late. Have you been waiting long?"

Without missing a beat, Luther said, with a completely smile-free face, "Yes, I have."

I thought, *Fuck. Me. This whole session just went to shit.* And then, as I had seen it several times before, I witnessed the magical charm of Lionel Richie. I don't even remember what he said to Luther, only the way he said it. Within five minutes, he had Luther laughing and practically ready to make Lionel the beneficiary of his will.

We went to the studio piano, where I sat and played the chorus of the song over and over until we worked out who would sing which harmony notes. I had already sung the melody of the chorus, so I asked Luther to double those notes, and Lionel sounded great singing the lower third harmony. I spent my early years as a background singer honing my high falsetto so that I could even occasionally double as a female voice, so singing the high harmony on this was a no-brainer.

We ran through the chorus a few times, finding the right blend, and had it done in half an hour. For the last chorus, Lionel came up with an extra part, reminiscent of a street corner doo-wop group, and sang "baby, um-um, baby" on top of what we'd already recorded, and the session was over.

The song became another Top Twenty single for me in 1994. It was an even bigger hit on the AC chart, peaking at number 5, and MTV and VH1 gave the music video a lot of plays.

31

OPRAH, O.J., AND ME

I n 1994, the opening of the World Cup was held at Soldier Field in
Chicago. It was a really big deal, or at least the media and, more so,
the folks at Major League Soccer wanted America to think it was.
This was before we had Beckham or any celebrity players to pull our
attention away from the "real" American spectator sports. Soccer
was the sport we played in eighth grade, not the one we lined up
outside a stadium for and paid $50 to watch. But in 1994, there was
a movement to try to get Americans into it, and though it ultimately
failed, there was a brief period of huge buzz.

The Soldier Field opening spectacle was to be hosted by Oprah
Winfrey, and featured a performance by Diana Ross and an appearance by President Clinton. I was asked sing the National Anthem,
and everyone in my camp was thrilled because I had a new album
out, and the media were expecting a television viewing audience of
30 million. *Massive* exposure.

I was asked, encouraged even, to lip sync the anthem, as other
big-name singers had recently done at the Super Bowl to avoid
audio mishaps. But that's cheating, so I said, "No way. I'm singing
it live." I decided to do an a cappella arrangement featuring four

background singers (including my mom!) that I prerecorded and sang live to.

On June 17, we all arrived and ran through the song without any issues and waited for the live broadcast to begin. Soldier Field was packed to the rafters. The president was seated in a front-row box. Cameras and news and sports crews were everywhere. Oprah welcomed the huge crowd in the stadium and the massive television audience.

After she introduced a dance company, she walked back toward the tent, where they had chairs and air conditioning for her, but she ended up walking exactly where the production staff had explicitly warned her *not* to walk, and she went crashing through the floor of the stage like it was made of papier-mâché. I was standing about thirty feet away and saw this happen. There was no way I could have predicted this mishap, nor could I have reached her in time. In fact, I never even met her the entire day. (Not that I made an effort to do so.) And I'm only marginally ashamed to tell you now that as soon as I realized she wasn't hurt, I laughed my ass off.

About ten minutes later, the singers and I took our places, and Oprah, shaken from her trip into the bowels of the stage, introduced me. I remember looking around at the thousands of people packed into my hometown football stadium, on a gorgeous June afternoon, and really, *really* taking it all in. I felt so lucky to be there. I knew this was a big deal, and I was thrilled to be part of it, entrusted with our National Anthem no less.

I sang proudly, with less nervousness than I'd predicted, and felt like I pretty much nailed it. As I hit that high note on "freeeeeeeeeeee," the crowd erupted, and when I hit the last note—"braaaaave"—four fighter jets soared overhead at the precisely perfect moment. The ovation was big and sincere and brought a huge smile to my face. Having my mom up there with me provided an extra source of gratitude.

My father was in Los Angeles and had been working there, so he couldn't be with us. He would watch the live telecast and had made me promise to call him as soon as I finished, so he could give me props for what he was confident would be a solid performance. As soon as I was offstage (walking *only* where the stagehands had instructed) I dialed his number.

"Hello?"

"Dad, what'd you think? Was it great?"

"Uh, pal, I didn't see you."

"What? What do you mean? How come you didn't see me?"

"Richard, *nobody* saw you."

"What are you *talking about?* I just *did* it!"

"So, you don't know what's happening?"

"No. What the hell?"

"They just cut into the broadcast. O. J. Simpson is in a white Bronco leading police on a high-speed chase!"

So, it turned out that literally as Oprah was saying my name, televisions everywhere were hit with "We interrupt this program to bring you this special news bulletin." And they stayed with the infamous Bronco chase until it was over, hours later. Hardly anyone in the country saw the soccer game, let alone me singing the anthem.

Maybe that's what I get for laughing at Oprah falling.

"THROUGH MY VEINS"

I t was barely past four in the morning in Osaka when the hotel room phone rang. *This better be important,* I thought as I wrestled with my sleepy disorientation. I was on tour in Japan in July 1997, playing several cities there over two weeks. Finally, I cleared my throat and picked up the phone.

"Hello?"

It was Cynthia. She gave me news that no one ever wants to hear. My father had been in a car accident. Immediately, my heart started pounding and I felt a little dizzy.

"*What?* What happened? Where is he now?"

"They didn't tell me much, babe. Only that it was a bad accident and he's been injured. I have the phone number of the trauma center in Las Vegas where he's been taken."

He had been driving cross-country from Los Angeles to our family vacation cabin in Minocqua, Wisconsin. This place was his favorite spot on earth, and when he bought it in 1974, it became his refuge from the pressures and pace of the jingle business, which he had dominated since the mid-1960s. The sheer volume of music he composed over twenty-plus years is impossible to wrap your head around. But he also arranged and produced these compositions for every product and company from Kellogg's Raisin Bran and Dial soap to Oldsmobile and AT&T. Most days, he would record two or three separate sessions in a day. Sometimes more. It was a high-pressure business, but he thrived on the thrill of it. He did, however, realize a few years into it that he needed to step away from it occasionally to remain sane. And that cabin in Minocqua recharged his batteries.

In the late '80s, he and I shared the costs of updating the property and building a year-round house there. It sits by a small, private lake. He hadn't been to the house in a few years and was excited to go that summer. Knowing he was not the most focused driver, and that my mother would not be accompanying him, I asked him several times to consider flying to Milwaukee and making a shorter drive, but he was actually looking forward to the long drive from California and back.

A few miles outside of Vegas, he was changing lanes on the highway and somehow clipped the back of a truck. In trying to control the SUV he was driving, he overcorrected, causing the vehicle to flip several times. He was airlifted to the trauma center and was about to go into surgery when I finally reached the surgeon on the phone.

Before he could really start talking to me, he said, "Mr. Marx, please hold the line. Your father wants to speak to you."

My dad's voice came on the phone with the opening line, "I know. I've always gotta be the center of attention!" He sounded okay, which was a tremendous relief. He then said, "Pal, I'm pretty badly hurt, but this isn't life or death, I don't think, and I want you to promise me you won't cancel any gigs. Just stay in Japan and finish the tour, and I'll see you in a few days."

I had two more shows scheduled in Tokyo, but I was freaking out and wanted to come home. My dad knew this and made me promise not to cancel anything, at least not yet. We spoke for another minute and said our "I love you"s, and he handed me back to the surgeon, who said, "Look, he's got a lot of broken bones, and we have to make sure there's no internal damage, but sit tight and we can speak in several hours after the surgery."

I hung up feeling scared and very helpless but optimistic. I let my band and crew know what was happening and said for now it looked like we could go to Tokyo and finish the shows.

About six hours later, the surgeon called and said that while my father was stable, he was in worse shape than they thought. His heart was now in a very unstable rhythm. Battling obesity his whole life, my dad had had heart issues since age fifty, He had undergone a procedure mere months before this accident to shock his heart into a normal sinus rhythm. Ironically, it was the best he'd felt in years. Then this accident happened.

The surgeon urged me to come home as quickly as possible. I was on a plane within hours, flying twelve hours with no way of contact, and being as frightened as I've ever been all that time not knowing if my father was still alive. I couldn't sleep or eat, I couldn't read or watch a movie. I couldn't concentrate on anything but my fear. I don't think I moved in my seat the entire flight.

I landed around noon Vegas time, and ran off the plane dragging my bag behind me. I found the first cab outside and burst into the emergency room, clearly distraught until I found a nurse who had my father's chart information. I was told he was critical but stable. I remember the trepidation of walking into his room and fearing what I was about to see. He was asleep when I entered his room, and I just stood there, in shock. It was still my dad, but he was bandaged everywhere and had tubes coming out of multiple spots connected to the machines we see in every hospital TV drama. He was a very large man. Just over six feet tall but always somewhere between 215 and 250 pounds, depending on the success of the diet he was on. In this bed he looked so small. And broken.

My mother arrived later that day, and we spent just over three weeks there at his bedside, only occasionally leaving the hospital to get a quick coffee or bite, or sleep in an actual bed at a nearby hotel. While he remained stable, his condition never seemed to improve. He was intubated the entire time, unable to breathe on his own and unable to move in his bed, let alone walk.

My mother and I began planning his long road of rehabilitation when the doctors in Vegas suggested he be moved closer to my home in Chicago. I arranged an ICU-equipped jet to transport him to the best hospital near my home, a ten-minute drive away.

The second evening there, I was with him in his room until almost midnight, talking about how he would start trying to walk the next morning with a walker. His mood was very subdued, but I knew that could be the strong painkillers he was on. Sitting next to his bed, I was looking at him when he turned to me and mouthed, because of the tube in his throat, the words "I'm finished with music."

I stood up and leaned closer in to him. "What, Dad?"

He looked me right in the eye and mouthed it again. "I'm finished with music."

"Dad, you and I both know you'll never be finished with music. It's what you're about. Yes, this is going to be a long fucking road getting you back on your feet, but soon enough you'll be back writing and conducting. You'll be back to work."

He let my words hang in the air a moment before looking at me, and with the slightest smile that was more begrudging than accepting, he said, "Okay."

I kissed his forehead and said, "I'll see you in the morning for your rehab. Get some sleep."

I then went home to get some much needed rest, but for some reason I was totally unable to sleep. A little after six the next morning

I got a call from the ICU saying he was having some issues and I should get over there immediately. When I walked in, a nurse told me that he "didn't make it."

Everything went black.

I collapsed on the floor as her words swirled in my head, and the brutal and devastating reality attacked me that my father was gone.

My dad and I had, by any estimation, a truly remarkable relationship. We were best friends. We had each other's backs and trusted each other implicitly. We laughed a lot together, loved each other beyond words, and best of all, as he often reminded me, we had no "unfinished business" with each other.

He'd say, "If one of us gets hit by a bus tomorrow, we've shared everything. We've told and shown each other how much we love one another thousands of times, and you know how proud I am of you, and I know what I mean to you. That's a very rare thing between fathers and sons."

This immense gift was something that would help to heal me over time, but for most of the year following his death, I was in a severe state of grief. Nearly twenty-four years have passed, and I still miss him terribly, and always will.

Like my experience with romantic heartbreak, it was not surprising that my mourning worked its way into my songwriting. I released an album in 2000 called *Days in Avalon*, which contained two songs about my father. "Almost Everything" was a mid-tempo rock song that dealt more with my anguish and anger over losing him.

> Hand me the sun, say that I've won
> The world on a string
> And then I will have almost everything.

The other song was a simple chord progression that, in my head, sounded like a traditional country song, almost bluegrass. So rather than contort it into something it wasn't, I recorded "Straight from My Heart" the way I heard it internally. The lyrics I wrote were appropriately simple: basically a letter to my dad about how deeply I missed him.

> I will always try
> To hold my head up to the sky
> If only just to let you know
> That straight from my heart
> I still miss you so.

I was fortunate enough to have the brilliant Alison Krauss sing the harmony vocals, and she even flew to LA to perform it with me on *The Tonight Show*. I felt a sense of relief writing those songs and felt I had purged my sorrow.

Then one middle of the night three years later, I was in my home recording studio, and not even writing or recording. I was organizing the tape vault I'd had built that housed all my recordings over the years. I'm a night owl anyway, and it was not uncommon for me to be in the studio most of the night.

For some reason I still can't explain, and with no conscious provocation, I stopped what I was doing and walked to the grand piano in the middle of the high-vaulted-ceilinged room where I recorded. I began playing a piece of music that I felt was somehow writing itself. Within moments I had visions of my father's face in my mind. And about an hour later, I had written a song called "Through My Veins." It turned out I had a lot more to say to my father, and this song did the job.

But I've missed you hanging 'round
And the way we were together,
But I can let go now,
'Cause it's you running through my veins.

I recorded it not long after, and it remains one of my favorite songs I've ever written. While never a single or hit song, it became a fan favorite in my concerts and often receives a standing ovation. It's my ultimate tribute to my father.

33

"THE ONE THAT GOT AWAY"

In 1979, I was a sixteen-year-old dying to be a successful singer-songwriter, and I was also a musical sponge. It was a great time for music, and one song that I cranked up every time it came on the radio was "This Is It" by Kenny Loggins. I wasn't that familiar with Kenny's older stuff, except for maybe "Your Mama Don't Dance" by Loggins and Messina. But "This Is It" was such a different-sounding pop record, and Kenny's vocal blew me away. Within a week or so of hearing the single multiple times, I headed to my neighborhood record store and plunked down $8.99 plus tax on the album that contained "This Is It" called *Keep the Fire*.

The opening track, "Love Has Come of Age" solidified me as a full-on Kenny Loggins fan. Killer rhythm arrangements, great musicianship, and his insanely brilliant vocals. Kenny's immense vocal range, not only in terms of actual notes over several octaves but his phrasing and use of falsetto, inspired me greatly, and I would spend hours each day after school or in my car (a navy blue and silver two-tone Datsun 280 ZX with a T-top, baby!) singing along with every track from the album, emulating Kenny's vocals as perfectly as I could. I became aware over a month or so that singing along with Kenny Loggins was its own form of voice training, as I saw a dramatic improvement in my range and power and watched my own already formidable falsetto voice become what felt almost limitless. The following summer of 1980 brought us Kenny's smash hit "I'm Alright" from the film *Caddyshack*, and that became my new favorite song and vocal performance.

At eighteen, in the spring of 1982, I moved to Los Angeles to pursue my career. That fall, Kenny released a new album called *High Adventure*, which I bought the day it was released. Though Kenny has made some great music since, this album remains not only my favorite by him, but one of my favorite albums ever. Back then, like many music fans on a budget, I would buy an album and then record it on audio cassette so I could play it in my car. This was pre-digital audio and, looking back, it's amazing we could hear anything but hiss. Still somehow the preexisting hissy sound that comes with analog vinyl combined with the insanely loud white noise of cassettes didn't dampen my love for the music I was blasting in my car.

The *High Adventure* album became my new benchmark, not only for singing, but songwriting and versatility of style. Rockers like "Don't Fight It" and "If It's Not What You're Looking For" blissfully cohabitated with R&B-influenced tracks like the hit "Heart to Heart" and gorgeous ballads like "The More We Try." Again, the musicianship and arrangements were stellar, and Kenny was singing better than ever. I quickly memorized every nuance of every song on that record. And I could still recite it all today.

So when, in the early months of 1983, I was invited by Kenny's then-manager, Larry Larson, to see Kenny perform, I was psyched, to say the least. I'd met Larry a few months before through my attorney, and Larry had shown some interest in managing me. While that never materialized, he did bring me to see Kenny's show and I met him briefly afterward.

About a month later, I got a call at home from the producer David Foster. He was working on a demo of a song with Kenny and asked if I'd come down to the studio and sing some background vocals. I always did this kind of thing for David for free, not that he ever offered to pay me. He and I both knew this was great experience for me as a young up-and-coming songwriter, artist, and producer, and I did learn a lot from those sessions. I can't say I do things the same way in the studio as David or other producers I worked with, but it was like going to Record Production College.

I jumped in my car, drove to a tiny studio in the San Fernando Valley, and parked my Datsun next to the Mercedes and Ferraris in the small driveway. Kenny vaguely recalled meeting me with his manager, Larry, but greeted me warmly all the same. David and Kenny played me the song they were working on. It was called "Never Say Never," and they were going to try to get it placed as the title song to the upcoming James Bond film of the same name starring Sean Connery. I remember thinking it was a really good song, even with the very sparse demo production featuring David's keyboards and a drum machine.

Kenny taught me some harmony vocals on certain lines in the song, and he and I stood at the same microphone and recorded them. As I stood there, though concentrating on my vocal job at hand, I couldn't help but be acutely aware that I was standing next to my singing idol, working with him. It made more sense than I was even conscious of at the time. I've always had this ability to will people who've made an impact on me into my life. It's happened more times than I can count. It just took me a few decades to realize that I had been in control of it all along. What you think most about is what you will experience. Good and bad. And I was constantly focused on working with my heroes. And now it was happening. It still does, actually.

The three of us spent a couple hours recording the vocals, and as it was already late in the evening, David and Kenny headed home to their families and I went home to my apartment, incredibly wired by the experience of having sung with one of my vocal heroes. As he got in his car in the studio driveway, Kenny said, "Hey, let me give you my number. Maybe we can hang out sometime. I live in Santa Barbara, but I'm in LA frequently. Do you happen to play racquetball?" I nodded with a smile.

A couple of weeks later, I rang Kenny to see if he was going to be in LA anytime soon and to just maintain the connection that had begun at the studio that night.

"Oh, hey man," he said. "No, I'm not in LA soon, but I'm around in Santa Barbara. Would you want to drive up one day this week?"

So we arranged a time to meet at the local racquetball club where Kenny liked to play and spent the afternoon over a few matches followed by lunch at a nearby restaurant. He mentioned that the producers of the Bond film had never even bothered to respond to the song David and he had sent them, which both blew my mind and made me feel a little better about all the corporate bozos who had ignored me. He also asked me about my plans and what I wanted to do in the business. I told him I was happy getting work as a background singer but really wanted to be an artist and songwriter-producer.

The next time we got together a few weeks later, he asked to hear something I'd written. I had just finished a song called "Yours Tonight," an up-tempo pop-rock song with a techno groove in the stylistic vein of Michael Sembello's "Maniac," recently a massive hit. I scraped enough money together to go into Lion Share, one of the studios where I regularly worked as a background singer on big-budget albums. I hired a staff engineer there and arrived around 11:00 p.m. with my own keyboard and drum machine in my trunk. After an hour of setting up, I recorded the demo through the wee hours, finishing around sunrise. This was the only way I could afford pro–studio quality demos on much less than a pro-studio budget.

After an hour of racquetball at a nearby club, we drove back to Kenny's Santa Barbara home. A sprawling estate, it had a separate building set up as a recording studio. (I would build my own version of this years later.) Kenny put the cassette of my "Yours Tonight" demo into a deck that was built into a large desk that housed his other audio equipment. Remember, this was a few years before CDs were invented, so a cassette was as high quality as a home demo could get at the time. He sat next to me, listening, and as soon as the first chorus passed, he opened his eyes and stopped the cassette, mid-song.

"Good melody," he said. "But do you want to fuck with it?"

"What do you mean?" I asked.

"Well, I mean if you love it as it is, that's cool. But if you're interested in picking it apart, I have some suggestions."

I was immediately aware of the opportunity being presented to me. One of my heroes was offering his expertise.

I said, "Of *course*! I'm up for trying whatever you want to."

Kenny listened to the chorus over and over, at least ten times before saying, "I think it's really just an edit. There's this eight-bar section I don't think you need. Without it, the chorus is stronger and more memorable."

He then, using what was the most barbaric but efficient means under the circumstances, cut out the eight-bar section in question. Hard to explain here in writing but basically it went like this: I played the original demo on my own portable cassette machine, which we hardwired into the cassette deck in Kenny's studio. Then on the new, duplicate recording, Kenny lined up the spot where the edit would start, and when the end of the "about to be deleted" eight bars arrived on my cassette, Kenny pressed "Record" on the studio deck. Instant homemade edit.

He was right. The chorus was stronger without those eight bars. While nothing ever became of "Yours Tonight," it was like getting a free songwriting master class. I drove home to my apartment in LA that night and listened to the new edited version of my demo nonstop the whole way for ninety minutes.

Kenny and I continued hanging out pretty frequently, but I never again asked him for musical help. I felt to do so would be intruding on our burgeoning friendship. One afternoon in late 1983, we met for another racquetball match. I picked him up at his Encino house where he lived part-time, and as he climbed into the passenger's seat, he said, "Hey, before we go, would you like to hear a couple new tracks I just cut? They're for a movie coming out next year called *Footloose*."

He slid the cassette into my car deck and pressed Play. The bending, rockabilly guitar riff blasted from the speakers, and we cranked the title song loud enough that the car windows were slightly shaking. When the song was over, I said, "Dude, this is a really fun song." As a longtime fan, "Footloose" wasn't one of my favorite songs of his, but it was masterfully written by Kenny and my pal Dean Pitchford (who also wrote the screenplay to the film and all the songs in it). "I don't know about this one," he said. "I mean, it could be a hit, but I'm just not that crazy about it."

I turned on the car engine and Kenny said, "Wait, there's another one. Check this out." And on came another song from the upcoming *Footloose* soundtrack, "I'm Free."

From the first notes of the intro, I was totally into the song. It was darker and edgier than "Footloose," and Kenny's vocal performance was, and still is, astounding in its range and power. Also cowritten with Dean, I felt *this* would be the biggest hit from the film's soundtrack.

"I fucking *love this!*" I exclaimed as the song faded.

Kenny smiled and said, "Yeah, I really dig this one, too."

This was one of the defining moments that proved I'd have made a really shitty A&R person. "Footloose" was released as the first single behind the opening of the film in 1984 and became Kenny's first number 1 single and one of the biggest songs of the decade. "I'm Free" was released as the follow-up single and peaked at number 22. So, yeah. When it comes to picking hits, don't ask me. I also didn't even want to record what became my biggest hit, "Right Here Waiting."

Shortly before the film *Footloose* was released, I found myself walking with Kenny down Michigan Avenue in Chicago. I was visiting my parents, who still lived there, and Kenny happened to be doing a concert at that time. We went to a local racquetball club and played for an hour before heading for a bite. As we walked among the lunchtime crowds along the busiest street in the third largest city in America, I saw Kenny's face grimace and his demeanor darken.

I said, "You all right?" (It didn't occur to me at the time that if he'd responded with "I'm alright" that it would've been fucking hilarious.) He was silent a moment before saying, "Look at this, man. I've been making music successfully for over ten years. I've toured nonstop and done a bunch of TV. And no one fucking recognizes me."

I realized he was at least mostly right. If he was spotted, no one stopped him or made it obvious they recognized him. It felt so strange to me because Kenny was such a big star in my mind. I felt bad that this was bugging him and tried to appease his mood.

"Dude, no one expects you to be walking down the street like this. It's just not on their radar. That's all it is."

"Yeah. Maybe."

He was still unconvinced.

Within six months of that walk down the street, *Footloose* was the biggest movie of the year and Kenny's title song was number 1 and nominated for an Oscar. I called him a couple times just to congratulate him and found it odd that he didn't respond. I figured he was just crazy busy. He launched a big tour behind this newfound success and did a dress rehearsal in LA before leaving for the first gig. I still hadn't heard from him but his bass player, Nathan East, was a dear friend of mine and invited me to the LA show.

There were only a couple hundred people in attendance, and afterward I saw Kenny come down from the stage and start talking to some friends. I went over and waited to say hello. When he saw me, he went, "Oh, hey, man." It was a bit cold considering all the times we'd hung out, but I patted him on the back and said, "Congrats on everything, buddy. You really deserve all this."

With only a hint of a smile, he muttered "Thanks" and turned and started talking to someone else. I drove home wondering if I could have done anything at any point to offend him and came up with nothing. So, I was left to conclude that now that he was the biggest star he'd yet been, I just wasn't cool enough to associate with anymore. The more I ruminated on this conclusion, the angrier I became. And so I now very actively disliked my former vocal hero.

Three and a half years passed, and I was out on tour supporting my debut album. It was early 1988, and my career was hot. One day in some hotel I got a call from my manager. "Hey, Kenny Loggins's agent just called me. They want to know if you'll open for him a week from Friday in Milwaukee. You actually have that night off, so you could do it."

I immediately responded, "Kenny Loggins can go fuck himself."

Without going into detail, I told my manager there was bad blood between me and Loggins, and I wasn't interested. Then my manager said, "Well, do whatever you want. But apparently the promoter wants you on this bill very badly and is willing to make it worth your while."

So, the businessman in me agreed. Sure enough, after advertising me on the bill the next day, the gig had a great turnout, with many in the audience my own fans. My band and I arrived in the afternoon and did a sound check before I had to leave the venue to do an interview at a local radio station. I didn't see Kenny then, nor did I see him when I returned to do my opening set. Midway through my show, the crowd up and dancing and fist-pumping, I looked over at the side of the stage and saw Kenny standing there in the wings. He was smiling big and bopping his head to the beat of whatever we were playing.

At the end of my set, with the crowd going crazy, I ran off the opposite side of the stage and into my dressing room. A few minutes later, my tour manager came in and said, "Kenny's outside and wants to say hi."

I said, "Bring him in."

Kenny walked in and high-fived a couple of my band members before walking over to me as I sat on a couch, guzzling Gatorade. As he approached, I didn't get up. And I didn't smile.

He said, "Hey, man! Long time! You were great out there!"

Quickly accepting his handshake, I looked at him with a blank stare and said, "Thanks."

The room got quiet and the vibe in the room got extremely uncomfortable. Kenny stood there, and after a minute or two of brutally awkward silence, looked at me and said, "Well, congrats on everything."

Again, all I returned was, "Thanks."

He left the room and my saxophone player Dave Koz came up to me and, breaking the silence, said, "So . . . you guys are buddies?"

About a year and a half later I heard from a mutual friend that Kenny was going through a pretty tough time, both professionally and personally. For some reason I still don't quite understand, considering the circumstances, I picked up the phone in a hotel room somewhere on tour and called Kenny.

We spoke for about an hour, and after making it clear that I was calling out of concern, and hearing that yes, he was having a tough time but was essentially okay, we started to hash through what had caused the rift between us. I spared no language and told him everything I'd felt, and he listened without defensiveness or excuses.

He said, "It's all true, Richard. I wronged you. Whatever the stuff was that led to that, you never did anything to me that warranted me cutting you off that way. I apologize. I hope we can move past it."

I accepted his apology and we hung up, agreeing to try to stay in touch. A few weeks later, Kenny rang asking if I'd consider singing a few songs at a benefit he was hosting in Santa Barbara, and I gladly agreed. We didn't have time to hang out, but it was nice to see him.

A few years passed and, after accidentally running into each other a couple times at industry events, an opportunity came up where I decided to reach out to Kenny and ask for a return favor. It was 1999 and my father had passed away two years before. I had created a scholarship fund in my father's name at his music school alma mater, the DePaul School of Music in Chicago. The fund would provide a great education to exceptional music students who couldn't otherwise afford it.

To finance the fund, I put together a series of benefit concerts. The first one, held in 1998, featured myself along with my talented friends Michael Bolton, Kenny G, Fee Waybill, Kevin Cronin, and the great Luther Vandross. It was a huge success, and the following year I wanted at least one amazing musical guest. I asked Kenny, who immediately agreed to come.

We performed a few songs together with my band, and Kenny was amazing as usual. After the show I asked him if he'd like to hang out a bit the next day before he headed back to Santa Barbara. I was then living just outside the city of Chicago where the concerts were held. Kenny came to my house for an early lunch and stayed until leaving for his evening flight. After some food, we ended up sitting in my recording studio, talking about a million things. It wasn't like the old times when I was a teenage fan of his. It was two men who had quite a few things in common.

He mentioned that day that he was actually considering retiring. I said, "What? You can't. Singing is a huge part of who you are."

He stared at me and said, "Wow. That's so weird. I mentioned my retiring to my six-year-old son Luke the other day, and he said, 'But Daddy, if you stop singing, you'll die.'"

Kenny got emotional retelling me this conversation with his little boy, and I put my arm around him and said, "From the mouths of babes, right?"

Performing together at the benefit concert and the hang at my house the next day jump-started a new friendship between me and Kenny. Soon thereafter, he called me and said he was writing songs for a new album and wondered if I'd be interested in collaborating with him. I gladly accepted, and a few weeks later he came to stay at my house for a few days.

Arriving in the early evening, we had dinner and delved into a deep conversation about life, fatherhood, relationships, and more. This would become a pretty regular happening between us and still stands these days. I asked about his sons from his first marriage,

Crosby and Cody. I'd met both of them when they were little boys and now they were in their early twenties.

Kenny told me that he'd been estranged from Cody for well over a year, barely seeing or speaking to him. He explained that he felt Cody was the "casualty" of Kenny's divorce from his first wife, Eva, and that Cody had blamed Kenny for the bitterness that defined the aftermath. I could tell that Kenny was really heartbroken about the silence between him and his second child. We called it a night and agreed to try to do some writing the following day.

I woke up early, made my way downstairs to the kitchen, and sat alone accompanied only by a leftover iced coffee from the fridge. I normally prepare for writing sessions well in advance and had already compiled a few melodic ideas to bounce off Kenny. But then all of a sudden (as has happened innumerable times before and since), I heard this melody in my head. I walked down the long hallway to my studio, sat at the beautiful Yamaha grand piano that lived in the corner of the big tracking room, and began translating what was in my head to my fingers on the keys. I played it over and over and grabbed a handheld digital recorder (I had them stashed everywhere throughout my house and in my car) and recorded the idea.

Kenny came downstairs from the guest room above the studio about an hour later, and I poured him some coffee.

I said, "I just came up with a melody I want to show you."

We went to the piano, and I played and sang it using dummy "la-la" lyrics.

Kenny stared at me for a second and said, "Dude. That is so fucking . . . beautiful." He asked to hear it again, and this time, as I stopped playing, his face turned serious. "If it's okay with you, I think I'd like to write this about Cody."

I immediately knew two things. One: this would be a very difficult experience for Kenny, emotionally. And two: the melody I'd written begged for a topic like this.

Over the next several hours, we finished the melody together. My original melody was clearly the chorus, and we quickly wrote the verse, pre-chorus, and bridge melodies, finishing each other's musical thoughts effortlessly. But then we began the task of telling the story through rhyming lyrics. This had no choice but to be completely authentic. Kenny wanted to address his estrangement from his son, whom he desperately loved and missed terribly.

I said, "Maybe we should just talk about it. Tell me the whole story, and the lyrics will come from that."

As he spoke, fleshing out incidents and conversations over a period of many years, Kenny would regularly get to a part of a story and break down crying. Apologizing at first, then regaining his composure, he'd go on.

At this point in my life, I had three young sons myself. The very thought of this kind of thing happening between me and any of them was excruciating. As the afternoon and conversation wore on, as many tears as lyrics came. From both of us.

As we worked on one particular line, we wrote "And in this world of separate houses, someone's always missing someone, day after day, and year after year." We both took a minute to cry like little babies; then we'd look at each other and burst out laughing at the ridiculousness of two grown men in a room sobbing, before carrying on trying to finish the song.

The chorus of the song goes:

> Though you and I are distant
> Don't ever think I didn't want you

> Or miss you every day
> No matter where life takes you,
> Know that I'll still be waiting patiently
> For the day that you've forgiven me, my son,
> The one that got away

That last line seemed like the perfect title.

We finally finished the lyrics, and as we both wiped tears from our cheeks I said, "Well, all you have to do now is sing it. Good luck with that."

We both laughed hard at that moment, but half an hour later, as Kenny stood at the microphone inside the vocal booth, we soon realized it wasn't that funny. I had recorded a track of me playing piano and added some synthesized strings that sounded pretty close to a real symphony, adding a movie score–like emotion to an already heart-wrenching song. When Kenny was ready, I pressed Record and the track began. The opening line was:

> You were the quiet one
> Afraid to sleep alone
> Heaven knows I was lonely, too

On the first take, Kenny barely got out the words "quiet one" before he began crying, his voice choking with emotion. And I would stop recording until he could compose himself. It was the oddest vocal session I've ever experienced. Devastatingly sad and awkwardly hilarious at the same time. It was also, as you can imagine, a *very* long afternoon.

Finally, Kenny's vocal was done and we had a really beautiful demo of our song. As he left to fly back home, Kenny expressed his gratitude to me for burrowing through the emotional sludge needed to finish our song. I knew that no matter what happened with it commercially, it was meaningful. And important. I just had no idea how important at the time.

About two weeks later, Kenny called me to tell me that he'd just seen Cody for the first time in many months. Kenny had called him and said, "I need to see you right away," and Cody agreed. They ended up sitting in Kenny's car, where Kenny played him "The One That Got Away." They both cried very hard and hugged each other a good long time. It prompted a conversation that turned into understanding, forgiveness, and healing. It mended their relationship, which they enjoy closely to this day.

Songs are written by a multitude of people for a multitude of reasons. I've found in my experience that the best motivation for writing a song is to communicate something I couldn't otherwise or more effectively say to someone. So, when I'm asked to name a song I'd put in a time capsule, I'm hard-pressed not to choose this one. It might not be personal to me, but I couldn't be prouder to have cowritten it with a friend whose life was changed by its creation.

34

"IF YOU EVER LEAVE ME"
(BARBRA, PART III)

By any barometer, between 1987 and 1997, I had a good run. Sold a lot of records and had about twenty songs get into the charts, most in the Top Ten. Although I was almost universally hated by music critics, the hits kept coming, but more important, I never made a record or wrote a song I'm embarrassed by. Sure, some of those records have drum sounds that make me cringe now, but there's nothing I'd be ashamed to play you.

Even at the beginning of my breakthrough as an artist, I knew I wasn't the kind of personality who would sustain decade after decade of fame. The handful of artists who managed that all had one thing in common: they were focused on their image and paid great attention to maintaining and reinventing it. I, on the other hand, never really had an image to begin with. Except for my fluffy mullet, the only things that were really recognizable about me were my songs. They were always more famous than me, and still are.

My lack of image, or good PR, or whatever you want to call it, is also responsible for the fact that on a regular basis, I see people in my own audience, who have spent their money to see me, break into a look of surprise when I play "Hazard" or "Take This Heart" or "Way She Loves Me." The look on their face says, "Wait—he did *that song*?" I felt there was never a competent execution by the publicity people to whom my label and I paid millions over the years to connect the dots. It's not entirely their fault. I never had much of a "story" that journalists could write about. Happy guy, loves his family, loves writing and recording songs: zzzzzzzz. Where are the hookers and coke-filled nights of debauchery?

I also always hated the PR game and consistently refused to go to Hollywood parties or premieres. Even at music events like the Grammys or the American Music Awards, I was notorious for getting there exactly when I was needed and leaving the minute I was done. One night, I was a presenter at the AMAs, and I told Cynthia as soon as she saw me on the live broadcast, to put cookies in the oven, and I'd be home by the time they cooled. I handed the award to Bobby Brown or Billy Ray Cyrus or whomever, walked off the stage and directly into a limo, and was at my front door within thirty minutes.

It wasn't that I had immense disdain for that stuff. It was just that I found it, and most of the people involved, extremely boring. I'm generalizing, of course, but most famous people are pretty stupid. Think about it. In order for them to sustain their popularity, they need to focus 99 percent of their energies and attention on themselves. That leaves no time for listening to other people about *their* lives or reading about the world at large. Hence, they become intellectually stunted. And unless they're really funny, they make for mind-numbing conversation.

My popularity and power on pop and rock radio was on a rapid decline by the late '90s. I had always known that time would come, due to my lack of "image," so I was more prepared for the fall than some artists who really think it will never, ever end. The dilemma was that I still had a ton of music in me, and I felt my best work lie ahead. So, I dove right into a career in the background, just as I had started, and was lucky enough to get consistent work as a writer and producer for other artists.

One of these was my old friend Barbra Streisand.

Soon after her wedding to James Brolin, Barbra was starting to record a new album of love songs that celebrated her current state of happiness and asked to meet with me about writing a song for her. She was at a recording studio, and I dropped by to try to get an idea of what she wanted. As we talked about various concepts for love songs, I jokingly said, "You should do a song called 'If You Leave Me, Can I Come Too?'"

After laughing, she got a serious look and said, "No, wait: you could actually write that and make it not funny, but true. It's a really sweet sentiment."

And with that, the song I ultimately wrote and coproduced for her as a duet with Vince Gill, "If You Ever Leave Me," was born.

As we were talking, an assistant at the studio came in and said he was going to a local market and asked if anyone wanted anything. I had recently discovered Arizona Green Tea and was drinking it constantly. I said, "If they have any, I'll take a bottle of that, thanks." Barbra asked what it was and I told her it was my favorite beverage of the moment.

About two weeks later, I went to her home in Malibu to get her key for the song and work out the arrangement. A few minutes after we sat down at the piano, one of her assistants came in and asked if I'd like something to drink. I said, "Oh, maybe just some water, thanks." And Barbra said, "Wait. No. I knew you were coming, so I had them get that tea you like."

I stared at her for a moment and thought, *How in the world did she remember that? For years, I've heard all these stories about what a difficult, bitchy diva Barbra Streisand is, and I don't see anything but the complete opposite.*

Over the last few years, while I've done virtually *zero* work with her (although I did have the honor of being one of her opening guests at London's Hyde Park concert in 2019), I've spent time with Barbra socially and have had some wonderful evenings with her and Jim. My experience with her is that she's a sweet, thoughtful, insanely bright woman. Her talent is, as everyone knows, otherworldly. What I have experienced with her professionally is that she's an incredible and total pro who expects everyone involved with the projects she does to be prepared. She also has zero tolerance for bullshit.

The only times I've seen her frustrated are when she's either getting a verbal runaround from someone or dealing with people who are paid to be prepared and professional but are not. I think it's incredibly hypocritical that historically, when a man exhibits this kind of demand for professionalism, he is considered a perfectionist. When it's a woman, she's considered a temperamental bitch.

So I'm going on record here that if you bad rap Barbra Streisand's character in my presence, those are fighting words.

While producing the vocal on "If You Ever Leave Me" for her soon thereafter, I did have the experience of seeing her get very frustrated, but only with herself. Before she began singing her vocal on the song we were doing, we sat and talked for a few minutes. She mentioned that a book was about to come out about her, an unauthorized biography, which detailed accounts of her diva behavior and "bitchiness," but that they were all unfounded stories. She said, "There's even a story in there that claims once, years ago, I walked into a studio, looked over at the people on the right side of the room, and unceremoniously fired them. Can you imagine?"

A few minutes later, Barbra walked into the vocal booth and we started working on her performance of the song. She sang it over and over, and I would occasionally suggest ideas about phrasing certain words or notes, which is part of the job of a record producer. At one point in the song, she was struggling with a particular line, and I asked her to sing it a different way, and sang it for her over the talk-back.

She said, "Hmmmm. I like the way you do that. Let me try to do it my way." (She once said to me, "The truth is, I often don't 'sing' these songs. I have to 'act' them. If I can't 'act' them with my voice, it doesn't work." I thought this was a genius quote.)

She tried singing the line again, but it still didn't work. So she tried again. And again. At this point she'd been in the vocal booth for over an hour on this song, and I could see by her body language that she was getting frustrated. But I also felt we were dangerously close to having what we needed, so I kept saying, "*Really* close! One more time!"

After about the fifth time of me saying that, she said, curtly, "You know what? This just isn't working. I'm not getting it, and I'm feeling like I sound stupid singing this."

I pressed the talk-back and said, "You could never sound stupid singing anything. But I think you need to take a break."

And with that, she reached for her headphones and slammed them onto the music stand. She came through the door into the control room with a look of complete disgust and frustration, stopped cold, and stared right at me. The couple of people in the room—her assistant and the engineer—immediately became silent as a church, and after about ten long seconds, I looked at Barbra and said:

"Hey, wait a second—I'm on the *left* side of the room!"

35

"THIS I PROMISE YOU"

In 2000, I got a call from an executive at Jive Records.

"Hey Richard, how's it going? I'm calling to see if you might have a song for NSYNC."

NSYNC was massively popular at this point, having sold about 8 million copies of their first CD in America alone. I was bummed because at first I didn't think I had anything that was right. Losing an opportunity to work with the biggest group in the country at the moment would have been a major mistake, so I really racked my brain and went through a ton of old material to see if there was anything worth dusting off for them.

I soon remembered that I had recently written a song for a girl group made up of three Latina sisters. I had seen them perform at a wedding reception, and while nobody else in the room paid them any attention, I was blown away by their voices and stage presence. I had a few meetings with them and their father and had hoped I could sign them to a record deal and produce them. But the "business" part of it got way more complicated than it needed to, and I walked away from the idea.

In the midst of our discussions, however, it became clear that material was needed for them to record. So, I put on my songwriter hat and wrote a ballad that utilized three-part vocal harmony, with a mid-tempo groove (for those unfamiliar with music theory, that basically means: not too slow but not too fast), called "This I Promise You." Due to the complications with the contractual stuff with them, the song never went further than my own archive.

I went to my music room and found the demo. Listening to the song again, I knew it was perfect for NSYNC, and the next morning I sent it to the executive at Jive. He called a few days later and said, "We all love it, and the group loves it, and Justin Timberlake suggested that we get you to produce it. Are you interested?"

As they were the aforementioned biggest band in the country, I jumped at the chance to work with them, and it was one of the most pleasurable experiences I've ever had in my career. All five of the guys were gracious, focused, and kind.

But one thing that was immediately obvious was the incredible talent in Justin. It was clear even then that he was going to be a megastar the likes of which we rarely see. He had a fire in his belly that would not be tamed. He was constantly working on song ideas, arrangement ideas, vocal parts. It was really inspiring to even me, who'd been in the business fifteen years at that point and worked with all levels of talented and creative people. Everyone around him knew he was something special.

Making records is a blast for me, but for some it can be tedious work. There would be chunks of time while I was recording with one of the guys in the group and the other four guys would have that time to kill. Video games were already huge, and the lounge in the studio outside the control room had been outfitted with a big-screen TV and a video game console, where the guys would play against each other during their recording breaks. Not Justin, though. Instead of playing, any time he wasn't needed to record something, he would ask me, "How long 'til you need me again?"

No matter what I told him—"About an hour, just fifteen minutes," etc.—he would go into a studio next door to work on his own stuff. I had been in the midst of many big-time, high-functioning, and incredibly successful musicians before, and over and over again, I see it's that commitment and drive that makes someone really talented into a superstar. Justin is no different. Even at his young impressionable age, you could tell he was able to get around the tons of distractions thrown at him and focus on his craft.

And, as it turns out, I became a big footnote to his (and the band's) success. "This I Promise You" became a Top Five single on the *Billboard* Hot 100 and not only went to number 1 on the Adult Contemporary chart but remained there for thirteen straight weeks—a massive hit by any standard and one of my best-known compositions to this day. As I look back, even though it was tough to deal with at the time, I'm happy that things fell through with the group of Latina sisters for whom I'd originally written the song. It never would have found its way to NSYNC.

"This I Promise You" not only became a big hit, but it also became and remains an extremely popular wedding song thanks to lyrics like "Just close your eyes, each loving day, and know this feeling won't go away . . . until the day my life is through, this I promise you."

I know that up until this point, this story has been positive and, frankly, career-changing for me, especially the kismet of how NSYNC ended up recording this song and how I ended up producing it. If we're being honest, though, there is one thing I have to admit that kind of sucked about the NSYNC experience, and it had nothing to do with them. It had everything to do with their insanely crazed fans.

We had to record in a small studio in the middle of nowhere outside of Orlando, where the guys were based. The sessions lasted two days and nights, and by the end of the first night, a bunch of young girls figured out where we were recording and camped out in front of the building, hoping to meet the guys. Seeing this happening, we always planned to sneak the members of the group in and out of the back of the building through a secret door and into a limo. They were whisked away back to their hotels, homes, whatever.

I, on the other hand, would just park in the parking lot and go in and out of the main studio door right past all the craziness. I was in my late thirties, four years past my last radio hit, and was a good twenty years older than most of the young ladies there. I got the feeling I wasn't on most of their iPods, let alone walls.

A couple of girls came up to me as I came and went and asked, "Is Justin in there?" or "Will you please take this note to Joey?"

The final night we were recording lasted into the wee hours. We finally wrapped around 3:00 a.m. Lance Bass, who did the last of the vocals, was led out the secret door in the back. Feeling good about the work we had just put in, I threw my bag over my shoulder and walked through the front door and headed to my waiting car.

There were still, even at three in the morning, several young ladies sitting on the ground of the parking lot, praying for a glimpse of Justin or Lance or any of them. Being a parent, I wondered who the hell would let their teenage daughters be out here like this but was too tired at that point to judge.

As I opened my car door, a very pretty blonde of about twenty appeared from the group and approached me.

"Excuse me—"

I turned to her.

"Are you"—studying my face closely—"are you Richard Marx?"

I was shocked this young woman knew who I was, and frankly, pretty damned flattered.

With my best "Aww, shucks" demeanor, I said, "Uh, yes, yes, I am."

Her eyes flew open wide and she said, about fifty decibels louder than before, "Oh . . . my . . . GOD! My MOTHER LOVES YOU!"

36

"TO WHERE YOU ARE" (THE MISTAKE THAT WENT TO NUMBER 1)

I t's tough to explain just how hits are made and how some artists get big breaks while other artists just as talented never achieve any commercial notoriety. If you had told me back when I first met him that the skinny, pale, twenty-one-year-old opera singer from Los Angeles named Josh Groban would reach stratospheric heights in the music industry, I would have never believed you.

Shortly after I worked with NSYNC, I received another inquiry from a label. This time it was Warner Bros. They told me about Josh and asked if I had anything that might be right for him.

I had met Josh briefly about a year before this call came in. We were both at a charity event. I was there to sing a couple songs, as was he. Prior to seeing him, I had never heard of him but was soon totally converted. That night, I witnessed firsthand the unique qualities that contributed to Josh's successful career. Josh came out and sang this powerful, range-y, opera piece. Hearing this huge, booming Pavarotti-like voice barrel out of the mouth of a scrawny, shy kid seemed so odd to me. It's no wonder the audience went crazy that night and he went on to sell millions of records. His talent and voice are undeniable, but seeing him perform is so unexpected that I really think that's what drew people to him in the first place.

Someone at Warners had decided to try to cash in on this kid with the opera voice, and aside from the classical pieces they had recorded on him, much of it in Italian, they wanted to have a couple of original songs that would still fit the vibe of the album. On paper, selling this kind of music at a time when P Diddy ruled the charts was a challenge, to say the least.

I immediately realized that, if nothing else, it would be a fun exercise for me to write a song that was somewhat classical in style. I could incorporate chord changes I had never been able to use in writing pop or rock songs, and those chord progressions, in turn, would open up a new string of possibilities for a melody unlike anything I'd ever written.

I sat down at the piano and composed the music pretty quickly and really loved what I had written. It was reminiscent of various romantic classical pieces, but very much its own animal. The melody was dramatic and ranged from low resonant notes to big, high belting notes. It felt powerful, and "right" for Josh's voice. I toyed with a lyrical concept or two about young lovers who were being kept apart by circumstance, almost as if from an old *Wuthering Heights*-esque film, but I was in the midst of writing a lot of songs at that time and a little lyrically burnt out, so I decided to ask a lyricist to step in and write words to my melody.

I called my friend Linda Thompson. Linda, a still-beautiful former Miss Tennessee, had written lyrics to a big hit for Whitney Houston called "I Have Nothing," Natalie Cole's "Grown Up Christmas List," and the Barbra Streisand–Céline Dion song "Tell Him," among others. We had written a couple of songs together before that I thought were good, but for whatever reason, these had not found homes on anyone's records. I sent her a track of my song with me singing dummy "la-la" lyrics, and she called me from Los Angeles immediately to tell me she loved it and that she felt the music was telling her to write about her mother, who had passed away recently.

The next day, she e-mailed me the lyrics.

> Fly me up to where you are beyond a distant star
> I wish upon tonight to see you smile
> If only for a while to know you're there
> A breath away's not far to where you are

The song was called "To Where You Are." I sang Linda's beautiful lyrics to my track and sent the completed demo to the record company, who called a day or two later.

"Richard, Josh loves the song and so do we! We'd love you to come to LA and produce it, if you're interested."

I love producing and was totally up for it. I recorded the track at my studio at home in Chicago. I played piano, synthesized bass, and used computer-generated strings, which can sound great but never really match the real thing. What was I going to do, though? Hire a full orchestra to come to my house and lay down a string section?

As I developed the track, I had the idea to try modernizing this classical-sounding song with some drum loops, creating a hybrid of classical and modern pop. I thought it sounded amazing and unique.

About a week later, I flew to LA to cut Josh's vocal. I remember that the day of the session, LA was in the midst of a brutal heat wave. Temperatures were in the upper nineties, and even higher in the Valley and heading east toward Palm Springs. But when Josh arrived at the studio, he was wearing a turtleneck sweater. And it was black. I couldn't help but say, "Dude, what the hell are you doing wearing a turtleneck in this heat?"

"I know, I know," he said, "but I always have to keep my throat warm when I'm singing."

This was a level of dedication that was, frankly, lost on me, but I'm the idiot who never, ever, warms up my voice before singing. So, I guess that's why I'm not the guy they asked to stand in for Andrea Bocelli when he got sick and couldn't make it to a Grammy Awards rehearsal.

Josh had already recorded most of his album, so he was fairly experienced in the studio behind a microphone. We recorded take after take over a couple of hours as I would slowly but surely figure out the missing vocal pieces to the puzzle and Josh would supply them. One thing I've often found with great technical singers such as Josh is that the hardest element to achieve is the proper emotion. Someone can sing a line perfectly in tune and yet it leaves the listener cold because their voice is not creating the proper emotional effect. I urged Josh to think less about the notes he was singing and more about the feeling he was trying to convey. Little by little, his performance became both powerful and emotional.

With Josh's vocal recorded, I received another call from Warner Bros.

"Richard, we've decided to invest a bit more in Josh's album and are prepared to use a full orchestra on your song. Let us know when you can come back into the studio with them."

This was a way better alternative than my computer-generated strings. Within a week or so, we had our finished recording. I sat back and listened to it with great pride. And then I heard nothing from anyone for about six months.

I knew they were finishing the rest of Josh's album, but that's a little out of the ordinary. Typically, you hear something from someone, even just a "Great job: we will keep you posted" email, but I didn't hear a peep for half a year. I actually got to the point where I'd forgotten all about the song.

Then, one afternoon I got a call from a label guy. He wanted me to know that Josh's record had been complete for a while, and that a decision had been made along the way that my track would not be included. Josh had fallen out of "like" with it, felt it didn't fit the "legit, classical" nature of the album, and had kicked it to the curb. I was disappointed, but only because I was very proud of it and wanted it to be out in the world somewhere. It was still hip-hop and pop dominating the charts at the time, so I certainly never thought anyone would figure out how to sell Josh's music at that juncture in the business. So, I felt the news didn't hurt me financially.

The label guy said, "Well, wait: there's more. Josh sang last week at a charity function and in the audience was David E. Kelley, the writer and producer of *Ally McBeal*. Kelley came to us and said he's doing an episode of the show and wants to have Josh play a character who sings a song at the end, so he asked that we send him Josh's album so he could listen through and choose a song. We had a girl at the label dub Kelley a copy of the album, but for some reason, totally by mistake, she put your song at the end of the CD, and he apparently listened all the way through, got to your song, and loved it. I told him, 'David, there's been a mistake. That song isn't going to be on Josh's album.' And after a brief pause, David Kelley said, 'Uhh. I think it is.'"

The rest is history. The song went to number 1 within a couple weeks of the *Ally McBeal* episode, and though it never won any awards (or was even nominated for any), I'd like to take this time to thank a few people as if it did.

Thanks to Linda Thompson for writing a beautiful and moving lyrical tribute to your mother. Anyone who's lost someone they love can totally relate.

Thanks to my current manager and friend, Diarmuid Quinn, who was then head of marketing at Warner Bros., Josh's label, and who, once the song was on the *Ally* show, went to every length to get Josh all over television singing the song, certainly fueling it to number 1.

To David E. Kelley, for creating and writing one of the best television shows ever, *Picket Fences*, and for choosing "To Where You Are" for that episode of *Ally McBeal* and not accepting any other song in its place.

And most of all to that girl in the office at Warner Bros. who screwed up and accidentally gave Josh Groban his first hit and me another number 1 as a writer.

37

"DANCE WITH
MY FATHER"

No one tells you this when someone you deeply love dies, but you're pretty much a wreck for at least a year. And you never stop thinking about them.

When I lost my father, I "functioned" just fine. I recorded an album, did concerts, and organized benefits. I took care of my family and seemed okay on the outside, but emotionally I was curled up in a fetal position wrestling with a combination of grief and anger. Well-meaning friends and acquaintances sent me books, poems, motivational speeches, you name it. Nothing helped. On top of that, I found that many people who cared about me either didn't know what to say to me or said things that felt so clichéd and typical that none of it resonated with me.

Several months after Dad's death, I was having a particularly rough night. So, I got in my car and took a long drive. No radio, just me and my thoughts. Hours later, as I turned down my street to head home, my phone rang. It was Luther Vandross. He was calling to check in on me. I parked outside my garage, and we ended up talking for over an hour. Somehow, he knew what to say to make me feel better.

"Richard, I know how much pain you're in. But you've got to also think about what you had with your dad. Most people never experience a relationship like that. He wasn't just your dad; he was your best friend. And you had the music in common. He was so proud of you and he made sure you knew it! Think about how lucky you both were in that way. Ain't gonna hurt you any less, but try to balance those thoughts if you can."

I liked Luther very much and considered him a friend, but that phone call certainly made our friendship stronger.

Fast-forward six years later, in early 2003, and my phone rings. It's Luther.

"Richard, I have an idea for a song, and I need you to write it with me. It's called 'Dance with My Father.'"

Luther explained that while he had only faded memories of his father, who died when Luther was just twelve, his most vivid was of his dad coming home after work to their Brooklyn apartment and dancing around the kitchen with Luther, his mother, and sisters.

"He'd come home, and I'm sure he was tired, but he would put his arms around my mother in a slow dance and just sway with her back and forth. Then my sisters and I would have to get in on it, so he would put our little feet on top of his shoes and shuffle us around the kitchen, humming songs if the radio wasn't on. That's how I remember my father." He continued, "I know how close you were to your dad, and I wish I'd had the time with mine to have had the relationship you guys had, so we should write this together."

I told him I'd start a melody immediately and send it to him. At this point, we'd written songs he'd recorded before, including his Christmas single "Every Year, Every Christmas," and our method was not to sit in a room together and write, but rather I would write a complete piece of music with melody, send it to him, and then he would write lyrics.

Within an hour at the piano, I had the music for "Dance with My Father," including where the title line should be sung at the end of the chorus. I emailed a rough recording from my laptop to Luther, and the next morning he called and said, "I had more words I wanted to say than your melody allowed, so I modified it a bit. Hope it's okay with you because I fucking love this song!" Of course, I loved it, too. And within a few weeks, Luther recorded it for his forthcoming album, which was being overseen by the veteran industry executive Clive Davis.

About a month later, I was at my house when a FedEx truck dropped off a package. It was a CD with the final mix of "Dance with My Father." I took the CD right to my recording studio and cranked it up. The first thing I noticed was that instead of it being a completely new recording, the song started with the demo piano part I had sent him as a guide for a real piano part. But I was thrilled with the song, his amazing vocal, and the emotional power of what he was singing. I called him to tell him how much I loved it.

"Luther, this is fantastic."

"Oh, Richard, I'm glad you like it!"

"But I can't believe you took the piano part from that original demo I sent over to you. That was just something I laid down in one take as a guide."

"You're crazy. I loved the feel of that original piece. You could tell it was coming from a pure place."

"Well, if I knew you were going to use it, I'd have spent way more time on it!"

He laughed and before we hung up said, "Richard, I'm so proud of this song. This is my signature song. This is my 'Piano Man'!"

And I can't say that he was wrong.

Three months later, I received a call from Luther's business manager, Carmen Romano. My initial thought upon hearing his voice was that he wanted to tie down the publishing details of our song before the pending release of Luther's album, but instead his words were, "Richard, Luther suffered a stroke last night."

Shocked but already reliving in my mind conversations I'd had with Luther about his weight and overall health, I listened to as many details as Carmen had at that moment. One thing that was certain was that it was very serious. Luther had come home to his New York apartment and collapsed soon after. He lived alone, and he lay there on the floor until his housekeeper arrived the next morning. Had someone been there with him, the severity of the stroke could have been reduced by getting him promptly to a hospital. But he bled into his brain for many hours, and it was amazing he was even still alive.

I flew to New York to visit him in the hospital a couple of times. I won't share those experiences or conversations, as they're very private, but it was both wonderful and heartbreaking to see him. He was in pretty bad shape, but I felt he had a good team of physicians and therapists working with him, and we were all hopeful for a full recovery eventually.

On February 8, 2004, I attended the Grammy Awards, where our song was nominated for Song of the Year and Best R&B Song. Given Luther's condition, there would be no way for him to attend, let alone perform the song that night. A week before, I got a call saying that Céline Dion had heard and loved our song and would very much like to perform it at the ceremony. Céline's own father had recently passed away, and the song resonated with her deeply. Having immense respect for her talent and having met her a few times and found her lovely and kind, I was beyond psyched that she would be performing, but became even more excited when she asked if I would accompany her on piano. I stopped in Vegas the day before the Grammys, and we ran through the song together a few times on the stage of her residency at Caesar's Palace. Céline became very emotional when singing it the first time, but her reading of the lyrics (now taking on a personal connection for her) was incredible.

When the time came for our Grammy broadcast performance of the song, it was following OutKast doing their hit "Hey Ya!" with what seemed like seventy-three people onstage. Immediately after, Céline and I walked onstage to great applause. I began the song, playing the piano intro, and Céline sang the opening line, "Back when I was a child," when all of a sudden her microphone made a clicking sound and cut out. She looked at the audience, and then at me, with a face full of sheer panic and the knowledge that hundreds of millions of people around the world were watching. I stopped playing and fixed my eyes on hers with a look that said, "It's going to be okay. Just breathe." As a tech came running out to her with a new microphone, I motioned to the audience with my hand as if to say, "Live TV, folks. Let's try this again and show Céline some love!" Closing her eyes momentarily and shaking off the technical debacle, Céline delivered a flawless performance and got a standing ovation, as I knew she would. When she exited the stage, I hugged her tightly and said, "You are such a fucking pro, and you *killed* it!" At that moment, the show's director, Ken Ehrlich came running up to us, profusely apologizing. I said, "Ken, the truly hilarious thing about this is that you just had OutKast perform the musical equivalent of the War of 1812 without a single glitch, but then you guys fucked up a piano and a vocal mic?"

Earlier in the evening, before the telecast began, the Grammys handed out a number of awards, including Best R&B Song to Beyoncé's "Crazy in Love." I had been optimistic Luther and I would win that smaller award, and pretty certain we would not win Song of the Year, the biggest award of the night. So, at the end of the actual ceremony, when presenter Carole King opened the envelope and said, "And the Grammy goes to Richard Marx and Luther Vandross for 'Dance with My Father!' " I was a tornado of emotions.

I was thrilled that we had won but also tremendously sad that Luther was in a hospital in New York and not sitting next to me at the Grammys. The love and respect for Luther in that room that night was palpable. Carmen and I went up onstage together, and Carmen read a "thank you" statement from Luther, which received a huge round of applause.

I stepped up to the mic and said, "I couldn't be more proud to have written this song with Luther. My friend. Who . . . I wish was here because he'd be whispering to me about what everybody's wearing." The audience laughed. "You all know Luther for his amazing talent, but I know that he's also one of the funniest, kindest people on the face of the earth." I thanked my family and ended with, "And most of all, to my father, who I know in my heart is up in heaven right now with Luther's dad, opening a bottle of champagne."

A few months later, I was in New York again and went to visit Luther. His progress had been extremely slow, and there had been some scary moments with his breathing and some minor infections, courtesy of a big hospital where infections are rampant. I walked in and hugged him, and we finally got to sit face-to-face and talk about the Grammy win and how thrilled he was about it. The last hour I spent with him was in the rehab facility's gym, where I watched his trainers still trying to help him regain his balance and mobility. I felt pretty useless, but I pitched in when I could and made him laugh a few times. We went back to his room and I hugged him good-bye.

The following July 1, I woke up and while sipping my morning coffee, clicked onto CNN's news website and saw the headline: "Luther Vandross Dead at 52." I hadn't seen or spoken to him in a couple of months but regularly checked in with Carmen Romano, who would basically say, "He's the same." I had come to believe it was unlikely he would ever be anything but a shadow of his former self, but I had no fear of his imminent death.

I immediately dialed Carmen, who said, "I'm sorry, man. It's true. He just quietly passed away early this morning." I hung up and spent the day mourning my friend and cherishing the laughs we'd had and the beautiful songs we'd brought into the world together.

For many of the years that followed, when I'd be asked to sing "Dance with My Father," I would decline. It felt wrong to sing it, for some reason. Maybe it was simply that it made me miss Luther, and I didn't want to feel that sadness. But several years ago, I had the epiphany that I was looking at it all wrong and that the right thing to do would be to sing it as much as possible and tell every audience I could about how cool a guy Luther was and how proud of our song I am.

So, that's what I do now at pretty much every show I perform Like my other hit songs, that one wasn't just mine and Luther's. It belongs to everyone.

38

THE PERFECT MAN'S IMPERFECTION

I n 2004, I got a call from a record executive in New York who ran a jazz and classical music label. I don't know him well but always liked him, and when we would occasionally bump into each other, he would say, "We need to work on something together." His call to me went like this:

"Hey, Richard, how's it going?

"Good, man. You?"

"All good. Are you insanely busy the next few days?"

"Yeah, but what's up?"

"Well, I have a project I need to discuss with you, and I want to fly you here to talk it over. I don't mean to be cryptic, but can you pick a day and just come here?"

"Oooookay. Sounds weird. I'm in."

A few days later I flew into JFK, and a car picked me up and drove me right to the Imperial Theatre on Broadway. I got out and saw an enormous photo of Hugh Jackman in a sequined, gold lamé shirt as Peter Allen in *The Boy from Oz*. The record exec walked up to greet me, and I said, "I'm really confused."

He said, "Just come inside and watch the show and then we'll talk."

Two hours later, the house lights went up, and he said, "What'd you think?"

I said, "Look, I'm not really a Broadway show guy, so I can't really speak to the show itself. But that guy, Hugh Jackman is amazing. What a showman."

He said, "Perfect. Come with me."

We headed backstage and were put in this tiny room off the dressing room area and about five minutes later, in walks Hugh. I had seen the first two X-Men films and loved them, and I had recently seen Hugh's romantic comedy *Kate and Leopold* and exclaimed to my wife, "That dude is our generation's Cary Grant." So, I was already impressed with him.

Hugh Jackman is one of those guys who so effortlessly puts everyone around him at ease, he could easily have had a career sitting on the UN. There's nothing phony about him. He's just genuinely kind and thoughtful. I'd love to say it's annoying, but it's not. It's admirable. So Hugh greets me like an old friend, telling me he'd been a fan of my work, and making sure I knew my songs had been big in his homeland of Australia. You see, with Hugh it's never about him. It's only about you, whoever you are.

He and the record exec explained that they had made an album with a renowned producer and not only had it turned out musically disappointing, Hugh had not enjoyed the process at all. But they felt strongly that the timing for an album was now and wondered if I'd be interested in taking on the producer job. I was flattered and, frankly, much more interested after meeting Hugh than I would have been if the exec had simply pitched it to me on the phone, so he's a smart guy.

We agreed to have me record some tracks in LA and then bring them to New York to record Hugh's vocals over a period of weeks while he was there on Broadway. The album would be all covers of standards, but I wanted the album to sound like it was done in a jazz club. Nothing too "produced."

I spent an afternoon with Hugh to choose songs and then flew to LA. The rhythm section I hired for the sessions was a stellar cast. Christian McBride on bass, Dean Parks on guitar, Peter Erskine on drums, and Billy Childs on piano. These are some of the greatest and most respected musicians in the world. As I drove to the studio for the first session, I was as nervous as I've ever been. Here I was, about to make a jazz record with amazing jazz musicians and I knew about half a percent above jack-shit about jazz. But I'd done my homework on these songs and was excited to hear some of my arrangement ideas fleshed out. The sessions went smoothly, with all those amazing players not only playing great, but also being fun to work with.

Over the following six weeks or so, I would fly to New York every Sunday, wait for Hugh to finish his evening show and come to the studio, and we would record his vocals until about midnight. He had Mondays off, so we would reconvene after lunch, sing until he was tired, and then I'd fly back to Chicago only to return for the same drill six days later.

Some days Hugh would do two shows in a day, and the schedule, along with the vocal workout he got in the show itself, made cutting vocals on these songs in the studio a dicey task. The poor guy was exhausted, and while the show was making it hard to get great vocals in the studio, all the studio singing was making it hard for him to sing onstage the following night. So, one day I said, "Dude, this is no way to make a record. Unless you strongly feel otherwise, I think we put this off until well after *Boy from Oz* is over." Hugh reluctantly agreed.

Though we stopped recording, the friendship we had developed only flourished as time went on, and I count Hugh as one of my closest friends. I don't know a classier, more soulful person. I tell people all the time, "How great is it that there's a real superstar we can all root for?"

In the last decade, Hugh's acting career has reached new heights. His role in the film version of *Les Misérables* earned him an Oscar nomination and a Golden Globe win. He also performed a one-man musical variety show on Broadway that earned him his second Tony Award.

When he decided to tackle that show, he rang me and asked if he could come to my house in Chicago and have me help him choose the right songs and do some arrangements on them, along with his musical director, Patrick Vaccariello. Patrick ended up doing the hard work, but I was thrilled to be a part of the origin of what became a three-month sold-out engagement on Broadway and then eventually a show that filled arenas around the world.

Hugh Jackman is one of those freaks of nature who can act, sing, and dance, all brilliantly. He's a learned fitness and diet expert who can transform his body into *Muscle and Fitness* cover model shape in a matter of weeks. His memory for people's names and details about their lives and families is unparalleled. He's also sensational at very tricky things like hosting the Oscars and the Tonys.

But luckily for all of us mere mortals, I'm happy to report there's one thing Hugh Jackman is *not* good at, and that's telling jokes.

Years ago, Hugh and I were sitting around on a break from recording, and I told him the following joke:

"What did the rapper say when two houses fell on him? Get off me, Homes."

Hugh cracked up. He loved that joke.

About three weeks later he called me. "Ricardo, I'm embarrassed to tell you this, but I was at a big star-studded cocktail party last night. It was a who's-who of entertainment, politics, and business. I ended up in a circle of about ten people, conversing, when I thought, *I'm going to tell Richard's joke and these people are going to laugh their asses off.* So, I say, 'I have a joke. What did the rapper say when two houses fell on him?' And the entire group stared at me awaiting the punch line, which came out of my mouth as, 'Get these homes off me!' After seconds of awkward silence, I finally said, 'Wait, no, that's not right, umm. Never mind.'"

So the good news, my friends, is that even Hugh Jackman has a flaw.

39

"GONE COUNTRY"

Thanks to my two uncles, by age eleven or twelve, I had become a such a fan of the day's modern country music that I barely listened to pop or rock music for about two years straight. I was all about Merle Haggard, Jerry Reed, the Gatlin Brothers, Waylon Jennings, and Lynn Anderson. It wasn't until early 1976 when my father sat me down and played me Paul Simon's *Still Crazy After All These Years* (the album that really made me want to be a songwriter) that I dove back into pop music.

Although my first hits as a songwriter were with Kenny Rogers, they were not really what I considered "country" songs, since Kenny was such a massive global artist who dominated the pop genre as well. Over the years I had not kept up too much with country music, so it wasn't until Shania Twain burst onto the scene in the late '90s that I started to listen to what else country radio was playing.

Shania was both massively successful and polarizing at once. She was gorgeous, and her songs had huge, catchy hooks that infused rock and pop elements into an otherwise country sound. Her producer (and then-husband) Mutt Lange had been the man behind such iconic albums as AC/DC's *Back in Black* and Def Leppard's *Hysteria*.

As her songs became more played and popular, the old guard of Nashville started to get nervous. Mutt and Shania were "outsiders" having huge success in a genre that always did things "the Nashville way." Country purists took issue with the pop and rock influences in Shania's recordings, and soon enough a controversy was created over whether she deserved to be played on country radio.

It was around this time that I started traveling to Nashville to write songs. My first collaborator was Gary Harrison. Gary was a lifelong friend of my then-wife, Cynthia, and I knew him socially. He'd already had a very successful career, having written hits for Trisha Yearwood and Martina McBride, and had then recently written the Country Song of the Year for Deanna Carter called "Strawberry Wine."

Gary had mentioned to me at a social dinner that he'd be open to writing with me anytime I wanted. It was 1998 and my career was in a bit of disarray. I'd mutually parted ways with Capitol Records, and the writing was on the wall: white, male, solo pop singers were essentially persona non grata at radio. It wasn't just me. Bryan Adams, Billy Joel, Elton John, and Rod Stewart weren't having pop hits either. After a period of panic and self-pity, I decided I would take some time to just write songs and try to have hits via other artists. I loved what was happening in country radio, so I started going to Nashville to try to become part of that music community.

The first song Gary Harrison and I wrote, "Easy to Believe," was promptly recorded by a new artist on MCA named Shane Minor. Shane didn't ever become a hit artist, but he's had a nice career as a songwriter for others. Although our song didn't make much noise, it was gratifying to have had it accepted by a country label so easily.

On one of my early writing trips I was asked to meet with a young trio of sisters from Utah who were making their debut country album. They were called the Violets when I met them, but soon switched to the name SHeDAISY. They sang beautiful three-part harmony, and one sister, Kristyn, cowrote all their songs. Tall, blond, and very beautiful, Kristyn was and is an exceptional lyricist influenced strongly by everyone from Joni Mitchell to the poet Rainer Maria Rilke. Kristyn and I got together and wrote "Still Holding Out for You," which was not only recorded for their debut album but was their fourth single from it, following three big country radio hits, including the number 1 "Little Good-byes."

So by this time, I'm going to Nashville frequently, writing with an array of new and established artists and writers and continuing to ingratiate myself within the Nashville community. My kids were quite young at that time and ensconced in school outside of Chicago, or else I'd probably have moved there at least for a while to see if it felt like a place I could call home.

On one particular writing trip, I was asked to attend an event that was part of Country Radio Seminar, or CRS. It's an annual convention in Nashville where the radio community mingles with artists and executives from Music Row to survey the state of the country format. That year, there was a panel discussion called "Pop Versus Country," which was to take on the controversy of whether records like Shania Twain's were making country radio sound too "pop."

I thought it was a fairly ridiculous topic, as Shania's incredible success was proving that not only did country fans enjoy hearing her on country radio, but also that she was selling more records than any other country artist in ages. I went to the panel discussion and sat in a small audience of about a hundred people. On the panel were a label executive, a program director for a big country station, and a young country artist who had just enjoyed his first hit single. His name was Brad Paisley.

I don't recall much of the panel discussion, as it all seemed like banal noise to me. "What will happen to traditional country music if the Shania Twains of the world take over the format?" That kind of silly rhetoric, all steeped in fear of something new. But when the question of "What is the real difference between pop and country?" was posed, it was Brad Paisley's answer that got my undivided attention.

Brad leaned into the microphone and said, "Well, country music is really about the *song* and the craft of writing. And pop music is really all about the production."

I could feel my ears turning red and the blood in my veins begin to boil. In one ignorant sentence, this kid was insulting an enormous group of songwriters. I thought, *What the fuck did he just say? Would he like to tell that to Paul McCartney? Or James Taylor? Or Michael Jackson? Or Smokey Fucking Robinson?* I stood up and left the seminar, shaking my head.

The next morning I was interviewed over breakfast by a writer from *The Tennessean.* The interview had been scheduled for a while and was to cover my country writing over the past year or so, and my then new album *Days in Avalon,* which I'd recorded mostly in Nashville.

As the interview was wrapping up, the writer asked, "Is there anything else you wanted to talk about?"

My inside voice told me to just say, "Nope, all good." But instead I said, "Actually, yeah. I was at CRS yesterday and heard something that kinda pissed me off." I went on to say that not only was Brad's comment incredibly disrespectful to non-country songwriters, but that it also implied that we don't take the craft of writing as seriously as he does. I closed by saying, "And, sorry, but it's also tough to swallow coming from a guy who's been famous for nine minutes."

Of course, the next day the article was printed with the headline "Richard Marx Slams Brad Paisley." After saying good-bye to me, the writer had immediately called Brad for a comment. Instead of saying something along the lines of "Yeah, that didn't come out right. I didn't mean any disrespect to other songwriters," Brad said, "I didn't mean to make Richard mad. I like his music. In fact, I'm the one who bought his last album."

True enough, *Days in Avalon*, my first attempt at releasing an album on my own label, had also been my first commercial flop. But his quip of a retort dodged the issue of what I perceived as his disrespect to a legion of songwriters, and it was lame as fuck. Obviously, Brad went on to have great success to this day. But I remember him, in the days of "pop versus country," making statements like, "I only want my records played on COUNTRY radio." And I would always think, "Yeah, dude, don't fucking WORRY!" With respect to his success, I've always considered Brad Paisley the poster boy for pandering.

A few years later I became friendly with a radio promotion guy at the DreamWorks label named Jimmy Harnen. Jimmy had had a hit in the '80s called "Where Are You Now" but had abandoned his performing career and was rising up in the promo ranks.

Jimmy called me one day and said, "DreamWorks is finishing the debut album by a Canadian band called Emerson Drive and we need a single. I found a song I like a lot, and the band is going to be in your town in a few days. I was hoping you'd meet with them and see if there's a way you guys could work together."

The band, along with Jimmy and his promo boss Scott Borchetta, arrived at my house a few days later. (A few years later, Scott launched his own label with a young fourteen-year-old singer-songwriter named Taylor Swift. Not sure whatever happened to her.) We wandered down to my recording studio and chatted awhile before Jimmy said, "Can I play you this song I found? It's called 'Fall into Me.'"

We blasted the demo on my studio speakers, and I instantly liked it, but I felt the end of the chorus melody was a letdown. I suggested a slightly different melody, which everyone in the room agreed made the chorus pay off more strongly. The band's guitarist, a very talented young lad named Danick Dupelle, then picked up one of my guitars laying against the studio wall and said, "What if there was an arpeggiated part over the chorus like this?" And within minutes, Danick and I were arranging the song.

Two days later, I flew to Nashville and we recorded "Fall into Me" in its entirety (all parts and vocals) and mixed it the next day. The track became a number 5 hit on the Country charts a few months later, giving me my first big country hit as a producer.

The rest of their debut album was produced by veteran country producer James Stroud, who also happened to be the head of the DreamWorks label. I met with James as "Fall into Me" was climbing the charts and recall him offering an offhanded comment about my work on the song being "not bad for a pop guy."

Emerson Drive went out on the road and worked hard, performing many concerts in bars and clubs, and set themselves up for a second album that would push them to the next level. Much to my delight, the band went to James Stroud and asked if the label would hire me to produce their entire next album. Stroud probably felt a bit slighted, but the band was adamant, so he agreed.

For the next six months, the band basically lived in my house. We wrote songs together. I brought in collaborators. I sent various band members off to write songs with great writers, and we finally chose twelve songs to record. I believed in this band and was completely committed to them. I ate, slept, and breathed focused on nothing but Emerson Drive.

As we headed into the homestretch of making the album, we got the incredible news that Shania Twain had chosen the band as her opening act on her upcoming tour. This would mean they'd be in front of massive audiences. We just needed to have the album ready and out within three months for the start of the tour. No problem! We were almost done, and I felt we had multiple radio hits on it.

We delivered the album six weeks later, and DreamWorks released "Last One Standing," a song I'd written with Fee Waybill, as the album's first single. As the song began to climb the charts, I noticed that there was still no release date for the album. Despite my concerned calls to the label, it became clear that DreamWorks was going to delay the release. I couldn't believe it. Neither could the band or their manager, all of us powerless to do anything.

DreamWorks waited until the Shania tour was over before releasing the album *What If.* They also rather half-heartedly promoted the single, which barely made it into the Top Twenty. And despite the album reaching number 12 on the country chart, sales were pretty bad and DreamWorks dropped the band.

I was absolutely crushed. Instead of nurturing and getting behind this young band of talented guys who had already dipped their collective toe in radio and sales success, Dreamworks just dumped them like last weekend's trash. I even flew to Nashville and met with other labels on behalf of the band, asking for them to be signed elsewhere, but to no avail. The whole thing turned to shit. And I got my first real taste of being collaterally fucked over by Music Row.

40

"BETTER LIFE"

A few months after the Emerson Drive debacle, I took solace when "Better Life," a song I'd written with Keith Urban, hit number 1 on the Country charts and stayed there for six straight weeks.

Keith and I met in Nashville in 2001. A guy who worked for the publishing company Keith was signed to thought we would make a good writing team, so on one of my regular trips to town, we got together at the company's offices one afternoon. I had heard his debut album the year before and liked it, plus I had done some work with keyboardist Matt Rollings, who had produced it.

Keith and I hit it off very quickly; for whatever reason, I have had a lifelong kinship with Australians. Maybe it's a shared sarcastic humor. It seemed clear we would be easy friends. Our writing, however, wasn't so effortless. I had come into the session with a musical chorus idea that I showed him and he liked. But after a couple hours, we didn't really have much more than that.

We took a break and had lunch down the street at a place I think is still there called Midtown Cafe and bonded further through a couple of club sandwiches and fries.

"You know, I do have to confess something to you, Richard." Keith said. "About ten years ago, my debut record came out in Australia on EMI."

"That's my label down there, too," I said.

"Yeah, I know. Here I am, a young act no one ever has heard of, ready to be put out by EMI, they have all these big plans, until—"

"Uh-oh. Until?"

"Until a guy named Richard Marx announces he's coming down for a tour to support his massive hit, 'Hazard,' in Australia. At that point, my record became a buried casualty," Keith said.

My face turned redder than the ketchup on the table.

"I'm . . . sorry?"

We soon changed the subject and went back to the publishing offices to try to finish our stubborn song. After another couple of fruitless hours, we agreed it just wasn't supposed to happen that day and that we'd stay in touch and get back together on my next visit.

A few months later, I returned and essentially the same thing happened. This time we got together at the house he was renting and started another idea, only to end up staring at blank legal pads with silence bellowing through the room. Instead, we shot a few games of pool and drank beer. And started telling jokes. It became one of those great memories where you're laughing so hard at each other that your sides ache and you can't catch your breath. I ended up heading back to my hotel late that night, with a decent beer buzz, but no finished song.

The next evening, Keith was playing a club in town called 3rd and Lindsley and asked if I'd be up for sitting in on a song with him. We decided on my first hit, "Don't Mean Nothing," and that we'd just wing it with no run-through whatsoever. It was actually a really fun and inspired performance with just two acoustic guitars. Someone filmed it and it's on YouTube to this day.

The following year, Keith's career broke into the big time with his follow-up album *Golden Road*. It yielded several huge country hits, including his number 1 "Somebody Like You." I was a little bummed out that I hadn't written a song on it, but we stayed in touch and would always grab breakfast or dinner whenever we were both in the same town.

Then another year later, he called me and asked if he could come to my house in Chicago so that we could try once again to write together. Super Bowl weekend was coming up and we decided it'd be fun to write a bit and hang out and watch the game. I picked him up from O'Hare Airport and upon his arrival to my house, he met Cynthia and our three sons. We had dinner at home and called it a pretty early night.

The next day, after some hanging out, we wandered down the long hallway to my recording studio. We each picked up an acoustic guitar and started playing some absentminded chords and riffs when Keith noticed the new instrument I'd bought: a banjo strung like a guitar. Nicknamed Ganjo, it was something Keith had used a lot on his breakthrough album. I'd loved the sound of it and decided to keep one at my studio. He picked it up, and within fifteen minutes we had nearly all the music for what became Keith's song "Better Life."

Historically, the music always comes to me first, and more easily. I've got literally thousands of melodies stored away that just haven't had lyrics put to them yet. Lyric writing is harder for me, partly I suppose because I am always trying to say something a little differently than I've heard it said before. I try diligently to avoid clichés. So, when it comes to cowriting with someone, it usually either just flows effortlessly or is painfully laborious. With Keith, the music always flows quickly, and the lyrics are like pulling teeth.

As I was singing the chorus we'd written, I just kept singing gibberish. Vowel sounds. It's what a lot of us writers do until we write actual lyrics. I kept singing, "Someday, baby . . . you and I'r gunna be da ones . . ."

And Keith said, "Oh, that's good, I like that!"

I stared at him. "You like what? I didn't say anything."

"No, yeah you did. You said, 'You and I are gonna be the ones.'"

"I did? Well, okay. But you and I are gonna be the ones who *what*?"

"No, no, it's just what you said. 'You and I are gonna be the ones.'"

"The ones who *what*?!"

"Richard, it's just 'we're gonna be the ones!'"

"Oh."

After that moment of divine inspiration, we got stuck again.

Even though we were in my million-dollar, state-of-the-art recording studio with every current piece of digital recording gear, we were recording the ideas for our song onto a small cassette tape recorder. I shit you not.

Keith and I both had these old-school tape machines because there's just something about the ultra-compressed sound when you listen back that replicates the radio. We were, however, out of blank cassettes. So we jumped in the car and drove to a Best Buy, all the way there and back singing our song in the car and coming up with lines of lyrics as I drove.

Though Keith had recently had big breakthrough success on the country charts, he wasn't yet the superstar he would become. As we were checking out at Best Buy, a girl came over to us and said to me, "Are you Richard Marx?" I acknowledged I was, and she then looked at Keith and said, "And are you Keith Urbane?" Keith smiled at her, then at me, and said, "Almost!"

We went back to my place and somehow still hadn't finished the lyrics to this fucking song. Keith had to leave the next morning to head back to Nashville, so we arranged to meet up when I came there to work a few weeks later.

Keith came to my hotel, and thanks to a chance to clear our heads and a change of scenery, we finished the lyrics quickly and easily.

> There's a place for you and me where we can dream as big as the sky
> I know it's hard to see it now, but baby, someday we're gonna fly
> and this road we're on
> you know it might be long,
> but my faith is strong
> it's all that really matters
> someday baby, you and I are gonna be the ones
> good luck's gonna shine
> someday baby, you and I are gonna be the ones, so hold on
> we're headed for a better life.

A month or so later, he had recorded the track for his album and was doing his lead vocal when I happened to be back in Nashville. I accepted his invitation to come to the studio and check it out.

It sounded killer and like a big hit song. I stayed an hour and then had to go meet someone at another writing session. As I was driving there, an idea came to me for Keith's track. It was basically a counter chorus at the end of the song, just one more new, catchy piece of information for the listener. I called Keith from the car and sang him my idea.

> Hey, we're gonna leave this all behind us, baby . . .
> wait and see . . .
> we're headed for a better life . . .
> you and me . . .

He loved it and went right into the vocal booth to sing it, adding a couple lines of his own. He also came up with a melodic ending to the section where he flipped up into falsetto and held this beautiful long note. I still get chills at that moment in the record.

Featured on his next album, *Be Here*, our song "Better Life" was the last single released from it. I was getting frustrated because I believed the song was really great and commercial, but either Keith's label or management kept passing it over as a single for other songs. I couldn't really argue because not only was it not my call, but the songs they were choosing were all becoming hits: "Days Go By," "Making Memories of Us." But then they released "Better Life" and it quickly went to number 1 and stayed there for six straight weeks. I had cowritten my first number 1 Country song since 1984.

About a year and a half later, Keith called me and said he was finally off the road and if I had any time in the near future, he'd like me to come to Nashville and try writing a new song or two. Within a few weeks I booked a flight and headed down from Chicago.

Keith had recently married Nicole Kidman, and they'd moved into a beautiful home just outside of town. I'd regretted not being able to accept his invitation to their wedding in Australia due to my work schedule, so I brought along a wedding gift to their new house and after a coffee and some small talk in the kitchen, we wandered into the living room and grabbed guitars.

As usual, we hovered around a few random musical ideas for about an hour, occasionally and temporarily zeroing in on a melody he responded to, or a groove idea, but nothing was forming into a coherent song. Back to the kitchen for more coffee and a chat, and I remembered that I'd had an idea for him I'd forgotten to mention. Not really a melody but a vibe.

"Do you know 'Stay (Faraway, So Close!),' by U2? I was thinking we should write something for you in that zone." Keith stared at me. "Dude, that's so fucking weird. Just yesterday I played Dann [producer Dann Huff] a bunch of songs for inspiration, and that was one of them."

A very common practice among those of us who make up songs for a living is to use other existing songs as inspiration. As long as you're careful not to outright steal someone else's idea, it can be a great way to discover new songs you might not have written otherwise. There may be some songwriters out there who say they never do that, but they're lying.

So, we picked up our guitars and started playing a rhythm part and chords that sounded like a distant cousin of the U2 song. At some point within the gibberish that occurs while searching for actual lyrics, I absentmindedly sang, "Everybody . . . needs somebody . . . sometimes."

Keith said, "Wow, that sounds great with that melody and chords."

"Yeah, but it's an old Dean Martin song. Plus, it's trite. As fuck," I said.

"One man's trite can be another man's universal message. And that Dean song is a million years ago. I like it, Ricardo."

Complete non sequitur, but at this juncture I should point out that ever since I moved away from home at eighteen, person after person has invariably nicknamed me "Ricardo." Not sure why, but it's what everyone calls me, with the exception of my mother, my wife, and Fee Waybill, who has always referred to me as Ricky Boy.

Keith and I finished "Everybody" in about ninety minutes. Usually, it takes Keith and me days to finish a song if we ever even *do* finish an idea. This one felt good, and right, quickly.

With Nicole out of the country making a movie, Keith asked if I wanted to go hang out later, and that evening we ended up at the Ryman Auditorium to see James Taylor play a solo acoustic concert. I've seen James in concert several times over the years and have met him. He's a consummate performer, incredible songwriter, and a gracious guy.

Keith and James shared a manager at that time, so we saw the show and stopped backstage to say hi afterward. James greeted us warmly, and when we mentioned we'd been writing together that day, he said, "Well, well. I certainly look forward to hearing what the combination of you two will bring us this time."

Keith dropped me at my hotel and said, "Ricardo, I gotta tell you, man. I fucking *looooove* the song we wrote today. We nailed it. Thank you, brother!"

I was thrilled, not just because I, too, liked the song, but because I had great respect for Keith as a musician and considered him a friend. I really wanted to deliver for him as a collaborator.

A few weeks passed and I knew Keith was starting to record his new album, but I'd not heard from him about when he planned to record "Everybody." Another week or so passed, so I called him and asked how recording was going. "It's going great, man. But hey, listen, I'm not going to record 'Everybody.' It just doesn't hold up for me."

I recall muttering something like, "Hey, bro, no worries. Just checking in." But inside I was bummed out. Not as much for creative or financial reasons, but personally. In fairness, I myself have had several instances of writing a song (alone or with someone else) and being pretty into it at first but then deciding against recording it later. Maybe the song just didn't wear well, or maybe it didn't really fit the direction of the album.

Coincidentally, I was soon due in the studio myself with Keith's producer, Dann Huff. Dann and I had known each other a long time but had never worked together, and I asked if he'd be into cutting a couple tracks with me. I went to Nashville, and we had a meeting to listen to a stack of my new songs and choose two to record together on me as an artist, with the two of us producing. The first song I played Dann was one I'd just written by myself called "Loved." Dann flipped over it.

"We've gotta do that one," he said. "That's a really great song."

After listening to two or three more songs, I saw on my laptop the MP3 of the recording of Keith and me writing "Everybody."

"I hadn't thought of this, but Keith and I wrote this about a month ago. I love it, but I guess he's not into it anymore."

"Wow. Really? It's killer. He needs something like this. But, hey, if he's not doing it, you should."

The next day we began a two-day stint at Blackbird Studios in the Berry Hill area outside Nashville, and we recorded both songs with a brilliant array of session musicians. Steve Brewster on drums, Jimmie Lee Sloas on bass, Tom Bukovac and Dann on guitars, and I played piano. By the end of day two, both tracks sounded like near-finished records, and I was thrilled with them.

Dann called me early the next morning. "Hey, I'm seeing KU [as in Keith Urban] today and I want to see if you'd mind if I play him what we did with 'Everybody.'"

"Ummm, no. Fine with me."

About three hours later the phone rings. "Ricardo. Keith here. Dann just played me the track. I'm an idiot. I'd really like to cut it. Is that okay?"

Of course it was, despite the approximately $10,000 I'd already invested into my own recording of it.

Keith included "Everybody" on his *Love, Pain and the Whole Crazy Thing* album. It was the last single lifted from the disc and became a Top Five Country hit.

Keith's career went straight into the stratosphere soon after that, and deservedly so. Aside from his exceptional talents, his work ethic and relentlessness are on par with a select few. A few years went by where we saw little of each other and he did not reach out to cowrite with me. His albums continued to do very well, and I was working pretty hard at both rebuilding my touring career and advancing my writing and production for an array of other artists.

Then one day soon after the devastating floods that put much of Nashville literally under water, Keith rang me and said, "It's been awhile. We should get together and write. You up for it?"

I headed down to Nashville a few weeks later, and we met up at a rehearsal studio called SIR. Nearly all of Keith's guitars had been damaged or destroyed by the flooding that overwhelmed a local storage facility that housed his and several other country art-ists' equipment. Keith had to borrow a guitar from a friend for our writing session.

We caught up on each other's lives for a few minutes and dove into throwing ideas around. Keith had a drum machine brought in and programmed a simple up-tempo groove, and in no time we started playing and singing what became the verse to a new song.

> I can't sleep
> Ain't no sleep a-comin'
> I'm just lyin' here thinkin' 'bout you

This under an arpeggiated guitar riff reminiscent of the Police's "Mes-sage in a Bottle." After an hour of fleshing out the verse, the gibberish of the chorus that followed became Keith singing, "It's gonna be a long hot summer . . . and we should be together . . ."

From there we started calling out images of summer. A girl's pretty bare feet up on a car dashboard, singing loud to songs on the radio, tanned skin. We had a pretty good start of the chorus lyrics by the time we had to call it a day. We agreed to meet up again about two weeks later in Chicago where I was living. Keith had a gig opening for the Eagles there. We would steal an hour or two on his tour bus and finish the lyrics.

When I arrived at Soldier Field that afternoon, I was directed to park next to Keith's bus. We had just opened up our legal pads to work on lyrics when there was a knock at the door and onto the bus walked the one and only Joe Walsh. He was coming by to say hello to Keith and had no idea I'd be there.

I hadn't seen Joe since that day in 1986 when he was kind enough to play the guitar solo on my first hit, "Don't Mean Nothing." We gave each other a big hug, and he sat and talked with me and Keith for a few minutes before he seemed to notice the legal pads. "Hey, you guys, I hope I didn't interrupt something!" We explained we'd agreed to get together to try to knock out lyrics to a new song but that we were both *thrilled* to see him. "No, no! You guys get back to it! We can yap about nonsense later!"

I don't think it was more than twenty minutes after Joe left the bus that Keith and I had finished the lyrics. But we both agreed the song needed a bridge, and with Keith's pending sound check and show, we were out of time.

"We can finish it on Skype!"

Ah, the advancements in technology. Who needs to be in the same room to cowrite anymore?

A few days later, I flew to Brazil where I was performing in a few cities there. My first stop was Rio, and my hotel suite came equipped with a drop-dead gorgeous panoramic view of the Atlantic. I opened the sliding glass door and sat on my balcony, breathing in the beauty, when both a melody and lyrics arrived in my brain. It was the bridge to "Long Hot Summer."

The only place that I wanna be is . . .

where you are . . .

'Cuz any more than a heartbeat away is just . . . too . . . faaaarrrr

I sang this little fifteen seconds of inspiration into my phone and texted the file to Keith. Within an hour he texted back, "It's perfect, Ricardo. I'm cutting this song tomorrow!"

"Long Hot Summer" was released as the third single from Keith's *Get Closer* and went to number 1 on the Country singles chart in October of 2011. It became my fourteenth number 1 song as a writer, and also gave me the distinction of having written a number 1 song in each of four different decades.

I'm not a greedy man, but I do hope to see a fifteenth number 1, and sixteenth, and as many more as I can get.

41

A SUCCESSFUL MARRIAGE

'm a true believer in the idea that anyone's personal life, whether they choose to be in the public eye or not, is something to be shared solely at that person's discretion. There have been many celebrities who have routinely made the details of their relationships fodder for the tabloids and for their fans, and that's their prerogative. It's also their right, no matter how often they've been open about that stuff, to choose to keep something private. Unless it involves illegal behavior, there's no "right to know."

Since my career began in the '80s, I have been fiercely private about my personal life. I was never in the tabloids. I was never on *Behind the Music*. I enjoyed the fact that my songs were world famous while I personally carried on a pretty normal existence.

In 2014, I received some tabloid attention for the first time when Cynthia and I decided to divorce after a twenty-five-year marriage. There was no announcement by us. No press release. Nothing. Unfortunately, divorce proceedings are a matter of public record, and there are people who make their living scouring court briefings looking for the names of celebrities. Pretty gross, to me, but whatever.

Within forty-eight hours of our filing, my manager received a call from a reporter in Chicago looking for a comment. I gave none. In the years since our divorce, I have spoken very little about it and even then only in general terms. I have no intention of ever deviating from that.

People get married, and people get divorced. There's nothing novel about either decision. Sometimes marriages are immediate disasters, sometimes they last forever, and sometimes, believe it or not, marriages last just as long as they are meant to.

I had a conversation a few months after my divorce with an acquaintance I've known for many years. He said, "I still can't quite get over the shock that your marriage to Cynthia failed." I looked at him, then around the room, gathering my words carefully, took a deep breath, and said, "We were married for twenty-five years and had three sons who have all become exceptional young men. If you call that a failure, I'm not sure what to tell you."

For me, the year between Cynthia and me separating and finalizing our divorce was one of immense pain, fear, and confusion. It was also one of discovery, excitement, and deep enlightenment. I had never really known an adult existence as a single man. And though being free to date women was a bit like being let loose on a playground, it was the time I spent alone and nurturing my relationship with myself that was most valuable.

I spent days on end listening to lectures and voraciously reading as many books on "the soul" as I could find. Ultimately, it was one written in 1903 by a British philosopher that changed my life forever. James Allen's *As a Man Thinketh* was the catalyst that enabled me to finally understand that one's life is truly and inextricably connected to his thoughts.

A man's mind may be likened to a garden, which may be intelligently cultivated or allowed to run wild; but whether cultivated or neglected, it must, and will, bring forth. If no useful seeds are put into it, then an abundance of useless weed-seeds will fall therein, and will continue to produce their kind.

I read this book over and over, committing myself more each time to the dedication of improving the selection of my thoughts. Sure enough, my inner turmoil began to ease, and the darkness and depression inside me became more like manageable visits rather than a permanent residence. I still keep a copy of it on my night-stand and have gifted it to many friends, all of whom have gratefully benefitted from its pages.

In time, communication between Cynthia and me became more comfortable and our common concern for our boys' well-being is a bond we will share forever. We had some wonderful years in our marriage, and I consider her a truly kind and exceptional human being.

Despite all living very near me in California, my sons still have a close and loving relationship with her and also have a lovely and unique bond with Daisy, whom I'd say they consider more of a good friend than a stepmother. Our family dynamic is pretty damned functional, and not a day goes by when I'm not consciously grateful for it.

42

"EYES ON ME"

I have no problem admitting that I've always been an unashamedly romantic guy. I love romance, and I love the process of seduction, though with Daisy I would discover that in the right love affair, the seduction never has to end. Most of my songs are about women. Women I've loved, women I've married, women I've been fascinated by, and women I've never even met. They say an artist needs a muse, and I've had several in my lifetime. But never before have I experienced a level of captivation as the one I have with Daisy.

Out on a worldwide concert tour in the early '90s, I ended up spending a rare afternoon off in my hotel room somewhere in the continental United States and, as millions of others did every day, turned on MTV. That particular day I spotted a new VJ named Daisy Fuentes. She was hosting the *Top 20 Video Countdown*, of which I just so happened to be a part.

Daisy was stunning. Physically, as gorgeous as it gets, but she had this other quality that exuded through the TV screen. She seemed cool. And funny. And unlike anyone else on TV, let alone MTV.

From that day on, I would turn on MTV more often than I ever had before, hoping to catch her shift. Months later, I appeared at an album-signing event at a big record store, and after the long line of fans had passed by me to get an autograph or photo taken, the store manager said, "Feel free to grab a few items to take home. On us." I gratefully browsed the store and helped myself to a few albums I wanted to check out, and as I was leaving I distinctly remember passing a rack of celebrity calendars. There, staring at me, beckoning me really, was the face of Daisy Fuentes. The calendar featured fourteen of the most gorgeous and sexy photos I had ever seen. It didn't surprise me to learn that it was one of the store's bestsellers.

Strangely, despite Daisy's massive success on MTV as host of the countdown and then *House of Style*, not to mention many other shows on the network, and my near constant presence appearing on various MTV performance shows, our paths never crossed.

Until May 2013.

Daisy and I had interacted on Twitter the year before, as we both follow the former MTV VJ, Martha Quinn, and found each other in a tweet thread. We'd exchanged some funny quips and she seemed as cool as I'd always suspected. The following spring, I played a show at LA's Grammy Museum that was filmed for broadcast, and I invited several LA-based friends to attend. I sent a DM (direct message) to Daisy on Twitter to invite her as well, and she happily accepted. She sat in the front row along with a friend who accompanied her, and we briefly met backstage afterward. Her presence was unlike anyone's I'd ever met. Stunningly beautiful, obviously. But she had an energy that was certainly reminiscent of what I'd enjoyed when watching her on MTV decades before, but now mixed in with an elegance and grace that was unique unto her.

I was in the process of separating from Cynthia, and though I was captivated by Daisy, it wasn't until months later when I moved from Chicago to Los Angeles that I got in touch with her and asked her to dinner. It wound up being a three-hour gabfest over dinner at the Sunset Marquis Hotel restaurant in West Hollywood. It seemed that in addition to our natural attraction to each other, we just couldn't seem to run out of things to talk about. (I'm happy to say that is still the case, if not even more so.)

She was hosting a music competition show on Telemundo called *La Voz Kids*, which was like *The Voice* in Spanish with all the contestants between the ages of seven and fifteen. The show filmed in Miami. A month after that first date, I asked if I could come visit her for a couple of days. She said she had very little free time, but if I was cool with keeping myself busy most of the day, she'd be able to have a dinner or two with me. I simply wanted to be near her, so any time I could spend with her was valuable to me.

I checked into the same hotel where she was staying in a room a few floors below hers, and around six that evening, she texted me that she had just returned from filming and would love to have a drink with me before dinner. I picked her up at her room and we headed down to the bar and ordered martinis (our go-to cocktail to this day: Belvedere, straight up, no vermouth, olives, thank you very much) and launched into another wide-ranging discussion.

One of the ninety-three questions I asked her was, "What music do you love?" And I was somewhat taken aback with not only her answer, but the immediacy of it. It was as if she'd been prepped. She said, "I love Burt Bacharach."

Now, here was this drop-dead gorgeous woman who'd been on MTV during its heyday, who was always cranking up Jay-Z in her Rolls-Royce, and knows the words to almost every pre-1999 Bon Jovi song, professing her love for Burt Bacharach. I was already incredibly smitten with her, if not fully in love. And that answer shifted my attraction to her into another gear. As someone who considers himself primarily a songwriter, I have intense regard for the songwriters before me who shaped the landscape of modern music. And Bacharach is at the top of the list.

I have always channeled my emotions into songs. I'm a fairly articulate man, but I can't really *say* exactly what I'm feeling as well as I can write it in a song and sing it. It was a mere couple of weeks after I started dating Daisy that I found myself writing songs about her and what I hoped our relationship might become. The first song was called, "Like the World Is Ending."

> I wanna watch you cross the room
> Be the one you're walking to
> See our shadows fall down this bedroom wall
> In neon blue
>
> Touch me like you can't let go
> Burn into me soft and slow
> Prove to me you're not pretending
> Kiss me like the world is ending

I think it's one of the sexiest songs I've ever written, and it was a direct result of the fever-pitch level of seduction in which I was engaged with her. I was trying to sweep her off her feet. I was trying to constantly impress her. It turned out that while she was charmed by this relentless and impassioned courting on my part, she was really more interested in trying to discover who I really was. That took a minute.

A few months later, we had become closer, and while I was fully and completely in love with her and wanting to be in a committed relationship, Daisy was not yet on the same page. Still, we were having a lovely time together.

One night I went to her house to take her out to dinner. We had a quick drink there and were about to leave for the restaurant, and Daisy said, "Just give me a minute to freshen up" and stepped into the bathroom near the front door. I stood there in silence for maybe thirty seconds before singing a melody out loud. "Da-de-daaaa-deda . . . da-de-daaaa-deda . . . da-de-daaaa-deda . . . da-de-da." As usual with my songwriting, I could hear the *entire* finished music in my head. With strings, piano, nylon string guitar—everything. It was as if I'd rehearsed it. I knew that what was in my head was really beautiful.

Just then I heard a click as the bathroom door opened and Daisy said, "What was *that* you just sang?"

I said, "I don't know, it just happened."

She said, "Wait. *You just made that shit up in your head just now?*"

I said, "Yeah. That's what I do."

The next day I was at my house and went to the piano and worked out the melody and chords. I had imagined in my head the previous night a chord change I'd never used in a song before. I've found historically that the less I write at or with an instrument, the better my melodies and chord progressions are. You see, if you write with a guitar or at the piano, no matter how proficient you may be, you're limited to writing what you're able to play. But as a singer, just imagining music in my head opens up endless possibilities.

Now, it was all about the lyrics. I tend to struggle and slave over lyrics whereas music comes to me fairly easily. And the more excited I am about a new melody, the more pressure I create for myself to meet the challenge with the lyrics. In this case, I not only wanted to write an amazing song: I wanted to really impress my muse.

A day or so later, I was alone in my bed about to drift off into slumber when I remembered a text exchange between Daisy and me from about a month prior. I had traveled with my kids, mother, and several friends to Italy where I'd rented a house in Tuscany to celebrate my birthday. I had desperately wanted Daisy to join me, but we both agreed it was too soon in our relationship for a trip like this with my sons.

She was home in LA, and we texted each other every day, with me sending her photos of the gorgeous home and countryside around it. One day, I texted her and asked if she'd send a photo back to me. Not in a dirty way, although I'm certainly not shy about requesting sexy photos of her these days. I just wanted to see her exquisitely beautiful face. She obliged with a selfie from the set of a photo shoot she was doing. The photo definitely had the desired effect. I was almost frozen by how stunning she was, as I still am now.

I texted her back, "My God. You're the most beautiful thing I've ever seen. I . . . can't . . . even . . . breathe."

And she responded, "I live to take your breath away."

Hence the lyric in the bridge of the song (ultimately titled "Eyes on Me"):

> I don't know why
> I don't know how
> But you're burning me from the inside out
> And now I live
> Oh, I live to hear you say
> It's you who lives to take my breath away.

"Eyes on Me" was included on the album I recorded soon after writing it. The album is called *Beautiful Goodbye* and features quite a few songs inspired by or directly about Daisy, my pursuit of her, and our courtship.

The title track, we actually wrote together. I had written a piece of music I loved but had no idea for a lyric. I played Daisy the music track and she said, "This is so good! And hauntingly sexy."

I said, "The only words I keep singing are in the beginning of the chorus: 'Oooohhh . . . maybe this was meant to be a memory . . .'"

She looked at me for a second and very matter-of-factly said, "*Everything* is meant to be a memory."

I said, "Shit! Yes! So much better."

"You know, if *you*—Mister Love Song King—could write a breakup song that wasn't sad or forlorn but was basically a celebration of a love affair that simply ended, that would be cool."

And she started saying phrases to illustrate her idea.

I said, "Daisy, that's all really good. We should write these lyrics together."

"I don't know how to write songs!"

"But you're kind of writing it right now. Let's grab a bottle of wine and sit at a table and just figure it out."

And the next evening we did just that. Her lines are my favorites, by the way.

> No regrets, come to bed
> I'll set all your worries free
> Come with me, it's what you need
> Shut your mouth, just let it be
> Just let it go and let it be

I love this song not simply because I believe it to be well crafted but because I've never heard one quite like it.

Six months later, Daisy costarred in the video for "Beautiful Good-bye," which was also somewhat of a "coming out" for us as a couple. Before the video, and even for more than a year after it, there were no photos of us together anywhere. Not until our wedding announcement. We kept our relationship private, as we've both individually kept our lives, historically. I can't deny, however, that for quite a long time, part of me wanted to shout my love for her from the rooftops. I'm glad I can do it now.

Daisy and I married in December of 2015. Looking into her eyes the first time truly felt as if I'd been struck by a lightning bolt. And five years and a marriage license later, I'm still as captivated. Probably more, actually. I've never felt happier or more in love.

And I can tell you that my current state of bliss was an initially unconscious telepathic pulling of her into my life that began twenty-five years ago but became a meticulously conscious act of attracting our souls together after I met her. It was beyond "courting," although I definitely pursued Daisy in as chivalrous and persistent way that I could. But I've always had the ability to will people into my path.

4 3

"ALWAYS"

Soon after Daisy and I got married, we were home cooking dinner in our kitchen (and by that I mean she was cooking a delicious feast, and I was attentively filling her martini glass and gazing at her longingly, but I digress) when from our trusty Sonos speakers came Diana Krall's cover of "The Look of Love." We both absentmindedly hummed along until I said, "This song is so perfectly written."

"It's a Burt Bacharach song, right?" Daisy asked.

"Yeah, and I remember when we were dating, I asked you what music you love and you immediately answered with his name. I've always wanted to write a song with him."

"So, why haven't you?" she asked. "You've written with so many great writers."

I said, "That's a really good question. And I just decided this second that I'm going to."

The next morning I sent a few emails out to people I thought might have a current contact for Burt, and one friend emailed back with the number of his tour manager and assistant, Sue Main. I texted Sue straight away and explained who I was and that I'd be so honored to write with Burt sometime if he had any interest. Within a few hours she responded:

> Hi Richard. Of course I'm very familiar with you and your work, as is Burt. He is interested but is touring quite a bit and working on a new Broadway show, so not sure when we can put you two together. But if you can be patient, let's try.

My insecurity thought it *might* be a very kind brush-off, but it seemed genuine enough, so every couple of months I would check in with her. Nearly every time I reached out, she would respond with a variation of "Still not a good time, but let's keep at it." I was not deterred. In fact, more than once, when Daisy might ask if there was any progress, I'd say, "Not yet. But I know I'm going to write with him. And it's going to be great."

Finally, in November 2018, I received a text from Sue. I hadn't reached out in a while, so it took me a second or two to recognize her name. "Ahh, it's Bacharach's assistant!"

She wrote, "How's next Thursday?"

For a split second I had the usual, "I can't believe it!" reaction, but I quickly settled into "You knew this was going to happen."

Suddenly, however, I was met with a request that I didn't expect. Sue emailed and asked if I could send over either a completed or partial lyric. "Burt writes music to lyrics," she wrote. In my years of reading various stories about Burt, I knew he was not a lyricist, but I didn't remember reading about his creative process. So, when I pictured myself writing with him, I pictured us sitting in a room together, writing the melody and chords together and then me going off somewhere and writing lyrics to whatever music we came up with. In all my years of writing songs alone or with collaborators, that's basically how I've done it. Occasionally I'll have a title or a lyrical concept before any music is written, but that's a very rare occurrence. For me, the musical ideas generally flow easily, and then I try to figure out what the music is trying to *say*. But I would *never* think of writing lyrics first and then putting music to them.

Elton John has always done it that way, writing all those iconic melodies to words Bernie Taupin had given him prior. And long before that famous writing duo, Rodgers and Hammerstein did it the same way. I read an interview with Richard Rodgers who said, "The very first lyric Oscar finished was 'Oh, What a Beautiful Mornin',"' and when he handed it to me and I read it for the first time, I was a little sick with joy because it was so lovely and so right. When you're given words like 'The corn is as high as an elephant's eye,' you get something to say musically."

So, despite having never worked that way, I poured myself a tequila on the rocks and sat down in a comfortable chair in my house, and within five minutes words began to reveal themselves in my head.

> I wonder if I ever passed you
> In a crowded room somewhere
> I'm sure I would've noticed
> If I'd seen you standing there
> 'Cuz I've been searching for you
> Long before I ever saw your face
> And this love I've found in you
> Is the love I wish I knew
> Always

I stopped there, not simply because I wanted to see if this was something that Burt would be inspired by, but also because if he *did* like it and write a melody to it, I would then need to write another verse that could fit whatever melody he created.

I emailed the verse to Sue, and the next day got a phone call from Burt. I was in a meeting and missed the call, but he left a voicemail.

"Hi, Richard. It's Burt. Got the lyric. Good lyric. I've written something to it I'm anxious to show you. See you tomorrow. Looking forward to seeing you. [Several seconds' pause.] Really good lyric."

Hearing that voicemail was pretty amazing. The next day, I arrived at Burt's beautiful home and after a brief round of small talk in his office, he sat at his piano and played and sang the melody he'd written to my verse. It was gorgeous. And classic Bacharach.

I went home and by the time I slid into bed next to Daisy that evening, I had finished the lyrics. The song is a love letter to her. About how I wish we'd found each other so much sooner in life, but that all we can do is cherish every second we have together now.

A couple of weeks later, Burt and I recorded a demo of the song at a studio in Malibu. Our good and mutual friend Greg Phillinganes came in and played piano at my request. Though I could've easily laid down a decent piano track, I'm no Greg Phillinganes. No one is, frankly.

Daisy came by the studio, and I had the beautiful experience of singing the vocal while looking at her through the window of the vocal booth as she sat next to Burt. It really was quite a thrill. There I was singing this love letter to her via a melody written by Burt Bacharach, who was not only one of *my* heroes but someone whose music had strongly impacted *her*. And the three of us were all together in that room.

44

"LIMITLESS"

By the mid-'90s, there was an entirely different mind-set perpetuated by the music industry, and that was the "burnout factor." If you released too many singles or put out albums too frequently, the audience would tire of you and your career would be toast. So, artists began releasing new albums after a three- or four-year break, sometimes longer. I adapted easily to this new practice as it simply gave me more time to not only write songs for whatever my next album would be, but songs I could pitch to or produce on other artists.

Still, there was always a distinct moment when my brain said to me, "It's time to make a new album." Over the last two decades, I have sometimes gone five, six years or more between albums, but there's always that "moment" when making a new album is the mission.

That wasn't the case following the release of *Beautiful Goodbye* in the spring of 2014. Though it was a moderate success, the thought of making another album was never on my mind. I hadn't made any type of "recording retirement" decision—not consciously at least, though now I wonder if calling that album *Beautiful Goodbye* was more than coincidence. I just found that year after year would pass, and I was touring constantly and enjoying my new life in Malibu with Daisy. I also wasn't signed to a record label and had basically decided that I would devote the rest of my career to performing shows around the world and trying to find new opportunities I'd never pursued.

I started a podcast called *Songtalks* in which I interviewed musicians and celebrities about the music that affected their lives. I hosted a show on SiriusXM called *Inside My Head*, where I played some of my favorite songs by all types of artists and told some backstories about them. I was still writing songs here and there but always with or for other artists and with no intention of making a new album myself.

Then, in early December 2018, I decided I would write a song as a gift for Daisy on our upcoming third wedding anniversary, which is December 23. I wrote "Love Affair That Lasts Forever" within an afternoon. The title was inspired by a framed photo Daisy has had for many years. It sat on the counter of the master bathroom of the Hollywood Hills home where she lived when I met her. It is a headshot of Andy Warhol with his quote "I wonder if it's possible to have a love affair that lasts forever." I wanted to write a song that answered that question with a resounding and unwavering affirmative.

The song finished, I needed to record it fairly quickly to have it ready to present to her by our anniversary. I called a friend of mine, Michael Jade, who's a great arranger and keyboard programmer and has a studio in his house. We finished the whole track in a matter of an afternoon, and as I drove home, I must have listened to it in my car twenty times. I was quite proud of the song and my vocal performance and couldn't wait to play it for Daisy on our anniversary. But as I pulled into my driveway, I also totally unexpectedly had that "moment" I told you about: I realized this was the first song of my next album.

This would be the first time I would write and record an album with absolutely no thought of the reception it would receive. No thought of commerciality, format, genre, critical acceptance, or chart position. I just decided to start writing and recording songs that I felt were well written and that I enjoyed listening to myself. As the writing process began to reveal itself, I remembered the song I'd written a month after my marriage to Daisy called "Last Thing I Wanted" and thought it would be good to include on this new album as I hadn't remotely tired of hearing it over the past two years. I also decided to include "Not in Love," which I'd written with the incredibly talented Sara Bareilles a few years prior, and a song from 2014 called "Let Go" to which I'd written the music with the DJ and producer Morgan Page (who has had a very successful career in the EDM world) and the lyrics with Daisy.

There was absolutely no consistency between these songs or, frankly, *any* of the songs I was writing and recording for this new album. Some songs were very modern-sounding pop, some were more electric-guitar-driven "country-esque," and then there was a simple, naked piano-vocal track like "Not in Love." I didn't care about the varied genres. The thread of consistency would ultimately just have to be my voice.

I wrote two songs with my son Lucas. Over the past few years, Lucas has really come into his own as a songwriter and producer. Earlier in his writing career, he would routinely send me new songs he'd just written, and on very rare occasions I'd suggest a slight change, maybe a different lyrical line or a production idea. But for the most part I was just genuinely blown away by the work he was doing and finally called him and said, "Uh . . . how about writing a song with your old man?"

I went to his townhouse and up to his bedroom, which is also his studio. I had an idea to write a breakup song despite the fact that I was immensely happy and in love with Daisy. Just because you may be currently in a very content place emotionally doesn't mean you don't remember the pain of being dumped or of falling out of love. We writers can call upon any life experience and write about it as if it's happening to us all over again. Lucas and I wrote a really catchy and cool piece of music within an hour and then set about coming up with lyrics.

I mentioned that in the modern age of technology, when someone breaks up with you, or a relationship begins to turn sour, it's become instinctive to go read through the texts between you and that other person, looking for clues as to when and how it went wrong. I said, "Maybe the first line should be 'Looking through the last ten days of texts you sent.'" Lucas loved that line and chimed in with "Wondering if all of what you said is what you meant."

Within the next hour or so we had not only finished "Another One Down," but Lucas had created an incredible music track in his computer, and I was standing in front of a microphone singing what would become the actual finished vocal. It was an effortless and fun collaboration, and we had the same experience a few weeks later, writing a song called "All Along." You can imagine my level of pride and joy at having created songs I truly love with one of my sons.

Right around that time, my manager, Diarmuid Quinn—whom I'd first met back when he was the head of marketing for Warner Bros.—had a meeting with BMG, one of the last remaining major record labels, about it taking over my previous ten years of digital content. During those years I'd recorded and released several albums independently, and BMG wanted to make those albums more visible on the various streaming and downloading platforms like Apple Music and Spotify.

As the meeting with Diarmuid was ending, one of the BMG executives asked if I was recording anything new these days. Diarmuid said, "He is and it's really good stuff. Wanna hear a track?" He played them "Let Go," which they loved and asked to hear more. He then played them "Last Thing I Wanted," and they asked if we'd be interested in teaming up with them to release the new album. We worked out the terms of the deal fairly quickly, and I was now a BMG artist.

As I neared the completion of the new album, I decided to name it *Limitless* not only after one of the new songs, but as a metaphor for what I feel is my capacity to grow, learn, and become a better person. I had eleven songs finished and mixed and felt the album was done.

As we started thinking about album cover art and release dates, I went back to doing the mundane chores of life like responding to countless emails and deleting old files from my laptop. One afternoon as I was doing the latter, I came across a folder on my desktop labeled "Demos." In that folder were about seven songs I'd written over the last decade that had never found homes on any of my indie albums or with outside artists. One title in the bunch was a song I had no recollection of, whatsoever. It was called "This One."

Rather than just drag it to the trash, I clicked the icon and listened to it. By the first chorus I remembered it was a song I'd written with my pal Matt Scannell about eight years prior. By the last chorus, I had tears in my eyes because it moved me so deeply. Why had I forgotten this hauntingly beautiful song? Why had I not recorded and released it? It's *gorgeous*!

A few minutes later, when Daisy came home from walking our dog, I played it for her. She flipped out over it.

She said, "That's a really incredible and special song. You have to put it on the new album."

After listening a few more times, I decided that despite hearing a couple squeaks of my fingers on the guitar strings and a piano sound that I wish had been chosen differently, the track was magical and I'd add it to the *Limitless* album just as it was. I've since performed "This One" quite a few times in concert, and the reaction from every audience is as powerful as I've ever experienced.

NOVEMBER 2020

The *Limitless* album was released on February 7, 2020, and I set out on the road a week before to do a monthlong tour to promote it. In that month, I would do eighteen shows in eighteen cities along with a stopover in New York to do *The Today Show*. The week of the album's release, the first single, "Another One Down" was in the Top Fifteen of *Billboard*'s Adult Contemporary chart and the album itself hit the number 2 spot on the iTunes Pop Album chart, right behind Taylor Swift and her album *Lover*. It was quite a rush to see the album received so well, and I felt that on it were some of my best compositions, which could give the album legs to justify promoting it all year.

During the last week of my US run of shows, the news began being dominated by reports of a mysterious and potentially deadly virus that seemed to have begun in the wet markets of Wuhan, China. At the time, some precautions were recommended, but the threat of the virus becoming a genuine problem in the United States was downplayed as only a remote concern.

When the news of the virus began disseminating across every news channel, I still had a couple more shows to play on the West

Coast, and I took it upon myself to use caution when it came to inter-acting with people. I usually meet fans after every show, whether it be in what we call a VIP Meet and Greet (where folks have arranged to come backstage and take pictures with me) or when I see a group of fans hanging around my limo and I go over and shake hands and snap photos. Regardless of the situation, I stopped shaking hands or hugging people, explaining that as much as I'd like to, we should all be careful until we have a clear picture of what this virus is and how it spreads. Everyone was very understanding, and I practiced this safety precaution at the last few gigs, including in San Francisco, where I wrapped up the US run on March 1.

I flew home to Malibu the next morning but with no time to relax as I was still in full "promotion mode" with an appearance in LA at the Grammy Museum and then flew back to New York where I would perform on *Live with Kelly and Ryan*. Two days later, I was scheduled to fly to Estonia, where I would begin a twenty-two-show European tour to include shows in London, Paris, Amsterdam, and Germany, among other territories. Daisy had joined me in New York solely to steal some time alone together before I headed to Europe. I'd be gone five weeks, and we had never been apart for more than two. The plan was for her to meet me in Paris at week number three and stay with me through the end of the tour and we would fly home together.

Within that forty-eight-hour window in New York, the news media was in full red-alert mode about what was then called the coronavirus. The reports were harrowing. While the United States had only a small number of cases, Europe was a hotbed of infection. When I read there was an outbreak in Estonia, where I'd be arriving in two days, I called an emergency phone meeting with my manager and my booking agents. The situation with the virus seemed to be heading in a frightening and potentially dire direction, and although

I wasn't really concerned about my safety but more for the safety of audience members gathering to see me as the virus continued to escalate by the hour.

In a collectively pained decision, my team and I decided to postpone the entire tour. Despite mine being one of the first tours to reschedule shows due to the virus, the European promoters were incredibly understanding and had moved virtually all twenty-two concerts to the end of the year. I was and am deeply grateful for their collective cooperation, especially knowing it was a costly decision for them. They would now have to eat the costs of having promoted the shows on their original dates and spend even more money getting the word out about the newly rescheduled ones.

The next morning, Daisy and I flew home to Los Angeles and immediately sequestered in our Malibu house. So little was known in those early days and weeks about how serious the virus could be and, more frighteningly, how it was transmitted. Was it airborne? Could you get it from touching a grocery bag? We chose to listen to the scientists and medical experts from day one and took every safety precaution we could to avoid contracting the virus, especially as the case numbers began to surge and the death toll skyrocketed. For two months, I didn't physically see my sons or my mother, and when we finally did, it was at our home, where we wore masks and stayed socially distanced. Daisy and I never ate at a restaurant or even stopped at a coffee joint for nearly six months.

My tour dates indefinitely rescheduled, the realization hit me like a truck that I basically had a year off. Throughout my life, I've been described as everything from a "workaholic" to a "go-getter" to "extremely driven." I wouldn't disagree with these assessments. I love what I do, and I've never been someone to take extended breaks from my work. In the past few years, I have learned to truly embrace and enjoy vacations with my wife and can spend two weeks in a beautiful locale (we like beaches with warm waters), and I don't get antsy to get back to work. After a while, though, I feel not only the inherent need to earn and nurture my career, but also the wanderlust that's been part of my psyche my entire adult life. I feel the need to be in motion.

Now, with the coronavirus stopping the world in its tracks, I had no choice but to be still. The first couple of weeks consisted of a constant thirst for information. Daisy and I read and watched anything we could to try to stay informed and knowledgeable about the virus. One evening, as we were reading about the antibody tests that people were taking to see if they'd ever been exposed to the virus, Daisy said, "I'm now wondering if when you were so sick eight months ago, you had Covid."

I said, "It was last October. There were no cases in the US until January." To be certain, we researched further and found more than one article stating there may have been isolated cases as early as October. I called my doctor, who agreed that my October symptoms were very much like those associated with Covid and arranged for Daisy and me to take the antibody test. A few days later, both tests returned a negative result. So, back to careful isolation we went.

When it became clear this initially self-imposed quarantine was going to go on much longer than planned, I started to feel a need to fill my time creatively. I obviously couldn't do concerts, and without a studio in my house, I couldn't safely book studio time somewhere and record new songs. Instead, I began filming conversations with various entertainer friends on the Zoom app, asking them about how they were handling this scary and confusing time. I would then post the videos on my social media platforms and on my YouTube channel. I called it *Social Distancing* and after a month or so, the web series started getting attention from various press outlets. I found myself in a new and unfamiliar role: interviewer. I actually really enjoyed talking to all these people, as most were friends and acquaintances like Kenny Loggins, Rick Springfield, and Olivia Newton-John. But then I started getting requests from publicists asking if their clients could do the show. At that point, I was now finding myself quite busy preparing and researching guests, booking them, and recording and posting the finished interviews.

In addition, I launched a weekly mini-concert series, also on my social media and YouTube channel, called *Beachin'*. In each episode, I would perform three songs acoustically from our Malibu living room. It was the next best thing to performing live for my fans, and they seemed to really enjoy the performances. It was fun for me because it offered the opportunity for me to play not only the hits, but also songs of mine I rarely or never played in concert.

I was now home, sequestered in our house and, like many other people, unable to work, but also juggling multiple activities and commitments. Daisy joked that I was busier than before the Covid crisis. For about six weeks straight, I kept a solid schedule of *Social Distancing* and *Beachin'* episodes, along with walks on the beach with Daisy and our dog, Bette Davis; and evenings of martinis and long talks about life and the universe.

Until the day after Memorial Day, when everything stopped.

I had recorded a *Beachin'* episode in the afternoon, and Daisy made us a typically delicious dinner that evening. It was about nine o'clock, and I sunk into our living room sofa, scrolled through my Twitter feed for a few minutes, and dozed off. Daisy said I looked so comfortable she didn't want to wake me and figured I was taking a catnap and would join her in our bedroom soon.

I awoke about an hour later and immediately felt a familiar and unwelcome sensation. Cold chills. The thought that my never-diagnosed mystery illness might be returning flashed briefly in my mind before I chose to shun it, saying to myself, *It's nothing. I'll wake up in the morning feeling perfectly well.*

I woke up in the morning feeling worse. I started coughing within minutes of opening my eyes and felt hot, cold, and clammy all at once. I took my temperature and saw a reading of 101.6° staring back at me. Although Daisy and I had been ritualistically careful about not seeing anyone and following all the guidelines to prevent Covid, we had a few days before agreed for the first time since our quarantine to have my sons, Lucas and Jesse, and their girlfriends come over for a visit. They, too, had all been careful and pretty much stayed at home for months. When they arrived, we wore masks and we didn't hug (a strange new custom given how demonstrative we've always been with each other), and they only stayed a few hours. As I coughed and felt my fever burning, I wondered if I'd contracted the virus from one of them or even from touching a grocery bag of delivered food over the past few days.

Daisy felt totally fine, but I immediately stayed away from her despite her optimistic assurance that this wasn't Covid. I decided to wait another day to see if it was simply some twenty-four- or forty-eight-hour bug, but by that evening my fever was spiking to over 103°, and I felt like a building had fallen on me.

I called my doctor, Rob Huizenga, the next morning, who immediately said, "Sounds like Covid, for sure. Come in for a test right away and *stay away from Daisy!*" We decided she should be tested, too, so we masked up and drove to the doc's office with Daisy driving our SUV and me sitting two rows behind, with the windows down. Dr. H had created a coronavirus testing station in the parking lot of his office building, and he and his nurse met us outside to do the swab tests.

Rob has been my physician since I was nineteen years old, and we became great friends early on, socializing often. Rob pulls no punches.

"Ricardo, this test is going to come back positive. I have no doubt that you have Covid, and I don't want you to worry because we'll treat you immediately, and you're already in amazing health."

At the time, Daisy and I still owned two homes between which we would regularly divide our time, and I immediately isolated from her as we awaited our results.

The test came back negative, as did Daisy's. Rob was shocked but explained that a negative Covid test has a 30 percent chance of being a "false negative" and urged me to take another test. I was still feeling awful with a severe cough and high fevers, so Rob, who lives only ten minutes from us, stopped by the house where I was sequestered and administered a second test in the driveway.

Two days later, that test also came back negative.

"I'm telling you, you have Covid!" he exclaimed. "There's still a slight chance of a second false negative, so let's get a chest X-ray to at least rule it out, and maybe do a third test. But I'll bet you my practice it's Covid!"

I should have held him to the bet. My chest X-ray was totally clear, and my third Covid test was negative. It was *not* Covid. My relief turned immediately to fear.

"Then what *do* I have?"

Thus began a rerun of the past October with me getting my blood tested for every virus, disease, and infection known to medicine. I also had MRIs of my entire body and brain to see if anything revealed itself. Nothing did. But this time, unlike my October illness, which lasted about two weeks, this fever was not going away. After week three, I started feeling better. Less fatigue and little to no fever during the day, but every single night at around seven o'clock, I could feel a change in my body, and every single night I'd have a fever of 101° or higher.

This prompted concern from Rob Huizenga as well as the specialists who were now involved in diagnosing my illness. The nightly fevers lasted forty-three straight nights before finally leaving me alone. It was frustrating not only to have no diagnosis, but to be steadily feeling better and better despite the fevers.

I started taking walks with Daisy and Bette, which turned into easy to moderately challenging hikes, and before I knew it, I felt 100 percent fine, working out and totally back to normal, but still the fevers would come. Hearing sentences like "We need to rule out lymphoma" and "It's possible this is an infection in your heart" were unnerving, but they forced me into a perspective about life that would benefit my psyche to this day.

My health is literally everything. I've been incredibly fortunate in my fifty-seven years on earth to have had very little in the way of maladies. My hips gave out after years of running around stages and jumping off the tops of pianos, and I had them replaced in 2013. Other than that, I've been in near-perfect condition. I work out every day and eat a plant-based diet, and other than indulging in martinis and some top-shelf tequila (and an occasional vegan doughnut), I'm a very clean-living guy, and I definitely took my good health for granted.

That second illness also made me confront the fact that keeping myself busy all the time was simply a lifelong habit and one that didn't really serve me. Could I just take this time off and relax? Not do an interview show or mini acoustic concerts or write songs or record in the studio? Just . . . be? I needed to find out, and I'm eternally grateful that I did.

Between my own hits as a singer-songwriter, and my hits as a writer and producer for others, I have a track record anyone should be proud of, or at least somewhat impressed by. I'm so grateful for the run I have had. It's never lost on me how fortunate I've been. So, it's always somewhat baffling to me when I hear or read things that essentially say, "Whatever happened to . . . ?" or "Is he even alive?" It's not even that I'm offended personally. I'm confounded by the mind-set of people who say or write those kinds of things about *any* successful artist or actor or author.

I remember an interview with Burt Reynolds in 1997, when his work in *Boogie Nights* was nominated for an Oscar, putting him back in the headlines after an already spectacularly successful career. He said, "Show business has a strange distinction. In all other walks of life, people are remembered for their greatest moment, their greatest achievement. In showbiz, people are only remembered for their most recent."

Here's the deal: about 1 percent of people who write songs have a hit, let alone a slew of them. Same thing with people who act. Maybe 1 percent make an actual living, and fewer become famous. For an author to write a bestseller, the odds are colossally against them. So, I find it odd that people ask "Whatever happened to . . . ?" because my feeling is, "Isn't the success I had *enough*?" It is for me.

As I write these words, I have a peace of mind that had long eluded me. That peace doesn't come from working hard or creating prolifically. It comes from listening to my own breathing, meditating, and being as present in each moment as I can be. It's an easier task when I'm forced into a long period of being off the road and out of the studio, as there are minimal distractions to pull me away from the act of simply living my best life. I feel like, to quote the late novelist Tom Wolfe, "a man in full." My sons are healthy, I've found the deepest and most rewarding relationship I've ever known with

Daisy, and I feel proud of the work I've done and optimistic about the work I may still do.

Every single time I write a new song, I get that same rush I always have. It's still a completely magical experience. One minute there is nothing; the next, there is this creation that will live on long after I am gone. I'm humbled by that concept alone, but then to have been gifted over and over with the euphoria that comes with seeing and hearing thousands of people sing these songs I made up in my head right back to me. That's a feeling I couldn't truly describe if I wrote a thousand pages.

I love being known as a songwriter. When I travel internationally and have to fill out customs forms, in the box labeled "Occupation," I never write "Performer" or "Singer." I always write, "Songwriter." I consider writing songs to be an elegant and noble profession.

And I plan to never retire.

ACKNOWLEDGMENTS

Daisy Fuentes: There's nothing I could write here that I haven't already said to you. You have made me happier than I've ever been. I worship and adore you.

Brandon, Lucas, and Jesse: To be able to say that my best friends are my own spawn may be the greatest gift a father could know. I love you even more than you could comprehend.

Sincere thanks to: Diarmuid Quinn, Matt Scannell, Fee Waybill, Hugh Jackman, Bobby Colomby, Bruce Gaitsch, Cynthia Rhodes Marx, Roe Conn, David Cole, Mike Landau, Humberto Gatica, Bernie Gudvi, Ivan Brailsford, Rob Huizenga, Chip Matthews, Wayne Isaak, Lionel Richie, Alan Silfen (the great photographer who introduced me to Lionel and took this book's cover photo), Terry Williams, Barbra Streisand, Linda Thompson, Olivia Newton-John, Dave Novik, Marissa Matteo, Keith Urban, Dave Grusin, Jimmy Harnen, Scott Borchetta, Allison Jones, Geoff Bywater, Martha Quinn, my BMG family, Sean Manning and the S&S team, Sam Walton, the Brijbag and Fuentes family, all the musicians who have contributed their talents to my work, and all the songwriters with whom I've spent time trying to catch lightning in a bottle.

GUILDERLAND PUBLIC LIBRARY
2228 WESTERN AVENUE
GUILDERLAND, NY 12084
(518) 456-2400